12/03

TRANSLATED TEX

This series is designed to meet the ...
medieval history and others who wish to broaden their stud, ...
source material, but whose knowledge of Latin or Greek is not sufficient
to allow them to do so in the original language. Many important Late
Imperial and Dark Age texts are currently unavailable in translation and it
is hoped that TTH will help to fill this gap and to complement the
secondary literature in English which already exists. The series relates
principally to the period 300-800 AD and includes Late Imperial, Greek,
Byzantine and Syriac texts as well as source books illustrating a particular
period or theme. Each volume is a self-contained scholarly edition
including an introductory essay on the text and its author. Notes on the
text indicate major problems of interpretation, including textual
difficulties. Translations are by individual specialists in the field.

General Editors:
Gillian Clark, University of Bristol
Mary Whitby, University of Liverpool

Editorial Committee:
Sebastian Brock, Oriental Institute, University of Oxford
Averil Cameron, King's College London
Henry Chadwick, Oxford
John Davies, University of Liverpool
Carlotta Dionisotti, King's College London
Peter Heather, University College London
William E. Klingshirn, The Catholic University of America
Michael Lapidge, Clare College, Cambridge
Robert Markus, University of Nottingham
John Matthews, Yale University
Claudia Rapp, University of California, Los Angeles
Raymond Van Dam, University of Michigan
Michael Whitby, University of Warwick
Ian Wood, University of Leeds

Cover illustration: Part of the base of a gold-glass beaker in the British
Museum, c. fourth century AD

A full list of titles in the Translated Texts for Historians series is available on request. Recent titles are shown below.

Optatus: Against the Donatists
Translated with notes and introduction by MARK J. EDWARDS
Vol. 27, 304pp., 1997, ISBN 0-85323-752-2

Bede: A Biblical Miscellany
Translated with notes and introduction by W. TRENT FOLEY and ARTHUR G. HOLDER
Vol. 28, 240pp. including line diagrams, 1998, ISBN 0-85323-683-6

Bede: The Reckoning of Time
Translated with notes and introduction by FAITH WALLIS
Vol. 29, 352pp. including 7 line diagrams, 1999, ISBN 0-85323-693-3

Ruricius of Limoges and Friends: A Collection of Letters from Visigothic Gaul
Translated with notes and introduction by RALPH W. MATHISEN
Vol. 30, 272pp., including 10 illustrations from the Codex Sangallensis 190, 1998, ISBN 0-85323-703-4

The Armenian History attributed to Sebeos
Translated with notes by ROBERT THOMSON
Vol. 31 (2-volume set), 240pp., 224pp., 1999, ISBN 0-85323-564-3

The Chronicle of Pseudo-Joshua the Stylite
Translated with notes and introduction by FRANK R. TROMBLEY and JOHN W. WATT
Vol. 32, 240pp., including 3 maps and 2 plans, 2000, ISBN 0-85323-585-6

Antioch as a Centre of Hellenic Culture, as Observed by Libanius
Translated with an introduction and notes by A. F. NORMAN
Vol. 34, 224pp., 2000, ISBN 0-85323-595-3

For full details, please write to the following:
All countries except the USA and Canada: Liverpool University Press, 4 Cambridge Street, Liverpool L69 7ZU, UK (Tel +44-[0]151-794-2233, Fax +44 [0]151-794-2235, email J.M.Smith@liv.ac.uk, http://www.liverpool-unipress.co.uk). **USA and Canada:** University of Pennsylvania Press, 4200 Pine Street, Philadelphia, PA 19104-6097, USA (Tel 215-898-6264, Fax 215-898-0404).

Translated Texts for Historians
Volume 6

The Book of Pontiffs
(*Liber Pontificalis*)

The ancient biographies of the first ninety Roman bishops to AD 715

Revised edition, translated with an introduction by
RAYMOND DAVIS

Liverpool
University
Press

First published 1989
Revised second edition published 2000
Liverpool University Press,
4 Cambridge Street
Liverpool, L69 7ZU

British Library Cataloguing-in-Publication Data
A British Library CIP Record is available
ISBN 0-85323-545-7

Printed in the European Community by
Bell and Bain Limited, Glasgow

CONTENTS

THE BOOK OF PONTIFFS

PREFACE

It is a pleasure to record how unstintingly I have been assisted at every stage of this work by friends and colleagues. Above all Dr Margaret Gibson's patience and endurance in reading and criticizing various drafts of everything in this volume have been of inestimable help. I am also much indebted to two other members of the editorial committee of this series, Dr John Matthews, under whose guidance I originally began research into aspects of the LP and who has never failed to encourage me, and Dr Henry Chadwick, whose sagacity has removed blemishes and added jewels in the introduction and the glossary.

I owe much also to the Master and Fellows of University College, Oxford, and particularly to Mr George Cawkwell, to the Director, Librarian and staff of the British School at Rome, where amongst other work part of this volume was prepared, to the British Academy which contributed to my support whilst I was there, to Dr Samuel Barnish, to Mr Jonathan Doria Pamphilj and Dr Anthony Luttrell. They deserve and have my gratitude, as do my colleagues in Belfast: especially Professor Alan Astin who has advised me on the introduction and encouraged me throughout, Dr Brian Campbell, Dr Margaret Mullett, Dr Clemence Schultze (who generously made her word processor available for the completion of this work), Dr Brian Scott, and Dr Anna Wilson, who have all helped in the elucidation of obscurities in the text, and Miss Janis Boyd who introduced me to the art of word processing and herself typed much of the first draft of the translation. I am also grateful to Mrs Sandra Mather of the University of Liverpool for her skilled work on the maps. It goes without saying that for errors which remain I bear sole responsibility.

PREFACE TO REVISED EDITION

This volume has now been fully revised in the light of years of further study, of the work involved in preparing the two volumes in which I translated and commented on the rest of the LP down to A.D. 891 (see Bibliography), of the comments of reviewers, and especially of discussions with my former colleague John Curran. The translation has been carefully emended, and in places the underlying text has been reconsidered. Some changes have been made to achieve even greater consistency in the use of equivalents for technical language, and (be it

acknowledged) to remove some errors. As in my two later volumes, the
Vignoli section numbers have been inserted (on these see the end of the
Introduction). In the translation the presentation has been redesigned in an
attempt to distinguish more clearly the status and value of additions to the
standard LP text by the use of different fonts. The glossary has been
revised, and extended by about a third in length. The bibliography has
been revised and extended. Appendix 3 now contains even more material
from the epitomes of the first edition. My greatest sorrow is that Alan
Astin and Margaret Gibson, to both of whom I owe so much, are no
longer alive to see this work.

INTRODUCTION

The *Liber Pontificalis* is the title now universally given to the collection of Latin biographies of the Roman bishops once generally cited as the work of Anastasius, librarian of the Roman see in the ninth century; in fact this title occurs in no good manuscript—the work seems originally to have had none. It is just over a century since Louis Duchesne issued the first volume of his magisterial edition. It is not too much to say that his vast labour (to which Mommsen paid tribute in his own edition a few years later) made the material contained in these biographies fully usable for the first time to students of Christian archaeology and art, Roman topography, and the social and economic history of Italy and the papacy in the late antique and early medieval periods.

It is hoped that this volume will make the contents of the first 90 lives in the *Liber Pontificalis* (hereafter, LP) available in a reliable form to readers unable to cope with its often extraordinary Latinity. For the increasingly fuller biographies from A.D. 715 (the point to which Mommsen's published text goes) down to 891 (where the LP properly so called finally breaks off) the reader may now refer to my *Lives of the Eighth-Century Popes* and *Lives of the Ninth-Century Popes,* published in this same series, which provide translation and full commentary. The present volume covers about one quarter of the total text, but it would be impossible to provide an extended commentary within the limits of a single volume. Duchesne's commentary is several times longer than the text itself, and the century since his work was published has produced a vast amount of material which would need to be added. Nor has there been scope to provide more than the bare minimum in this introduction and in the glossary to guide the reader on the value and reliability of the work. Readers interested in the activities of a particular pope will consult a work such as Kelly's *Oxford Dictionary of the Popes* to complete and correct the material given by the LP; and for a full commentary on each of the biographies readers will turn to Duchesne's commentary (in French). The bibliography should be consulted for details of these and other relevant works. Reasons of space have also precluded any index of the huge number of personal and place names in the text; the glossary and index of churches may supply the deficiency in part, but the reader wishing for more should consult the index of Mommsen (covering the lives here translated) or that in the third volume of Duchesne.

EARLY PAPAL CHRONICLES

The origins and history of the Roman bishopric evoked interest at a very early date. The work of Eusebius in the early fourth century preserves the successions of bishops at Alexandria, Antioch and Jerusalem, as well as Rome. No doubt these lists were all much earlier compilations but only for the Roman list is there evidence to prove its existence as early as the second century (it is given in the fragments of Hegesippus and in Irenaeus). The succession in the prestigious see at the imperial capital was of deep interest soon after the middle of that century, in part because of the crucial role it played in polemics against gnosticism with its notions of private succession. But it is not clear what exact position was held by the owners of the earliest names on the list before a monarchical episcopate had emerged at Rome.

As time passed the list was continued and chronological indications were given, with the curious consequence that for much of the third century papal chronology can be reconstructed more exactly than that of the Roman emperors themselves. This list reaches us in two forms, in the 'Index Catalogue' (see p. xx) and, more importantly, in a section of the work of the anonymous 'Chronographer of A.D. 354'; the latter form is known as the 'Liberian Catalogue' after the bishop, Liberius, who held the see at the date this Chronography was completed. Apart from the names of the bishops and the chronological indications, the Chronographer gave, albeit very sparingly, some additional historical information.

THE LIBER PONTIFICALIS

This information was included almost verbatim in a later work by an author who found in it inspiration to search out (or sometimes, it must be acknowledged, invent) additional material. In this way he not merely brought the information down to his own times but also transformed what had been little more than a catalogue of names and dates into a real series of biographies, which later writers would in turn continue.

His sources of additional information were clearly limited—snippets of Rufinus and Jerome, and a fair amount of apocryphal material: but amongst this farrago he was willing to include matter of great value which would not otherwise have been preserved, most notably the endowment catalogues (church plate, lighting equipment and landed estates for revenue) of a large number of churches founded from Constantine's time onwards in Rome or elsewhere in central Italy.

His finished compilation he foisted on to his readers as the work of Damasus, bishop from 366 to 384, and prefaced it with two letters: one from Jerome requesting information on the Roman bishops and a reply from Damasus introducing the lives that follow. Those letters (translated before life 1) are certainly apocryphal. The extraordinarily bad imitation of the epistolary style (which the translator has made no attempt to reproduce) is alone enough to exclude Jerome and Damasus as authors.

Rejection of those letters removes any evidence that the LP was first compiled in the fourth century. When did the compiler put pen to paper? The dating arguments are complicated, and a brief summary of them will be given later (pp. xlvi-xlviii). For the moment it is enough to state that the LP went through two editions not far apart in time. The earlier of them contained the lives down to A.D. 530, and was presumably completed soon after; it does not survive as such, though we have two epitomes made from it (extracts translated in Appendix 3). The second edition (the one here translated) reworked the earlier lives and continued the series to the middle of Silverius (536-537); it was produced no later than the 540s.

The work was then left aside, it seems, for two or three generations before anyone took it up again. It may have been in the time of Honorius (625-638) or shortly afterwards that continuations were again made to the work long suspended. From this point on there is no real doubt that we are dealing with a series of contemporary additions. Each life was added to the LP soon after its subject's demise. Some continuators did not wait even for that: the Venerable Bede (who is the first author ever to cite material from the LP) uses material from the biography of the pope who was still alive at the time Bede was writing. In this way the LP was kept going through to 870 (the already mentioned librarian Anastasius may have been one of its last continuators; there is also a brief fragment dealing with the events of 885-886). Much later, efforts were made to continue the work even further, but nothing could then be done for the popes from the late ninth century to the middle of the eleventh beyond the provision of a catalogue with little more than their names and the length of their tenure of the see. With subsequent developments, which took one form of the LP as late as 1431, we are not here concerned. The large number of surviving manuscripts vouches for the work's popularity in the middle ages. From the time of Bede onwards it became the source for much western medieval knowledge and prejudice about the earlier history of the church: most of Dante's information on the early popes is derived from it, directly or otherwise (compare *Inferno* XI 8 with life **52**, that of Anastasius II).

THE COMPILER AND HIS CONTINUATORS

Who was the original sixth-century author and who were the continuators? The manuscripts offer no guidance beyond the impossible attribution to Damasus. At any rate for the lives translated here the writers remain anonymous. There is little doubt that all were Roman, if not always by birth, at least by affection and domicile. They have not merely an interest in, but a positive enthusiasm for, the bishopric of whose occupants they are the chroniclers. Their product, certainly no work of literature, excludes members of any cultured literary élite; their Latinity equally rules out men of great education.

Where the information they give must depend on written sources and not on contemporary knowledge or legend (as particularly with all the material on church buildings and repairs, and the gifts and endowments made for their upkeep) the sources are of a kind that can mostly easily be supposed to have been available to relatively junior officials (the 'middle management') in the papal bureaucracy, whether laymen or, more probably, minor clerics—precisely the kind of men whose level of education would have been enough to enable them to do their day to day jobs but not to write literary Latin. Our authors are best imagined as humble clerks (conceivably, keepers of archives at the Lateran *vestiarium*) working for the Roman church and devoted to it, interested in its history though lacking the knowledge to see that history in its full context, concerned about the honour of the bishopric and the damage which emperors and even some of its own incumbents seemed to do to it, and taking sides ('the Roman populus usually does' is the comment on the events of 687 at **86**:2) in disputes over papal elections.

Disputed elections and their consequences may have provided one element in the motivation of the compilers, if affection for their church was not enough to justify their labours. There existed an earlier series of papal biographies down to Symmachus (498-514); only the last life has survived intact (translated in Appendix 2), but it is enough to show that its author's sympathies lay entirely with Symmachus' defeated rival Laurence. The LP's first compiler took the opposite point of view, so his account shows no contact with this 'Laurentian Fragment' (whether he used material from the lost earlier lives we cannot say). Perhaps he decided to take up his pen precisely to display his prejudices. The composition in the early sixth century of two sets of papal biographies which take opposing points of view can be no coincidence. Factional strife was nothing new to the streets of Rome; that it should now focus on papal elections (first in 366) need not surprise. But the events of the early sixth century were traumatic: the dispute between Symmachus and Laurence for possession of the see split the clergy and Roman senate. There were wider political ramifications; Symmachus had been elected by those dissatisfied with Anastasius II's efforts at a rapprochement with Byzantium (whence the view taken of this pope in the LP), and at first king Theoderic supported him. But the pro-eastern faction did all it could to achieve his replacement by Laurence, and when Symmachus fled back to Rome rather than face charges before Theoderic at Ravenna it seemed like an admission of guilt, and in 502 the Laurentians persuaded Theoderic to appoint a visitor to the see. Although a synod acquitted Symmachus, the grounds on which it did so (that it was not competent to pass judgment on the pope) would not please everyone, least of all Theoderic, who did not interfere when Laurence returned to Rome. For four years Laurence held the Lateran and all the Roman churches except St Peter's, while Symmachus was confined by street violence as a prisoner in the Vatican. It was only because by 506 Theoderic was taking an anti-eastern political stand that he ordered the surrender of all the churches in Rome to Symmachus; Laurence tactfully withdrew.

As we shall see (p. xxiv), the dispute gave birth to literary forgeries designed to support Symmachus' claim. There is no reason why Laurence should not have been similarly supported in his claim to hold the authentic tradition against Symmachus. We know that until its destruction in 1823 St Paul's basilica included Laurence in its famous series of papal portraits, and it may be that the series was originally painted in his time to assert his place in the papal succession. The Laurentian Fragment was produced after Symmachus' death, but as it makes clear there were those who had never been reconciled to him. It is easy to suppose that the victorious side would also continue its propaganda. Here, surely, is the niche in which our pro-Symmachus LP belongs. And when the compiler of the LP's second edition decided to extend the lives beyond 530, he too may have been influenced by partisanship: he had supported Dioscorus against Boniface II (530-532) and makes no effort to disguise his antipathy to the victor.

Where they are recording strictly contemporary events the compilers betray their lack of access to the higher circles, the actual participants in events and the real decision-makers of the Roman church. Typical in this regard is the lengthy and highly circumstantial account of the Sixth Ecumenical Council, at Constantinople in 681, given in life **81** (Agatho). Calendar dates are given for the various sessions of the council, and the chief events at each stage are carefully noted: the whole could almost be mistaken for a summary of the Acts of the Council (except for the delightful remark about the descent of black spiderwebs symbolizing the collapse of filthy heresy). But when all this is compared with the genuine Acts of that Council, we find that while many of the dates are correct, many others are omitted, and that while many genuine events are narrated, they have been assigned to the wrong dates. Much of the detail is inaccurate, yet in general terms the LP's account does reflect knowledge of the actual events. The explanation seems to be that the contemporary continuator had listened to an account given by a perhaps junior member of the Roman delegation to the Council after his return home, and the informant had produced a version based on inadequate notes supplemented from memory. Now the real Acts of the Council were soon available at Rome (**82:2**); but our compiler's status in the church was not one which gave him access to this material.

For the real history we go to the Acts. But the LP's account retains a very particular value: in it we see what might become commonly known at a lower clerical and social level—the very kind of knowledge which would do more to form public opinion than the precise truth would ever do. Similarly no one today believes that Constantine was cured of leprosy by pope Silvester and baptized by him at Rome (**34:2,13**); but the story was believed throughout the middle ages and to the end of the sixteenth century, if not later—without it, the inscription still on the base of the Lateran obelisk and the murals in the Lateran Baptistery are incomprehensible. The LP is the earliest account of the story and provides proof that (whatever its ultimate origins) this was the popular version at Rome by the early sixth century. What was believed, whether of recent events or of the more distant past, is of as much importance to the historian as the truth.

THE VALUE OF THE EARLY LIVES

With that point in mind we may now begin to appreciate the LP's value. Signs that the original author has firsthand acquaintance with the events described begin only at the very end of the fifth century. The lives from Leo I (440-461) to Anastasius II (496-498) contain some curious muddles which are best understood as material half remembered from oral tradition, for instance, the confused account of the Council of Chalcedon in 451, and the various references to the schism of Acacius, patriarch of Constantinople. What are we to make of other material in these fifth-century lives, and of all the material in those of popes who had died long before the lifetime of the first compiler?

THE TOMBS OF ST PETER AND THE EARLY ROMAN BISHOPS

The description of St Peter's tomb rebuilt by Constantine as a five-foot copper cube (**34**:16) could still be taken as genuine until the Vatican excavations of the 1940s showed that the rather cramped space beneath the high altar of the basilica could never have afforded room for any such construction. But the LP's account retains value—negatively, as showing that by the early sixth century all genuine knowledge of what lay below the surface had been lost, but perhaps positively, as reflecting a guess made and popular belief about the subterranean levels consistent, presumably, with what was then visible at surface level—and this long before the reconstruction of the whole area of the shrine about 591 (alluded to in Gregory I, **66**:4), let alone before the whole shrine was pillaged and largely destroyed by the Saracens in August 846.

In this context we should also consider the LP's references to the pre-Constantinian shrine. The author evidently believed that Peter had been buried where the shrine later stood, and he describes (**1**:6) this location as on the Via Aurelia close to the Triumphal territory (i.e. in the rather wide sweep of territory west of the Tiber bounded on the south by the Via Aurelia and on the north by the Via Triumphalis), and to Nero's palace on the Vatican (perhaps a reminiscence of the Circus of Gaius and Nero and adjoining buildings—Constantine's basilica would eventually overlap the site of the Circus, though it did not, as was once thought, make use of it as foundation for two of its walls), at the temple of Apollo (unexplained; the fact that a shrine of Cybele stood somewhere in the area is irrelevant, and it should be recalled just how small an area around St Peter's has yet been excavated). He then tells us that Aneclitus (**5**:2), whom he dates A.D. 84-95, was responsible for the *memoria* of Peter, along with burial places for the bishops. Now it has long been known that some kind of tomb or memorial stood on the Vatican before Constantine's time; Eusebius cites the Roman priest Gaius, who lived around 200, as mentioning the 'trophies' of Peter on the Vatican and of Paul on the Ostian Way. And the excavations which refuted the LP's description of the Constantinian shrine did reveal that a shrine was built on the spot around 165; no doubt this is what Gaius was referring to, and no doubt this provided the focus round which the architects of Constantine's basilica had to work. The date 165 would fall historically in the pontificate of Anicetus (even if the Liberian Catalogue and the LP date him 150-153); hence it has been assumed that as late as the sixth century a tradition survived that Anicetus built the shrine, and that the LP confused him with the similarly named Aneclitus. Such a use of LP material is unsound. Certainly its author believed there was a shrine before Constantine's basilica was built; but he had no clue who constructed it. His reasoning was this: it must have been built as soon as possible after Peter's crucifixion; it ought to be attributed to an individual whose name he knows; he knows no names of Roman Christians in the first century apart from the bishops; it might be thought unseemly for a bishop personally to build a shrine; the work must therefore be assigned to one who only later became a bishop; but Peter's immediate successors (Linus, Cletus and Clement) had already, according to our author's scheme of things, been ordained bishops by Peter and were thus excluded; Aneclitus was next on his list. He no more knew that the shrine had been built in the time of Anicetus than he knew that his Aneclitus was in any case a mirage—a duplication of Cletus made long before his time.

Nor did Aneclitus, Anicetus or anyone else provide burial places on the Vatican for Peter's successors. The LP's author had genuine records of the burial places of the bishops from the early third century: these details came to him from calendars included, like the Liberian Catalogue, in the compilation made by the Chronographer of 354 (see p. xii), and could have been confirmed from whatever form of the Hieronymian Martyrology was known at Rome in his own time. For the earlier popes he was at a loss; only two could be accounted for. Legends had already wrongly identified Alexander (**7**) with one of a group of martyrs culted on the Via Nomentana on 3 May, and of Clement (**4**) it was believed that he had been exiled to, and died in, the Crimea (this remains unexplained: it may be that there was a genuine martyr there named Clement who came wrongly to be identified with the pope—this is yet another case where familiarity with legend remains important: the whole story is depicted in the surviving ninth-century murals at S Clemente in Rome). Failing information, the author could have remained reticent about the unknown burial places. That was not his method. 'Formulaic' material throughout the lives, when not available, should be supplied. Where could be intrinsically a more suitable location for the early burials than the site on which Constantine would one day build St Peter's—the precise location of so many papal burials from the time of Leo I in 461 and thus *in the compiler's own time*? The excavators in the 1940s and subsequently have found nothing around the apostle's shrine to confirm the statements in the LP, and any expectation that further excavation (were it possible) will one day uncover these early burials is misplaced. Were it to happen it would merely mean that the author made a lucky guess.

THE COMPILER'S CHRONOLOGY

Since the author had genuine information about the calendar dates of most papal burials (from the same sources) from the early third century, it was desirable to complete the earlier lives in this respect too. No record existed (in all probability none was ever kept) of the dates on which the early bishops had died. Dates could be supplied for Clement and Alexander thanks to the liturgical observances referred to above. The joint festival of Peter and Paul on 29 June would conveniently start the list; the author was not to know that this was not a genuine anniversary. (See Appendix 1; the origin of this celebration remains obscure, and the notion that on 29 June 258 there took place a transfer of relics to the shrine on the Via Appia has little to commend it, despite the legend assigned in the LP to the time of Cornelius, 251-253, about a transfer away from that location.) The remaining information did not exist; the author appears simply to have scattered the names around the calendar. There is no discernible principle, no known earlier source, and no way that the dates can be reconciled with the lengths of each pontificate given in the LP itself in years, months and days. Eventually these invented dates, with minor variations, would be used by Ado, the ninth-century bishop of Vienne, when he thought it desirable that the martyrology he was compiling should contain the names of virtually all popes down to his own time about whom there was no positive evidence of a lack of sanctity; and from Ado the dates passed into many medieval calendars. It was only in 1969 that they were expunged from the Roman Calendar—so long lasting was the ingenuity of our compiler.

The Liberian Catalogue comments that from the martyrdom of Xystus II on 6 August 258 there was an interval till the following July before a successor was chosen; meanwhile priests were in charge. Later on we are informed that after Marcellinus there was an interval (*cessauit episcopatus*—episcopal government ceased) of 7 years 6 months 25 days during Diocletian's persecution. These statements seem to have inspired in our compiler the idea of finishing every life with a statement of the length of the ensuing vacancy; he used that Latin formula, but to him it meant no more than 'the see was vacant'. His figures are simply invented; they cannot be reconciled with the other data given, any more than with reality, at any rate until the early sixth century. Even for the interval after Xystus II, though preserving much of the information from his source, he reckons the vacancy as a mere 35 days. Could he count?

It may be remarked here that problems were caused to our compiler by the existence of a source other than the Liberian Catalogue for the early chronology, the so-called 'Index Catalogue', perhaps of fifth-century date. Variant figures from this permeate at least the second edition of the LP and the situation is not made any clearer by the efforts of some later copyists to modify the chronological system. The translation makes no attempt to draw attention to such variants, or to their agreement or conflict with reality; it has seemed sufficient to translate what the compiler probably wrote and leave readers to make their own comparisons with the dates now generally accepted, inserted at the head of each life.

OTHER 'FORMULAIC' MATERIAL

Each bishop is regularly ascribed a place of origin, and the name of his father is given. This information does not occur in known source material. For the bishops of the compiler's own time, these details may have been easily obtainable (the paternity of **50**, Felix III, is correct), and St Peter could be safely ascribed to Bethsaida in Galilee and made son of John (i.e. Bar-Jona) on New Testament data; everything in between is probably fiction. In the one verifiable case before the sixth century, that of

Innocentius (**42**), the LP is wrong about the father's name: Jerome (*Ep.*
130.16) tells us Innocentius was the son of his predecessor Anastasius I.
Statements, often still made, that Victor (**15**) was African (and may
therefore have preferred the use of Latin in a Roman church which then
still used Greek), or that Damasus (**39**) was Spanish, should not be
accepted. In passing we may note the façade of studious research the
compiler tries to present when he acknowledges his inability to trace the
ancestry of Hyginus (**10**) and Dionysius (**26**). At times he could clutch at
straws: Xystus II (**25**) had long before been wrongly identified with a
Pythagorean philosopher named Sextus, an idea which reached our
compiler from Rufinus, and similar reasoning provides the same
profession for Hyginus.

Much the same should be said of the statements about the numbers of
ordinations performed by each pope. Those for Leo I (440-461) are not
plausible (**47:9**), and it is even less likely that any earlier ones are genuine.
But from the latter part of the fifth century onwards we may well have
reliable and usable statistics. A good picture can be made to emerge;
around 500-530 we can see what replacements were needed to keep the
deacons and priests of the Roman church at full strength before the Gothic
wars and the horrors then brought on Rome, whereas from the seventh
century the emerging picture is one of a much smaller establishment of
priests (the deacons were always supposed to be seven in number). The
compiler evidently believed (and here he may have been correct) that until
the time of Simplicius (468-483), the local ordinations were performed
only in December; he is referring to the Ember Saturday falling in that
month. These Ember days were groups of three days set aside for fasting
in a particular week at each of the four seasons of the year; the LP
attributes this to the third-century pope Callistus (**17:2**, where the spring
ember days are ignored: the compiler believed that fasting at that season
would already be required because of Lent, which he had already
attributed to Telesphorus, **9:2**). The December observance originally had
no connexion with the preparation for Christmas—Advent was a later
idea. Later on ordinations at the other Embertides are mentioned,
particularly at that of February or March (i.e. the Saturday at the end of
the first full week of Lent). The calendar date given for the ordinations in
683 incidentally proves that the summer Embertide was not then kept at
Rome in the week immediately following Whit Sunday.

The ordinations of bishops, on the other hand, were not confined to any
one time of year. The pope claimed the right to consecrate at Rome all

bishops at least for 'Suburbicarian' Italy (the more southerly of the two divisions of Italy); and lives **82**, **84**, **89** and **90** show the claim extended to Ravenna, Sardinia, Corsica and Ticinum (Pavia). Consequently the fact that the number of bishops consecrated, unlike the number of priests ordained, tends to increase with the passing of time can be used as an indicator of how far the popes were able to exercise the right claimed.

On one matter the original compiler was not willing to chance his arm with fiction. In the Liberian Catalogue he found synchronisms between the popes and the reigning emperors; these he generally copied, though not for Urban (222-230) where there was an obvious conflict with a story making that bishop a contemporary of Diocletian. The series reached down to Liberius (352-366) as the contemporary of Constantius II (337-361), though the latter's name has been confused with that of Constantine. He then unfortunately synchronized their respective successors Damasus (from 366) and Julian (died 363); some manuscripts prudently remove this. Wiser counsels then prevailed (he could be too easily caught out) and synchronisms with kings and emperors are resumed only near his own time (in Felix III, **50:**1). For the same reason, the dating of the bishops in terms of Roman consuls is not continued beyond Liberius, until it is resumed with Symmachus whose dates, 498-514, are correctly given in terms of consular years (**53:**5).

THE EARLY POPES AS MARTYRS

The unfortunate truth is that too little was known in the compiler's time about the history of the Roman Church before Constantine for him to flesh out the material of the Liberian Catalogue in an adequate fashion. He could, perhaps, have made more use of martyrological material: from calendars and itineraries we know the names, burial places and anniversary days of a large number of Roman martyrs in the imperial persecutions of Christianity from Decius to Diocletian, from 250 to 305. But we know little more than that. 'Passions' were not written for Roman martyrs until reliable history had been overwhelmed by legend to such an extent that the writings emerging from the middle ages contain little trustworthy material beyond names, anniversaries and burial places. Of the earlier period we know even less; the cult of martyrs was slow to develop at Rome, and without a cult not even the barest details were remembered. But it is clear that the popular view by the sixth century was that a great deal of information was known: the legends had already taken over, supplying and supplanting history. Our author used what he could, even if impossibilities resulted: Urban, as we have seen, is made a contemporary of Diocletian, a synchronism wisely excised in many later manuscripts. Much more existed than was used; too often he could not attach stories closely enough to the lives of particular bishops. But where a pope himself was a martyr (or was believed to have been one), or where he was closely connected in reality or legend to a martyr (as pope Urban with Valerian and Caecilia), something could be used by the LP's compiler.

It is here that the LP is excellent evidence for popular belief in the early sixth century. The compiler uses some of this material in forms clearly not unlike those which have come down to us; in other cases he uses earlier forms of later legends; in others he uses material of the same kind which has not otherwise been preserved (as with Marcellinus, **30:3**, where the names of his martyred companions are nowhere else recorded, but could be genuine). It is even possible to trace the developments. In the second edition of the LP all the popes down to Marcellus are claimed as martyrs except Aneclitus, Hyginus, Pius, Soter, Eleuther, Zephyrinus, Urban (a *confessor*) and Dionysius. Their turn would come in later legends. But the epitomes of the first edition show that slightly earlier in the sixth century a martyr's crown had not yet been assigned to Anicetus, Eutychian or Gaius. In sober history, the only successors of Peter in the first three centuries who may have been martyrs were Telesphorus (if a remark of Irenaeus, *adv. haer.* 3.3.3 = Eusebius, *HE* 5.6.4, really refers to martyrdom), Callistus (victim of an anti-Christian pogrom?), Pontian (died unpleasantly in exile in Sardinia), Fabian (a prominent early victim of Decius' persecution), Cornelius (died in exile), Xystus II (beheaded in 258 shortly before his archdeacon St Laurence) and Marcellinus (controversial: even if he did not sacrifice to the pagan gods as the LP claims, he may have been somehow compromised: perhaps he handed over the scriptures and the title deeds to Roman church property a little too quickly—before, as Eusebius, *HE* 6.32.1, obscurely and perhaps coyly remarks, he was 'overtaken' by the persecution of Diocletian).

There is no point in deploring the mendacity of a compiler who was prepared to invent material to fill the lives before his own time. We should rather be thankful that he gave the lead to the continuators who would preserve analogous and genuine information in the later lives. The historian thus has to discount a great deal of fiction in the earliest parts of the LP. But the material retains its value for bringing us into contact with beliefs held in the early sixth century by those of no great learning, with the developments taking place in the genre of hagiographical literature and with the working methods of a chronicler at that time.

THE SYMMACHAN APOCRYPHA

It should not be supposed that all is plain sailing after the end of the persecutions: we have already noticed problems about Constantine's baptism and the shrine of St Peter. It would still be a century and a half before the compiler could call on living memory to help him. Consider the use which he makes of the Symmachan apocrypha. This material was forged about 502 to support Symmachus' claim to the papacy against that of Laurence, by producing, with other matters, 'historical' precedents for the claim that councils were not competent to pronounce judgment on the incumbent of Christendom's first see: Symmachus' refusal to accede to the council which attempted to depose him could thus be justified. The principle enunciated (*prima sedes a nemine iudicatur*) would be of considerable interest to later canon lawyers, and the LP is our proof that within a generation these forgeries had come to be accepted as genuine history. Our compiler inserts material from them (with no discernible polemical motive) at what he will have believed were the historically correct points in lives of the fourth century (Marcellinus and Silvester; hence the fictitious councils held under Silvester depicted in the murals at S Sebastiano on the Via Appia outside Rome) and in that of Xystus III (where the story of Bassus, **46**:1-2, is total fiction, though Bassus was a historical individual). But that is not the end. The forged material contains various disciplinary canons supposed to have been passed by church councils; the LP is quite prepared to wrench these from their already fictitious contexts and scatter them on no apparent principle through a large number of the lives. In addition he seems to have had more material of this kind not known to us (or invented by himself); this he treats in the same way.

The result is that no material of this kind in the LP before the sixth century can be trusted unless confirmed elsewhere. This can sometimes be done: in the life of Siricius (384-399) the author does allude to the earliest known papal decretals, issued by that pope. But in many cases we are in the dark. Anachronisms abound. It is no surprise that an author who claims that pope Dionysius, as early as the third century, had been a monk, can also state that Soter in the second century had legislated against monks touching the sacred vessels. To us, of course, the compiler's procedure seems not merely aggravating but dishonest. The sixth century would not have seen it that way: if challenged whether Linus in the first century had really issued a decree about women covering their heads in church, our compiler might have replied that the requirement anyway goes back to St Paul, but more probably he would have said that it was the immemorial custom of his own time and that, if not Linus, some other early pope must have been responsible—did it really matter which? This to us unhistorical way of looking at things would last until relatively modern times; most relevantly it is seen in the False Decretals produced in the mid ninth century and destined to have such influence throughout the latter part of the middle ages. And the False Decretals themselves owe some of their inspiration and material to the LP (it is no coincidence that consular dates assigned in them to fictitious early papal letters are only genuine when the consuls are mentioned in the LP).

THE LIBER PONTIFICALIS AND THE LITURGY

The importance, then, even of fictitious material in the LP can be immense. But the historian in search of facts has to treat all uncorroborated material with great care, and this has not always been done. Let us take some examples from the LP's statements about liturgical changes.

The profoundly obscure description of eucharistic ceremonial said to have been introduced by Zephyrinus (16:2) may have some value either for the compiler's own time, given the lack of any other such description before the seventh century, or as evidence for what the sixth century believed early ritual was like; but the passage is not reliable for pre-Constantinian ceremonial as such. The detail about patens made of glass is interesting, since they were obsolete in the compiler's day; but his statement that it was the next pope but one who made patens of silver is equally worthless. The introduction into the Roman mass of the *Gloria in excelsis* is attributed to the early second-century bishop Telesphorus (9:2), along with the invention of midnight mass at Christmas. We can merely say that they were customs already ancient in the compiler's time. The author believed that the mass contained no reference to the Lord's passion until the time of Alexander (**7**:2); he may have been aware of the tradition known to Gregory the Great (*Ep.* 9.26) that the apostles consecrated by using the text of the Lord's Prayer alone—a notion underlying the late interpolation at the end of St Peter's life (**1**:6). The addition of the *Sanctus* is attributed to Xystus I (**8**:2, though not in the standard text; it is included in the translation, bracketed, as a gloss from the first edition). Many liturgical scholars think that a date in the first part of the fifth century is appropriate, but it is most hazardous to pinpoint Xystus III (432-440) on the grounds that the LP's author 'must have' assigned the change to a pope of the right name, albeit of the wrong number.

Similarly, Celestine (422-432) begins with what seems to be a statement that this pope introduced the Introit (Entrance Chant) at the beginning of mass (the LP surely cannot seriously mean that all 150 psalms were to be sung before every mass); hence the statement gets into handbooks on liturgy. But even at that date it is not totally secure: the most we can safely conclude is that the practice was well established in the papal liturgy by the early sixth century and no one then living could remember its introduction. Yet the passage does reveal one valuable point—that in the compiler's time, and as long as anyone could remember, the first lesson read was (normally) from St Paul: the now popular theory that the Roman mass in the fifth century had three (or more) readings, with the Old Testament read before the Epistle, flies in the face of this evidence.

Again, the remark near the end of Leo I (**47**:8) that this pope added the words *sanctum sacrificium etc.* (near the end of the second prayer, as usually paragraphed, after the consecration of the wine in the Canon of the Roman mass) does in all likelihood reflect the fact that at some date between the time of St Ambrose (who gives an earlier text of these prayers, and claims that he follows Roman practice) and the latter part of the fifth century, this section of the Roman eucharistic prayer was recast and in the process those words were added. Leo may have been responsible, but we cannot be totally certain; and in passing it may be questioned whether Leo's later reputation as a liturgist has any basis independent of this single remark in the LP.

When, however, we come to the statement that Gelasius (492-496) was a liturgical author, we can accept it without reservation: we have reached the period of the compiler's personal knowledge. With the attributions of liturgical changes to particular popes by the later continuators of the LP there is no problem. Gregory I (**66**:3) did add *diesque nostros in tua pace* *disponas* (to the second prayer before consecration of the bread); but the LP does not reveal whether he did anything else of this kind, particularly whether he played the slightest role in the development of the chant which came to bear his name (though see the interpolated passage in Honorius noticed below); and Sergius I (**86**:14) did add the *Agnus Dei*. Whatever reliability the various liturgical notes in the LP possess, their existence at least stopped medieval commentators attributing the entire Roman liturgy to St Peter.

It is worth drawing attention to one passage, admittedly an interpolation found in only two eleventh-century manuscripts (and therefore bracketed in the translation, **72**:6), which has not been much noticed; it takes a keen eye to spot it in Mommsen's apparatus and Duchesne does not give it at all. Honorius (625-638) is said to have instructed monks to omit *Alleluia* from the third Sunday before Lent (Septuagesima). The rule of St Benedict (early sixth-century) had already excluded this joyful word from the monastic office chanted during Lent itself. But there was a strong tendency to anticipate Lenten observances; if this passage is genuine it provides a date at which an attempt was made to force monks into line with what the secular clergy were presumably already doing. But there is a problem: the same interpolation then imposes the Roman form of the office on monks during Easter and Whit weeks. If the ninth-century writer Amalarius is creditworthy, the Roman church of his time had not yet adopted in Whit week the shorter office which Amalarius knew in Gaul in his own time and which this passage of the LP seems to take back to Rome in the early seventh century. The original compiler of the LP may himself have advocated the lengthening of Lent; in his time it consisted of the six full weeks before Easter (Ash Wednesday and the next three days were a later idea); yet he claims that the second-century pope Telesphorus (**9**:2) instituted a seven week fast before Easter. That is not historical; but is he here pretending ancient authority for a stricter custom than that of his own day, for beginning Lent at what would later be called Quinquagesima Sunday?

CHURCH FOUNDATIONS AND ENDOWMENTS

Late manuscripts interpolate (**11**:4) into Pius the foundation legend of S PUDENZIANA, and hardly less legendary is the account in the original text of the origins of S MARCELLO (**31**:4); but both were founded no later than the fourth century. What follows is in a different class. Undoubtedly the most valuable material for the two centuries before his own time that the compiler has preserved is the series of church foundations and endowments which begin in Silvester (**34**:3) and mainly account for the much fuller scale of the lives from this time on. The Liberian Catalogue contains a brief reference to five foundations made by Julius (337-352), which seems to have inspired our compiler to include anything similar he could lay his hands on. Sometimes this would be no more than a reference to a foundation by a particular pope, but in many cases much more detail has been acquired from archival sources. The buildings themselves are not described, but much is recorded about their internal decoration. The compiler's source seems to have been more interested in the weights of gold and silver involved than in precise descriptions. Details are given of lighting arrangements and of the church plate provided; the reader should consult the glossary for an interpretation of the various items. What is more, this material includes, though only down to the time of Xystus III (432-440), details of the properties, land or buildings in Rome, Italy or elsewhere as far afield as the Euphrates, whose revenues were assigned by emperors or other benefactors for the upkeep ('lights' at **34**:12 should not be interpreted too narrowly) of the foundations. No records like this survive for anywhere else from so early a date; and this is the very period at which the church's material establishment was enormously expanding. Archaeology can often confirm the dating of the foundations themselves; and a few of the estates are known from later sources to have been church property. But, with the exception now of the Water Newton treasure, we have no surviving church plate from any date earlier than the sixth century; everything recorded in the LP's lists has been stolen or destroyed, and even where the buildings themselves survive their interior arrangements have been altered beyond recognition thanks to the destruction wrought in successive sacks of Rome and to the enthusiasm of restorers. It is certain that the data preserved are incomplete: some datable church buildings do not appear in the LP. For example, the foundation of the surviving basilica of S Sebastiano is not mentioned, though the type and date of the building are extremely close to what can be traced archaeologically of some of the basilicas that are listed (S Agnese, S Lorenzo, SS Marcellino e Pietro, **34**:23-27). And Siricius (384-399) includes no building works, yet quite apart from smaller late fourth-century buildings that might have been omitted as unimportant it is remarkable that there is no reference to the building of the new basilica of St Paul, fractionally larger than old St Peter's and surviving until 1823, which was undertaken on imperial initiative at precisely that time. But what emerges most strikingly from all the details we are given is the sheer scale of the munificence being shown to the church from the fourth century on.

THE CONSTANTINIAN CHURCH FOUNDATIONS

It is as well to stress, in view of the LP's undeniable faults in the fourth- and fifth-century lives, that this material is substantially genuine; and the same obviously applies to the early sixth-century catalogues and the usually briefer remarks made by the later continuators. Such problems as exist are almost entirely confined to the lists in Silvester, which form a lengthy block in the text (**34**:9-33; its incorporation has even caused the LP's compiler to repeat the ordination statistics for Silvester, **34**:8=34). But we can emphasize the extreme implausibility of a sixth-century compiler forging material of this kind and on such a scale. And how would he have known (**34**:19) that until late in the fourth century Egypt was still included, like Antioch and Cyrrhus, in the diocese of the East? How could he have conceived his ideas (**34**:25) that one estate had been taken by the *fiscus* in the time of the persecution and another provided so much revenue 'to the account (*nomini*) of the Christians'? Nor does the fact that the forged eighth-century Donation of Constantine owes some of its inspiration to this part of the LP mean that we should be sceptical of our material. At the same time there are points at which the fourth-century source material has been contaminated (we have already noticed the problems over Constantine's baptism and the description of the shrine of St Peter).

It is likely that the source document was compiled near the end of Constantius II's reign, and that the material in it is a summary of imperial munificence by the Constantinian family, not stopping at the death of Silvester in 335 or that of Constantine in 337. In its original form it may have made no reference to the name of Silvester or any other pope; and the emperor mentioned was not always or only Constantine himself. At the foundation of the original St Paul's a few manuscripts have preserved, coupled with Constantine's name, that of his son Constantius (who controlled Rome from 352 to his death in 361). The latter's name is bracketed in the translation (**34**:21): it is a contamination into the standard text, presumably from the first edition of the LP (and therefore from the source document). And Constantius, but not Constantine, is apparently spoken of (*domnus*) as still living. The name of Constantius, and indeed that of Constans (337-350), may once have occurred elsewhere; manuscripts confused such names only too easily, as in the second line of both Julius and Liberius (**36**:1, **37**:1) where Constantine (in Latin, Constantinus) appears for Constantius; compare also the confusion between Constantine's sister Constantia and his daughter Constantina at the foundation of S Agnese (**34**:23). The reference to a house at Antioch once belonging to Datianus being given to St Peter's by the emperor (**34**:19) cannot, given its value and Datianus' low origins (I assume the known individual of that name is intended), belong earlier than the last years of Constantius. The visit of Constantius to Rome in 357 (on which see Ammianus Marcellinus 16. 10) may have given an impetus to the completion of all the works involved, and thus in effect to our compiler's source material. Munificent activity by Constantius is all the more likely in view of the unpopularity he had acquired through his intervention in the affairs of the Roman church: the LP preserves in Liberius and Felix II (**37** and **38**) a garbled and partly self-contradictory version of these events. Such a dating will remove some of the difficulties in the document. Fragments of what was believed to be the True Cross, such as that referred to at the foundation of the Sessorian basilica (**34**:22), were 'widespread' by the late 340s (so the contemporary Cyril of Jerusalem claimed). An archaeological preference for dating the origins of S Agnese (note that Liberius was involved in the decoration of the actual tomb, **37**:7) to the 340s rather than earlier can also be accommodated.

The separate placing of the first endowment, that of the *titulus Equitii* (**34**:3), shows that it is not from the same source; and it goes awkwardly with the last endowment in Silvester, that of his own *titulus* (**34**:33), since the same foundation seems to be intended (S MARTINO AI MONTI). Some have suspected contamination by later material here, and indeed some manuscripts omit the section on the *titulus Silvestri*; it is however possible that the later church represented a combination of two earlier foundations.

The main series begins (**34**:9-15) with the foundation of the LATERAN BASILICA (S Giovanni in Laterano) and its adjacent BAPTISTERY ('Font'). Although the series of lists may not be in chronological order, it is likely that this was the earliest of Constantine's church foundations at Rome or anywhere at all; in the autumn of 313 a church council was held in the house of Fausta (Constantine's wife, but also sister of the recently defeated emperor Maxentius) at the Lateran; and the traditional date of dedication (9 November), though not recorded in any early source, may reflect a foundation made in Constantine's presence within a fortnight of his defeat of Maxentius at the Milvian Bridge (28 October 312), as the day fell on a Sunday (traditional for church dedications) in that year but in no other year in which Constantine was in Rome. The estates making up the endowment are all located in territory which had recently been under Maxentius' control—a thank-offering to the God who had given Constantine victory? Thus to the Baptistery are assigned properties in Africa, the Adriatic island of Cephallonia(?) and near Malta (if the corrupt 'Mengaulus' represents the island of Gozo). The endowment of the Baptistery is in fact so massive that it cannot all have been used to maintain the building and its services, more particularly as solemn baptisms were then only carried out once a year, on Easter night; in all likelihood we have here the imperial endowment of the bishopric itself—and the Lateran palace must have been begun on adjacent land not long after this. One of the estates had belonged to a *praepositus sacri cubiculi* (in a bracketed passage which may have come from the first edition), the earliest recorded instance of this title: a date under Constantius might here be more comfortable. Of the basilica itself more may survive behind the baroque facings of its seventeenth-century remodelling than has yet been found; at any rate the present building accurately reflects the dimensions and plan of Constantine's five-aisled church apart from the insertion of a transept in the middle ages and the extension of the choir in the late nineteenth century. The original Baptistery was rebuilt by Xystus III (the account at **46**:7 does not make the extent of Xystus' work very clear), in which form it still survives. If the LP is trustworthy, the two adjacent structures once contained the earliest recorded Christian statuary; the precise nature of the 'fastigium' in the basilica is still controversial, but the massive antique bronze columns now fronting the Altar of the Sacrament may have formed part of it. Many of the speckled green marble columns which once separated the side aisles and which medieval visitors regarded as one of the building's features have also been put to other purposes in the present building; others have found their way to Siena, and two are in the Palazzo Doria.

   Old ST PETER'S (**34**:16-20) did not survive the destructiveness of the Renaissance, though the vine-scroll columns mentioned in the LP (with six more added later) survive put to other uses in the present building. The estates listed are all (has the author omitted less exotic ones?) located in the east, territory controlled by Licinius until he was defeated by Constantine in 324. This provides a *terminus post quem* for the endowment though not necessarily for the foundation. The gold cross has long disappeared, and the garbled inscription recorded in the LP cannot be completed, but the mention of the emperor's mother Helena may be significant for dating; she seems to have spent the early 320s in Rome and to have died in 327 or 328, having received the title Augusta only in 325. The revenues are stated not merely in the usual *solidi* but sometimes also in various goods paid in kind: some of these cannot have been the produce of the estates concerned (e.g. balsam), others did not even come from within the empire (pepper, cloves); we have here a glimpse at an economy in which cash was not the only medium of exchange. Legends which made Peter bishop of Antioch before he came to Rome will account for the choice of property in that city. The districts of Antioch mentioned are genuine, and would hardly have been known to a late forger.

The foundation of ST PAUL'S WITHOUT THE WALLS (34:21) causes problems. There is no doubt that the basilica built in the 380s was not the first on the site, though very little is known of its predecessor. If traces discovered in the rebuilding carried out after the fire of 1823 were rightly identified, they confirm the complaints made by Theodosius and his fellow emperors that the old church was small and cramped. This makes it difficult to accept that its endowment was, as the text implies, marginally more valuable than that of St Peter's, and the names of some of the estates (Cyrios and Basilea, both simply meaning 'imperial', located in an unidentifiable town Aegyptia) do not inspire confidence. It has been suggested that we have here an interpolation made to suit the pride of the clerics who served the later basilica on this site and were unwilling to be outdone by their fellows at St Peter's; the order of the text at this point is also suspicious, and could suggest that the single estate located, suitably, at Tarsus is alone genuine as the endowment of the original small basilica.

The Sessorian basilica (34:22; SANTA CROCE IN GERUSALEMME) and the Lateran complex are (apart from the *titulus Equitii* or *Silvestri*) the only foundations of this series actually within the walls of Rome—and in both cases only just. At the date of these foundations it is likely that not even an emperor would take the risk of upsetting pagan susceptibilities by disturbing the monumental centre of Rome. The site of the Lateran had become available since (apart from Fausta's house) it had been the barracks of the *equites singulares*, the mounted branch of the praetorian guard which was abolished in 312. The Sessorian was an imperial palace (and survived as such into the sixth century). The foundation of the church there was in effect the creation of a palace chapel: an existing hall built about A.D. 200 was slightly altered to suit its new function. The building survives (though with an eighteenth-century façade and the interior totally remodelled) while little of the adjoining palace is traceable above ground level. The imperial occupant in the early 320s was almost certainly Helena: inscriptions of hers have been found close by. Given the reference to a fragment of the Cross at this basilica, the failure of the LP to mention her in connexion with this foundation is much to its credit: it is an indication not merely of faithful reproduction of its source, for the fact that the LP (Eusebius, **32**:2) has a different version of the discovery would not alone have been enough to prevent incorporation of the well-known legend which made Helena discover the relic (consistency is not our text's strong point), but also of the antiquity of the source—the first traces of any involvement of Helena in the story of the discovery occur only at the very end of the fourth century. Could it be that, with the diffusion of fragments of the relic, one reached Rome a generation later than Helena's death (in Constantius' entourage in 357?), and that its placing in an imperial chapel (itself not too surprising), a chapel with which Helena was known to have been connected, *gave rise to the entire legend?*

The next three foundations are of a kind which has only been interpreted in the last 30 years. The present S AGNESE is substantially the church constructed by Honorius early in the seventh century to cover her actual tomb, as the LP relates (**72**:3). There was an earlier shrine on the site, no doubt since the fourth century, but the foundation recorded by the LP (**34**:23) is that of a vast basilica a short distance to the southwest, whose ruined walls were once thought to mark the enclosure of an open-air cemetery. In a sense this was right (but the building was roofed); for it is clear from the absence of any trace of paving stones that the building had an earth floor and that its main purpose was for burials of those who wished to be laid to rest near the martyr. No doubt it was also used for purposes of worship on those rare occasions (such as the saint's feast day, 21 January) when the numbers attending made the tomb chapel inadequate. More distinguished personages buried there might have their own mausolea built on to the cemetery-basilica; and there is no doubt that this is what happened when Constantine's daughter Constantina was buried here, for alongside the ruins her circular mausoleum survives as the church of S COSTANZA. If this last building is intended by the reference in the LP to a baptistery, then the text of the source document has been contaminated; but note that Boniface I (**44**:3) conducted baptisms at S Agnese at Easter 419.

The case is the same with the basilica of S LORENZO FUORI LE MURA. Even if nineteenth-century inscriptions call the present basilica Constantinian, none of it is that early. The choir was built as a church over the martyr's tomb by Pelagius II (**65**:2, confirmed by that pope's inscription); it became a choir only when the nave (now restored after allied bombing in 1944) was added in the thirteenth century. Pelagius' building replaced what the LP (**34**:24) calls an 'apse' over the tomb; this was connected by 'steps for going up and down' (over uneven ground?) with the original basilica. This, the main fourth-century building at the site, was to the south of, parallel to, and larger than the present basilica, and except on special days its normal purpose was that of a covered cemetery. About the ninth century it fell into ruins (the massive shrapnel-damaged columns of the medieval nave a short distance to the north are almost certainly spoils), and all memory of it faded until parts of its ground plan were traced under the municipal cemetery in the 1950s.

So too with the basilica of the martyrs SS MARCELLINO E PIETRO. The ground plan has been traced, close to the modern church bearing the same dedication on the Via Casilina (ancient Via Labicana). Above ground there survives only a side chapel incorporated into a modern convent, and immediately to the east of the basilica the ruins of the rotunda in which Helena was buried, just as Constantina was buried at S Agnese. Helena's death in 327/328 provides the approximate date for the basilica. That far less survives here than at the two previous sites is because the cult of the martyrs at this location came to an end. Unlike those of Agnes and Laurence, the relics of Marcellinus and Peter were removed. According to Einhard's account they were stolen by unscrupulous German pilgrims, but others claimed that the relics were transferred into the city as part of that wholesale process whose beginning in the mid seventh century is recorded in the LP (**75**:4) and which continued into the ninth. Peter, Paul, Sebastian and Pancras were to be the only other exceptions; their shrines with those of Agnes and Laurence were the only extramural ones to survive to the end of the middle ages. Helena's own reputation for sanctity was not yet enough to save the site. In the twelfth century her sarcophagus 'of solid porphyry, carved with medallions' (in fact with scenes of battle—it may have originally been intended for Constantine himself until he moved definitively to the east), was purloined by a pope for his own use; with that of Constantina it is now in the Vatican Museum. It is evident from the endowment that Constantine was far less interested in the martyrs than in honouring his mother's memory. Archaeological evidence makes it clear that the site was imperial property already. In fact it had been the cemetery of the *equites singulares* whom we met above (p. xxxii); at the time it was set aside for the church, partly as the site for the basilica and partly to provide the endowment, it was the property of Helena, as the LP records (**34**:27, the farm Laurentum). The aqueduct mentioned is still a noteworthy feature along the Via Casilina when one leaves the Porta Sessoriana (now the Porta Maggiore), but the interpretation of the geography here is not helped by the unidentifiability of Mons Gabus. It may be that the other properties listed here were also Helena's; since it is out of the question that the whole of Sardinia was given to this church or that it could have produced only 1024 *solidi* in revenue, the text may be trying to say that the church received all Helena's properties on that island.

The four entries following relate to foundations whose connexion with Rome itself was either thin or non-existent, at Ostia, Albanum, Capua and Naples. The source document was clearly not concerned only with Rome; it may even have continued through other parts of Italy: our compiler would have had to draw the line somewhere. Ostia is described as near Portus Romanus, an otiose detail in a document compiled at Rome; and the foundation at Naples lists not merely a basilica but an aqueduct and a forum, hardly relevant in a document compiled for ecclesiastical purposes.

The basilica at OSTIA (**34**:28-29) has not been located; it has been suggested that it may lie in the unexcavated part of the ruins of ancient Ostia near the Laurentum gate. One Gallicanus is mentioned as cooperating with the emperor in the endowment: presumably the consul of either 317 or 330, of whom little more is known to history. But knowledge of his connexion with the emperor and with Ostia gave rise to many later legends; the LP contributed to these—it is not based on them. Ostia at least had some ecclesiastical contact with Rome: its bishop ordained the pope (**35**:2, confirmed by Augustine, *Breviculus Collationis cum Donatistis 3*. 16. 29), and as is recorded in some later lives he was assisted in this by others including the bishop of Albanum, which is the location of the next of these foundations.

The modern ALBANO LAZIALE is based on the settlement which grew up within the walls of the camp of the Legion II Parthica—the 'abandoned barracks' which, as the LP relates (**34**:30), made up part of the endowment for this foundation. The legion had still been at Albanum in 238; it is found in the east by 360; perhaps the transfer was not long before this endowment was compiled. Constantine, as at the Lateran and at SS Marcellinus and Peter, was finding new purposes for redundant military property. The site of the basilica seems to be that of the present cathedral of Albano.

Capua (**34**:31) is not the modern city of that name (ancient Casilinum) but the present SANTA MARIA CAPUA VETERE. The basilica has not been definitively located (it is not the great church of S Maria, probably of fifth-century date); the choice lies between the site of the present church of S Pietro in Corpo and ruins in the convent grounds adjoining S Maria delle Grazie. The recent identification here of a baptistery of possibly fourth-century date supports the latter location, but further work is needed at both sites to settle the matter. The occasion of the foundation could have been the fact that Vincentius, a priest from Rome and one of Silvester's legates at Nicaea in 325, became bishop of Capua about 341.

For the foundation at NAPLES (**34**:32) we are on surer ground: the northern part of a fourth-century basilica (known as S RESTITUTA) survives, though much altered, as a chapel attached to the Angevin cathedral. On architectural grounds a date shortly after the middle of the century is thought preferable to the reign of Constantine himself. Constantius' and his supporters' involvement in Italian ecclesiastical affairs entailed in or soon after 355 the replacement of Maximus, bishop of Naples, with the Arian Zosimus and it might have been to mollify local opinion that Constantius founded and endowed a basilica and provided a forum and aqueduct.

The difficulties caused by the final foundation in this series, the *titulus Silvestri* (**34**:33), have been mentioned already (p. xxx).

Mark's two foundations in 336 (**35**:3-4) are the basilica at the cemetery of BALBINA on the Via Ardeatina (the foundations were identified in 1991) and the church of S MARCO at the Piazza Venezia, the first recorded foundation close to the monumental centre of Rome.

OTHER FOURTH-CENTURY CHURCH FOUNDATIONS

Apart from a confused reference to the exile of Athanasius (turned into an exile of the pope) and some (historical?) statements on the development of the papal record office, the main interest in Julius (at **36**:2) is the record of five foundations given without details of endowment—does the absence of imperial involvement account for this? At any rate it fits awkwardly with the existence of the record office. The LP's compiler merely rearranges the order in which the five were mentioned in his source at this point, the Liberian Catalogue. The basilica by the Forum has not been traced: there is insufficient evidence for the claim that it was the site chosen in the sixth century (**62**:3, **63**:1) for the basilica of SS Philip and James (now SS DODICI APOSTOLI). The basilica across the Tiber is that of S MARIA IN TRASTEVERE; it may have been a reconstruction of a house-church connected with Callistus, martyred in 222 (cf. the LP's comment under that pope, **17**:3). Of the cemetery basilicas, that on the Via Flaminia is represented by the very meagre ruins of S VALENTINO. It is more than doubtful whether there was a martyr of that name; Valentine may have been the owner of the land, and the date 14 February may be that of the dedication of this basilica. Excavation in the 1960s somewhat clarified the situation at the CEMETERY OF CALEPODIUS on the Via Aurelia, where the second of Julius' extramural foundations was located and where he was buried, near the tomb of his third-century predecessor Callistus, to whom he perhaps had some devotion. The foundation on the Via Portuensis cannot yet be located with any certainty.

Apart from decorating the shrine of S Agnes, Liberius (**37**:7) founded a basilica close to the market of Livia. This has traditionally been taken as an earlier basilica on the site of Xystus III's great church, S MARIA MAGGIORE, often called the Liberian Basilica, and the LP's compiler believes this (**46**:3). Archaeology does not support it: there is no trace of pre-fifth-century Christian work at the site; nor does topography: it is not particularly close to Livia's market. A location at or near the later church of S Vito in macello ('at the market') has been suggested. Liberius' basilica seems to have been the basilica 'in Sicininum' at which the disturbances surrounding the papal election of 366 (the LP, **39**:1, reflects part of the story) resulted in over 100 deaths.

In Felix II (**38**:1-2) the LP preserves incidentally the true location of Constantine's baptism, but turns the baptism into a supposed second baptism of his son Constantius. The text claims that Felix constructed a basilica on the Via Aurelia but it makes the same claim (**27**:2^b) for Felix I. The reference must be to the known CEMETERY OF THE TWO FELIXES on that road; but it is highly unlikely that the LP reflects any genuine knowledge of the origins of the sanctuary. The information is merely guesswork by the LP's author or some only slightly earlier source. This biography presents many problems which cannot be fully treated here; it may be an early interpolation into the first edition of the LP (it is in the epitomes). At any rate its narration contains blatant contradictions with the preceding Liberius; most notably Felix has been turned into a martyr (in Liberius he dies in peace, which is true). Nor had Felix I been a martyr, despite the LP. False identifications with a martyr of the same name lie at the root of this, and these have assisted the wrong attribution of the cemetery on the Via Aurelia.

With Damasus (**39**:2,4,6[b]) we are on much surer ground. This pope's cemetery basilica and burial place on the Via Ardeatina are at the CEMETERY OF SS MARK AND MARCELLIAN only a short distance south of that of pope Mark at the cemetery of Balbina. His *titulus* in Rome is represented by the present S LORENZO IN DAMASO. This is a fifteenth-century building incorporated in the Palazzo della Cancelleria complex; the fourth-century church was on a slightly different site in the same area. The endowment is interesting as the first certainly non-imperial one and as showing what a Roman bishop thought most appropriate for the liturgical needs of a parish church in his time; whether the properties are those of his family cannot be known.

As noted above, Siricius contains no details of foundations; the surviving inscription of the emperors Theodosius and Honorius, not to mention extant imperial correspondence with the Prefect of Rome, guarantees the date of St Paul's. This is a signal that the LP's material is not the result of its compiler touring around the city copying inscriptions, but of his use of incomplete documentary material.

The foundation in Anastasius I (**41**:2) has generally been identified with S SISTO VECCHIO, though some doubts have been expressed: it is in the first, not the second, of the Augustan regions of Rome, though perhaps close to the boundary.

CHURCH FOUNDATIONS IN THE FIFTH CENTURY

One of the most interesting of the early foundations is that of the *titulus Vestinae* (the present S VITALE) in Innocentius (**42**:3-6), possibly the last of the 25 Roman parish churches to be founded. Few of these have actually been recorded in the LP, but the details given for this one are very valuable: we see something of the mechanics of founding a church by a will. Vestina herself is *illustris*, evidently the widow of some unidentified very senior imperial official. The task was entrusted to two priests and a deacon, whose activities are recorded elsewhere: they formed a kind of papal building committee at this time. The dedication was to be to the two Milanese saints whose relics had usefully been discovered by St Ambrose not long before this. Later legends claimed that these martyrs were sons of one Vitalis (whose remains were then found at Bologna); hence the present dedication. The church has been restored as far as possible to its fifth-century condition, though without the side aisles which were removed in the middle ages. When the building was finished, paid for by selling what was necessary of the foundress's jewels, the balance in hand evidently provided for the liturgical equipment (that baptismal equipment was required is proof that by this date baptisms within Rome were not carried out solely at the Lateran). The endowment estates are clearly a selection of Vestina's own rural and urban property. One she had acquired as a gift from her cousin. Many of the urban properties seem to have been located close to the new church, which was itself on the Vicus Longus; in one case the revenue, or perhaps the ownership, is 'in dispute' (*arbitrata*). Houses, a bakery and a bath are supplemented with part of the revenue collected from tolls on goods brought into Rome through the Porta Nomentana. This is interesting as evidence that the collecting of duty was not carried out by imperial officials but farmed out to private contractors. The figures (3 *unciae* = 3/12ths) show that the (annual) profit margin for all the contractors who had the franchise at this gate must have totalled very nearly 90 *solidi*. The LP also mentions the re-roofing of the earlier basilica of S Agnes, and the entrusting of that basilica, which presumably had no resident clergy, to the priests of the newly founded *titulus*.

Of Boniface I we are told about his modifications and gifts to a cemetery on the Via Salaria (**44:2,6**). The activities of Celestine are more interesting as they reflect the start of the restorations necessitated by the activities of Alaric in 410, an event which in Innocentius the LP had passed over in silence, but here 'the Gothic conflagration' can refer to nothing else. Which of the various basilicas of Julius (see p. xxxvii) received Celestine's attention is uncertain; something was done also to compensate for losses at the basilicas of Peter and Paul. As we shall see, much remained to be done; it took Rome some years to recover its nerve after the shock of 410.

But Xystus III (**46**) has in modern times given his name to the 'Xystine renaissance'. The new foundation of S MARIA MAGGIORE (see p.

xxxvii) is the last for which the details of a landed endowment are recorded in the LP; its interior still shows the magnificence intended to restore a sense of pride to the now largely Christian city. Much of the original mosaic work survives, and above the triumphal arch may still be read the inscription 'Bishop Xystus to the people of God'. The LP also records that Xystus secured the cooperation of the western emperor Valentinian III in various schemes including the replacement of the *fastigium* (see glossary) at the Lateran; as with its Constantinian predecessor, which the barbarians had removed (in 410), nearly a ton of silver went into this structure. Xystus showed concern also for the Constantinian complex at the tomb of St Laurence; but the new basilica to that martyr next mentioned and whose furnishings are listed (**46:6**) is that of S LORENZO IN LUCINA. The emperor's agreement was required for a specific reason: it was on imperial property, encroaching on the dial area of the *horologium* of Augustus, a massive sundial with an obelisk for its gnomon; the dial will have been useless if the obelisk had by this date been shattered.

Xystus also rebuilt the Lateran Baptistery, erecting the eight porphyry columns around the actual font; on the octagonal entablature supported by these columns his inscription may still be read. His devotion to his third-century predecessors, many buried at the CEMETERY OF S CALLISTO, is reflected in his tablet 'recording the names of the bishops'; fragments of it survive. Finally this biography tells us of the building of S SABINA on the Aventine by a bishop Peter. The compiler's knowledge is clearly not based on the surviving inscription there, which describes Peter as a priest and puts the foundation under the previous pontiff Celestine: if the LP is referring to its completion and if Peter had meanwhile achieved a bishopric, there need be no inconsistency. S Sabina is one of the most magnificent surviving buildings from fifth-century Rome. It is puzzling that the LP has no reference to the imperial foundation at about this time by the empress Eudoxia of her basilica (S PIETRO IN VINCOLI) housing the chains supposed to have once bound St Peter, which have been venerated there since this period.

Leo I (**47**) refers briefly to the foundation by Demetrias on her own estate of a basilica to St Stephen; its ruins and her dedicatory inscription have been discovered. Jerome describes the foundress as one of the world's wealthiest and noblest women. This is the earliest evidence for the cult of Stephen at Rome; his reputed relics had been discovered near Jerusalem in 415. After a muddled account of the Council of Chalcedon

(451), we are told of Leo's restorative work after the second catastrophe to hit Rome in this century, the sack by Gaiseric and the Vandals in 455 (curiously the personal initiative of Leo which had saved Rome from Attila and the Huns four years earlier is mentioned only after this). Gaiseric's activities had apparently included the removal of all the church plate from the 25 *tituli*. This time there was no imperial help for restoration work. The best Leo could do was to melt down 1000 lb of what survived from Constantine's donations of silver and use the bullion to make good what had been pillaged. The 'divine fire' which had damaged St Paul's will have been lightning.

Hilarus (**48**) is largely made up of details of minor works and donations. This pope seems to have seen his task as partly the completion of Xystus III's work at the Lateran Baptistery, and partly the replacement of more of what the Vandals had taken in 455. Two of the three small chapels he built on to the Baptistery survive, with his inscriptions on their door lintels, as do the huge columns intended to form a kind of narthex to the building, though they are not 105 ft high if that is what *hecatonpentaic* means; the description of his work at the font itself is somewhat opaque. Two buildings dedicated to St Laurence receive Hilarus' attention. These must be the building covering the martyr's tomb and the great basilica south of it (see p. xxxiv), and not either of the two *tituli* dedicated to the martyr (*in Damaso, in Lucina*), since the context is that of Rome's major churches, and only afterwards does the LP mention Hilarus' concern for the parish churches. This comes in the statement that he provided new plate to circulate round the *stationes* (Leo's replacements after 455 were perhaps inadequate); *stationes* were places to which liturgical observances were assigned on particular days, and although they should include the major basilicas it is clear from the numbers of objects provided by Hilarus (25 or 50) that our author is thinking of the 25 *tituli*. In view of what had happened in 455 all this valuable plate was to be kept in safety at the Lateran or S Maria Maggiore and taken to the *tituli* only when required.

Simplicius' activities included (**49**:1) the building of the surviving church of S STEFANO ROTONDO, whose function remains obscure, though it is further evidence for the spread of Stephen's cult to Rome. The building's design is that of contemporary martyr-shrines in the east (it may even be a copy of the Anastasis itself in Jerusalem, which then stood on the site now occupied by the Basilica of the Holy Sepulchre). But there is no evidence that any of the relics of Stephen discovered in 415 had reached Rome this early (though they reached Minorca by 416!); nor if they had is it likely that Roman sentiment would yet have felt happy about human remains being laid to rest within the city walls. The church is best thought of as a kind of cenotaph intended to encourage devotion to the first martyr; an eventual feeling that something was missing may explain why it was chosen in the seventh century (75:4) to receive the first relics of martyrs transferred into the city from the suburban cemeteries.

Simplicius' dedication of a church to St Andrew (S ANDREA IN CATABARBARA) on the Esquiline Hill is of particular interest as the first certain example at Rome (apart from S Croce) of the conversion of a secular building into a church. It had been built by Junius Bassus, whose son died in office as prefect of Rome in 359 and is the earliest person known to have been buried in St Peter's, where his sarcophagus still survives. The building was now made over to the church by the will of a Goth, Flavius Valila, who died between 476 and 483. The last traces of its ruins were destroyed in the 1930s. Valila has a further interest in that there survives a copy of the donation charter (the so-called *Charta Cornutiana*) which he drew up in favour of an unidentified church near Tibur (Tivoli), the town which was Simplicius' own place of origin (from about this point the LP's data on this are likely to be reliable). The contents of this charter bear a striking similarity to the kind of material so often given in the LP, but it includes many of the other requirements of worship which the LP lists omit (most obviously, books from which the lessons could be read).

The successor to Simplicius' church of S BIBIANA stands near ruins of third-century date which if the LP is right were part of a palace built by the emperor Licinius Gallienus (253-268). Simplicius is also stated to have provided a *scyphus* (see glossary) 'in the Roman church', an obscure expression which seems to refer to the Lateran and may be the first sign that this was now regarded as the seat of the bishopric, in fact as the cathedral of Rome.

OSTROGOTHIC ROME

The 'fall' of the western Roman empire and the passing of Italy into the control of barbarian kings, Odoacer (476-493) and then Theoderic (493-526), is not even noticed in the LP, so little immediate impact did it have on ecclesiastical or secular life in Rome; but the Arianism of these kings ruling over catholic subjects along with the ambiguous relations between the Ostrogoths and the emperor at Constantinople would have repercussions near the end of this period which are duly reflected in the narrative of the LP. And it is in this period, until 537, that we are dealing with the contemporary knowledge of the compilers of the two editions of the LP, as will be clear from what has been said (pp. xii-xiv) about the composition of the work. It is here that the LP comes into its own as a contemporary historical record of the first order. The narrative is that of eyewitnesses, and while criticism may uncover incompleteness and partisanship, it cannot disclose significant factual inaccuracy.

Contemporaries though they were, the compilers were clearly using written evidence for their material on donations; this material is so diverse, particularly under Symmachus and Hormisdas (**53** and **54**), that a full discussion here is out of the question. Cooperation with other donors, a praetorian prefect and (presumably) his wife, is recorded in the case of a church dedicated to St Peter 27 miles from Rome on the road to Trevi (**53**:10). Other churches at a distance from Rome are also recorded, including one at Albanum (**54**:1), evidently the surviving church there of St Peter, built out of part of what had once been the baths attached to the legionary camp (cf. p. xxxv). A further conversion of a secular edifice to ecclesiastical purposes is recorded (**56**:2) in the 'building' of the basilica of SS Cosmas and Damian overlooking the Roman forum. But the church which seems to receive most attention, particularly (as we should expect in view of current events, pp. xiv-xvi) under Symmachus, is St Peter's, where the LP's account makes it plain that the needs of pilgrims were met by laying out the *atrium* in front of the basilica and providing a public convenience (**53**:7); the structures for the poor at three of the great suburban shrines (**53**:10) may also be hostels for pilgrims. Gifts come from sovereigns, in particular from Clovis, first Christian king of the Franks, who, unlike the contemporary barbarian kings of Italy, had not chosen the Arian creed; though he had died in 511, his donation, surprisingly, is recorded under Hormisdas (514-523) at **54**:10, where too we see that the gifts of the heretic king Theoderic to St Peter were not refused. The gifts which arrive from the emperors Justin (**54**:10, **55**:7) and Justinian (**58**:2) reflect the theological rapprochement with Constantinople after the Acacian schism, to which the LP's references (**49**:3-4, **50**:2-4, **51**:2-4, **52**:2, **54**:2-9) are in their earlier part more than slightly misleading; suffice it to say that, whatever the compiler thought, Acacius himself died in 489.

ROME IN THE BYZANTINE EPOCH

The lives down to Silverius (536-537) maintain the high standard recently set. This biography itself falls into two parts: it begins by regarding Silverius as a far from ideal incumbent of the see, then changes tack entirely and presents his exile as martyrdom in language with scriptural allusions. There is an incompetent chronological join between the two parts: Belisarius had already reached Rome from Naples and defended Rome during the year-long siege by the Gothic king Vitiges, but the second part starts with Belisarius still at Naples. And the account of that siege given in the first part suggests that the author had not yet witnessed the two worse sieges Rome was to endure in the next decade. The next life, Vigilius, contains a good deal of circumstantial detail but also some extraordinary blunders: most notably, the two further sieges in this pontificate are conflated into one, a mistake which no contemporary could have committed. All this is accounted for by the history of the LP's compilation, for it was in Silverius that the second edition ended before later continuators began their work.

The Byzantine reconquest of Italy roughly coincided with this point. The devastation caused in these wars meant the end of ancient Rome in a far more real sense than the advent of barbarian kings had done; and for Italy as a whole, plague and then the Lombards would transform the economic and political scene. The LP's author shows no real consciousness of the wider picture, yet provides information and details of great help to the historian. Ancient institutions come to an end. At some point the Roman Senate ceased to meet and the Curia was turned into the church of S ADRIANO by Honorius (625-638). The LP records the last-known senator of Rome, either Honorius' father (**72**:1), or the father of his successor Severinus (**73**:1).

The lack of any further details on endowments until 625 is accounted for by the history of the LP's continuation; but some reference is made to foundations and restorations in these years. We have already mentioned the basilica of SS Philip and James (SS DODICI APOSTOLI, p. xxxvii, **62**:3, **63**:1) and the modifications at S LORENZO FUORI LE MURA in the 580s (p. xxxiv, **65**:2). Gregory's dedication (**66**:4) of S AGATA DEI GOTI refers to its transfer from Arian to Catholic use; naturally the LP had not mentioned its foundation by the Arian Ricimer over a century before, and this is the only hint in the LP that the end of Arian Ostrogothic rule in Italy had in the end meant the end of dissident Christians within the

city. Paganism, at least officially, had long been dead and in the early
seventh century we find that the PANTHEON is, with the emperor's
permission, converted into a church by Boniface IV (69:2). Among the
many details given in Honorius the most noteworthy is the building on the
Via Aurelia of the great basilica of S PANCRAZIO (72:5). This still
survives, and is a startling example of what could still be achieved in the
way of monumental architecture at this late date.

Many small details of foundations and renewals are scattered
throughout the following lives, but the successive continuators of the text
prefer not to give the kinds of catalogues of material the original LP was
fond of, at least not in the remaining lives translated in this volume. A few
of the churches mentioned are worthy of attention. On 22 February 683 a
church was dedicated next to S BIBIANA (82:5) to receive the relics of
martyrs transferred into Rome; that it was dedicated to St Paul is
confirmed by no other source and seems to be a misunderstanding. The
day corresponded that year to Sexagesima Sunday, when the papal liturgy
normally took place at St Paul's basilica; the regular texts for that day will
have been used, with their references to St Paul (see any edition of the
Roman Missal as late as 1969), and the LP's compiler may have assumed
that Leo II was dedicating the new church to the apostle. The basilica of S
AUREA at Ostia, restored at the end of the seventh century (86:13), was
not Constantine's building, but a church which stood in the town's
cemetery (the tomb inscription of St Augustine's mother Monica, who
died at Ostia, was discovered beside the church in 1945). The final
abandonment of ancient Ostia resulted in the fortification of part of this
area in the ninth century and in St Aurea's becoming the present cathedral
of Ostia. The various references to images and paintings in churches
(86:11,12, 88:1,2, 90:8) are to be seen in the context of Roman
opposition to the iconoclastic policy of Constantinople; and John VII's
evident concern (88:2) that his own appearance should be preserved for
posterity was successful.

For the rest of the period covered in this volume the Byzantine
administration under the exarch based at Ravenna impinges to a greater or
lesser extent on Rome. Rome would often be left, in practice, to its own
devices; it is the pope who is evidently responsible for the food supply
(see Sabinian, 67:1). An *apocrisiarius* would often represent the papacy's
interests at Constantinople. When officials from Constantinople or
Ravenna were present at Rome, their involvement could be unwelcome: in
640 they sacked the Lateran. In 537 pope Silverius was sent into exile and

died of his harsh treatment; in 653 pope Martin suffered much the same fate. But as the Italian militias and the 'judges' began to see that their future lay with Rome rather than with the east, the papacy gained strength: the imperial attempt to deport Sergius (687-701) ended in farce (**86**:7-9). In 663, for the first time in nearly two centuries, and for the last time, Rome saw a Roman emperor present in person; Roman reaction was mixed (**78**:2-4). It was good that he treated the pope and the shrine of St Peter with respect. But the 12 days of his visit saw the stripping of much of what was left of the city's ancient glory; the Pantheon suffered even though it was now a church. The LP avoids any judgment on the fact that all the bronze, left in Sicily on its way back to Constantinople, fell into the hands of the Arabs. From the mid sixth century the technical vocabulary, mainly military, of the new administration begins to appear in the text of the LP: *magistrianus* first at **54**:3, *scribo* first at **61**:4, *cartularius* first at **73**:1, *spatharius* first at **76**:6, *strategos* at **90**:4 (at **90**:2 the LP had translated this title), and *ducatus* (duchy) at **86**:7. At **86**:6 the LP shows off its technical knowledge with a word *scevrocarnalis* nowhere else recorded. Technical words to do with taxation are also used. For all these terms, the glossary may be consulted.

Similarly the LP provides evidence for the growing bureaucracy of the Roman church itself. As far back as the time of Julius (337-352) it was running offices keeping records and deeds of all kinds, not merely ecclesiastical, but including wills and the manumissions of slaves; the imperial term *primicerius notariorum* is used for the head of this office (**36**:3); eventually he has an assistant *secundicerius* (**90**:3). At **61**:5 there is the first appearance of a *vicedominus*. By **75**:2 there is a *sacellarius*, by **81**:17 an *arcarius* and also a *nomenclator*, the latter assisted (**90**:4) by an *ordinator*; from **83**:5 *mansionarii* occur, and at **90**:3 a *scriniarius* is found. By the point at which this volume ends it is this organization which is in effect ruling Rome, not merely the Roman church.

COMPOSITION AND DATE OF THE LIBER PONTIFICALIS

It remains to fulfil the promise made earlier to give a summary of the arguments concerning the two editions and the date of the LP. Duchesne has the credit for seeing that the solution to the origin of the LP depends on two main points. Firstly, the two epitomes (see p. xiii) evidently reflect a fuller text, a 'First edition', differing in a number of minor respects from the surviving standard text or 'Second edition', the one translated in this volume. One of these epitomes ends at 530; the other continues beyond that date, but abbreviates the standard text thereafter. Secondly, as noted above (pp. xvi, xlii-xliii), the author's firsthand acquaintance with events begins at the end of the fifth century and accounts for the quality of the early sixth-century lives. And it will be no coincidence that the first time he reveals a clear personal view about the conduct of a pope is with Anastasius II who in 498 'was struck down by God's will': the idea is that to prevent his Church's purity being compromised God took vengeance on a heretical pope (which presupposes that our compiler held a theory not much short of infallibility for a pope when teaching). There existed, then, an edition of the LP which ended at the death of Felix IV (**56**) in 530; though it does not survive, it is represented by the epitomes and, of course, by the use made of it by the second editor. Its date must fall between 530 and the date of the second edition.

When was the surviving second edition compiled? The author of this section still displays the quality and prejudices of a contemporary (he had supported Dioscorus' candidature for the papacy against Boniface II). But the peculiarities of Silverius and the inaccuracies of Vigilius already noticed (p. xliv) point to one conclusion. The work of the second editor, an opponent of Boniface II and Silverius, consisted of a revision of the earlier lives (to 530) and their prolongation to what is now the middle of Silverius. He will have completed his work before the siege of 546.

That the work was then left aside for some 80 years will explain the poor quality of Vigilius (the author was too distant in time) and the jejune character of the remaining lives in the sixth century: Gregory, though certainly the earliest account of this pontiff that survives, is particularly disappointing. But Honorius (625-638) contains many details of building works then undertaken, presented in a manner not followed in any of the lives since the first part of the sixth century, while the next life, Severinus (640) contains an account of the sack of the Lateran palace by two imperial officials which can hardly not be that of an eyewitness. From this point on we are dealing with a succession of contemporary continuators.

Study of the manuscripts confirms this picture of the continuation of the second edition. The earliest manuscript to survive (though it is not the best) is a badly damaged palimpsest at Naples, written in the 680s; it obviously could not have contained lives later than that point (even when it was still complete—the text now ends with Anastasius II at **52:2**). The best manuscript, at Lucca, is a century younger yet contains a significantly better text; it contains the lives translated here, and those from 715 to 795 appended on fresh quires and in a different hand. These two manuscripts belong to separate textual families, both families being represented by other manuscripts written later in the middle ages. (The full picture is rather more complicated than this: there are also many 'contaminated' manuscripts whose readings display features of both main traditions, and some which have readings which can best be explained as contaminations from then still surviving copies of the first edition.) It follows that the textual tradition had bifurcated by the 680s at the latest, and that the common ancestor of all our manuscripts can hardly have been less than a generation earlier than that date. In effect the textual history thus confirms a date around 640 for the first continuator of the second edition.

Such, in brief, is the case elucidated by Duchesne. It should be acknowledged that Mommsen, while conceding that the LP went through two editions, argued that both were compiled in the first part of the seventh century; thus he placed each edition approximately a century later than Duchesne had done. The quality of the early sixth-century lives showed, thought Mommsen, not a contemporary writer, but a later writer with good sources at hand for that period. Most of his arguments were easily rebutted, and Duchesne's dating has generally held the field, though some doubts subsist. The present writer believes that Duchesne's case is unassailable as far as the date of the first edition is concerned, and that Duchesne was probably right about the second edition also, though an early seventh-century date for this cannot be totally excluded. It should be stressed that (as Mommsen saw) this debate is one about literary history, and the historical reliability of those early sixth-century lives, or of any others, is not affected by it.

TRANSLATING THE LIBER PONTIFICALIS

The translation attempts to render what I believe the compiler of the second edition and his continuators were trying to say. There are a few minor departures from Duchesne's text, whose justification should be clear from Mommsen's text or apparatus, but otherwise preference is given, though not slavishly, to the textual tradition or recension represented by the Lucca manuscript. Duchesne and Mommsen were undoubtedly right to follow this text; where it differs from the other main recension (whose earliest representative is the Naples palimpsest), it can be shown wherever the comparison is possible to be closer to the first edition as now represented by the epitomes or to the ultimate sources used by the compiler. No attempt has been made to indicate the variants of this 'Neapolitan' recension which, despite the age of its earliest manuscript, is clearly inferior.

However *in angle brackets* I give some additional (but not alternative) material from later contaminated manuscripts. Such passages do not belong to the standard second edition. Down to 530 they may reflect the text of the first edition, and where this is certain or probable they are given within *angle brackets in regular type*. Even where (as must always be the case after 530) they are merely glosses and are printed in *angle brackets in small type*, they can contain material of historical interest. But it has not proved possible (except in Appendix 3) to incorporate into the translation material from the two surviving epitomes of the first edition. This would have resulted, as would the inclusion of variants within the second edition, in encumbering the translation either with footnotes of great complexity or with a system as confusing as the columns and diacritical marks used by Mommsen. This is not a substitute for a critical edition but a translation to aid the historian.

The minimum of editorial matter has been given *in square brackets*. They enclose insertions to provide connected sense where the original is corrupt or compressed, to correct some of the LP's slips (as where names like Justin and Justinian are confused), to give consular dates and indictions in their modern form, and at the beginning of each life to give the chronology now accepted.

The *section numbers* used within the lives are those of the 18th-century edition of Vignoli, and I have taken them directly from that edition rather than follow the partly inconsistent and incomplete versions of them given by Duchesne or Mommsen. Since Vignoli frequently followed the ordering of material in inferior MSS this has sometimes meant that his numbers here appear out of order (most notably in **81**, the life of Agatho), and in some places where Vignoli wrongly grouped material together it has been necessary to distinguish parts of his sections as [a] and [b]. Despite these difficulties, his system remains far more convenient than Duchesne's long pages. However, the *serial numbers of the lives* are those in the MSS and not those of Vignoli (who rearranged the order of some of the early lives, denied Felix II a number on historico-theological grounds, and apparently by accident used the number 85 twice; hence life **90** at the end of this volume is Vignoli's life 88).

I have tried to make the English readable, but there are places where the ambiguities of the highly idiosyncratic Latin make infelicitous English inevitable if the reader is not to be deceived. Nor would it have been appropriate to impose a style better than that of the original. I have regularized the spelling of proper names (Loomis even printed 'Batican'), but could not forgo the delightful Theodoliobollus (Elagabalus). I have often preferred to leave technical terminology in Latin (*italicized*, except in lists), partly because the reader, whose concerns are likely to be historical at least as often as they are literary, may prefer it, and partly because there are often no suitable English equivalents; for *amae* and *scyphi* Loomis's 'pitchers' and 'beakers' are not merely misleading but sound inappropriate in a liturgical context. The very frequent *presbyter* has been rendered by its derivative 'priest', while *sacerdos* has been left in Latin, since it often refers to a bishop; the rare *levita* is not ambiguous and appears, as of course does *diaconus*, as 'deacon'. *Cubicularius* is 'chamberlain' (except at **47:8** where the meaning is different), but most other technical words of Byzantine administration have been retained. I have aimed at consistency in my treatment of all such terms, and of all formulaic material and phrases, even at the cost of some awkwardness. The glossary should explain any terms that the reader finds unfamiliar and give the Latin equivalents for the English expressions adopted.

SELECT BIBLIOGRAPHY

THE LIBER PONTIFICALIS—TEXTS AND COMMENTARIES

Le Liber Pontificalis, Texte, introduction et commentaire, ed. L. Duchesne, 2 volumes (1886-1892). In these volumes Duchesne put the text on a new footing, and fully investigated the manuscripts, the date of composition and the sources used by the compilers; he also provided a commentary on the individual lives, the great length of which displayed enormous erudition. The volumes were reissued with a third volume containing Duchesne's further thoughts, other material in part updating the commentary, useful bibliography, and full indexes to all three volumes, by Cyrille Vogel (Paris, 1955-1957). See too C. Vogel, 'Le *Liber Pontificalis* dans l'édition de Louis Duchesne. État de la question', *Monseigneur Duchesne et son temps, Actes du Colloque organisé par l'école française de Rome (23-25 mai 1973)*, Collection de l'école française de Rome, 23 (Rome, 1975).

Gestorum Pontificum Romanorum vol. I, Libri Pontificalis pars prior, ed. Th. Mommsen, *Monumenta Germaniae Historica* (Berlin, 1898). Only the first volume, to A.D. 715, ever appeared. Mommsen provided no commentary as such, but his introduction (in Latin) confirmed Duchesne's results as far as the text is concerned, and challenged some of Duchesne's other conclusions, especially on the date of the work. The edition is of value for its more reliable reporting of textual variants in the manuscripts he had reexamined and for its indexes, but the printed text is marred by a thoroughly confusing use of diacritical marks to distinguish the textual history. See L. Duchesne, 'La nouvelle édition du Liber Pontificalis', *Mélanges d'Archéologie et d'Histoire de l'école française de Rome* 18 (1898), 381-417.

Anastasii abbatis opera omnia: Patrologia Latina, volumes 127-128, ed. J.-P. Migne (Paris, 1852). This reprints the Bianchini edition of 1718 with the text of the LP as received before Duchesne's edition, along with vast amounts of commentary (in Latin) including much taken over unaltered from the work of sixteenth- and seventeenth-century scholars.

li

J. Vignoli, *Liber Pontificalis seu de Gestis Romanorum Pontificum*, 3 volumes, the latter two completed by P. J. Ugolini (Rome, 1724, 1752, 1755); issued partly in competition with the Bianchini edition, Vignoli's edition contains an even worse text, but the Latin commentary is occasionally useful, and his section numbers are the most convenient system of reference.

L. R. Loomis, *The Book of the Popes (Liber Pontificalis), I to the pontificate of Gregory I, translated with an introduction*, Records of Civilization, Sources and Studies (New York, 1916). This work translates substantial excerpts from Mommsen's text (stopping at 590, not 604).

R. Davis, *The Lives of the Eighth-Century Popes (Liber Pontificalis): The ancient biographies of nine popes from AD 715 to AD 817*, Translated Texts for Historians Volume 13 (Liverpool, 1992).

R. Davis, *The Lives of the Ninth-Century Popes (Liber Pontificalis): The ancient biographies of ten popes from AD 817-891*, Translated Texts for Historians Volume 20 (Liverpool, 1995).

Dan Embree (ed.), *The Chronicles of Rome: an edition of the Middle English Chronicle of the Popes and Emperors and of The Lollard Chronicle*, Medieval Chronicles 1 (Woodbridge, 1999); contains a medieval translation of the 13th-century chronicle of Martinus Polanus, itself owing much to the LP.

O. Bertolini, 'Il 'Liber Pontificalis'' in *La storiografia altomedievale* (Spoleto, 1970), 387-455.

T. F. X. Noble, 'A new look at the Liber Pontificalis', *Archivum Historiae Pontificiae* 23 (1985), 347-358.

M. R. Salzman, *On Roman Time: the Codex-Calendar of 354 and the rhythms of urban life in late antiquity*, The Transformation of the Classical Heritage 17 (Berkeley, 1990).

For associated primary source material see particularly the bibliographies in C. Pietri, *Roma Christiana*, 1679-1683, for the fourth and fifth centuries, and in T. S. Brown, *Gentlemen and Officers*, xiii-xv and 228-231, for the sixth to eighth centuries.

MODERN WORKS—GENERAL

H. Chadwick, *The Early Church*, Penguin History of the Church vol. 1 (revised edition, London, 1993).

J. N. D. Kelly, *The Oxford Dictionary of the Popes* (1986).E. Duffy, *Saints and Sinners: a History of the Popes* (New Haven, 1997).

W. Ullmann, *A Short History of the Papacy in the Middle Ages* (corrected edition, London, 1974; new edition forthcoming).

W. H. C. Frend, *The Archaeology of Early Christianity, a history* (London, 1996).

C. Pietri, *Roma Christiana, Recherches sur l'église de Rome, son organisation, sa politique, son idéologie de Miltiade à Sixte III (311-440)*, 2 volumes, Bibliothèque des écoles françaises d'Athènes et de Rome, fascicules 284-285 (Rome, 1976).

C. Pietri, 'Appendice prosopographique à la Roma Christiana (311-440)', *Mélanges de l'école française de Rome, antiquité* 89 (1977), 371-415.

J. Herrin, *The formation of Christendom* (Princeton, 1987).C. Wickham, *Early Medieval Italy* (London, 1981).

J. Richards, *The Popes and the Papacy in the Early Middle Ages 476-752* (London, 1979).

P. A. B. Llewellyn, *Rome in the Dark Ages* (new edition, London, 1993).

T. F. X. Noble, *The Republic of St Peter: the Birth of the Papal State 680-825* (Philadelphia, 1984).

G. Cavallo and others, *I Bizantini in Italia* (Milan, 1982).

T. S. Brown, *Gentlemen and Officers. Imperial Administration and Aristocratic Power in Byzantine Italy, A.D. 554-800* (British School at Rome, 1984), with a very full bibliography, list of sources, and prosopographical index.

John F. Haldon, *Byzantium in the Seventh Century, the Transformation of a Culture* (revised edition, Cambridge, 1997).

E. Stein, 'Le période byzantine du papauté', in his *Opera minora selecta*, 501-535 (Amsterdam, 1968).

S. N. C. Lieu, *Manichaeism in the Later Roman Empire and Medieval China* (2nd edition, Tübingen 1992).

MODERN WORKS—SPECIFIC TOPICS

H. Chadwick, 'St Peter and St Paul in Rome: the problem of the memoria apostolorum ad catacumbas', *Journal of Theological Studies* n.s. 8 (1957), 31-52 (reprinted, H. Chadwick, *History and Thought of the Early Church*, 1982).

A. Amore, *I martiri di Roma* (Rome, 1975).H. Delehaye, *Les origines du culte des martyrs* (2nd edition, Brussels, 1933).

R. Davis, 'Pre-Constantinian Chronology: the Roman Bishopric from AD 258 to 314', *Journal of Theological Studies* n.s. 48 (1997), 439-470.

E. H. Röttges, 'Marcellinus-Marcellus', *Zeitschrift für Katholische Theologie* 78 (1956), 385-420.

A. Amore, 'Il preteso 'lapsus' di papa Marcellino', *Antonianum* 32 (1955), 411-426.

T. D. Barnes, *Constantine and Eusebius* (Harvard, 1981).

S. N. C. Lieu and Dominic Montserrat (edd.), *Constantine, History, Historiography and Legend* (London, 1998).

E. D. Hunt, *Holy Land Pilgrimage in the Later Roman Empire A.D. 312-460* (Oxford, 1982).

J. F. Matthews, *Western Aristocracies and Imperial Court A.D. 364-425* (Oxford, 1975; reprint 1998).

F. Marazzi, 'Le proprietà immobiliari della chiesa romana tra 4 e 8 secolo: reddito, struttura e gestione', *Le sol et l'immeuble* (Actes de la table ronde...Lyon 14-15 mai 1993), ed. O. Faron et E. Hubert, Collection de l'école française de Rome 206 (Lyon/Rome 1995), 151-168.

A. Lippold, 'Ursinus und Damasus', *Historia* 14 (1965), 105-128.

É. Demougeot, 'A propos des interventions du pape Innocent I dans la politique séculière', *Revue Historique* 212 (1954), 23-38.

W. Ullmann, 'Leo I and the theory of papal primacy', *Journal of Theological Studies* n.s. 11 (1960), 25-51.

P. Llewellyn, 'Le indicazioni numeriche del Liber Pontificalis relativamente alle ordinazioni del V secolo', *Rivista della storia della chiesa in Italia* 29 (1975), 439-443.

P. Wormald, 'The Decline of the Western Empire and the Survival of its Aristocracy', *Journal of Roman Studies* 66 (1976), 217-226.

G. B. Picotti, 'I sinodi romani nello scismo laurenziano', *Studi storici in onore di G. Volpe*, 2, 741-876 (Florence, 1958).

C. Pietri, 'Le sénat, le peuple chrétien et les partis du cirque sous le pape Symmaque (498-514)', *Mélanges d'Archéologie et d'Histoire de l'école française de Rome* 78 (1966), 122-139.

S. J. B. Barnish, 'The Anonymous Valesianus II as a source for the last years of Theoderic', *Latomus* 42 (1983), 572-596.

P. Goubert, 'Autour du voyage à Byzance du pape S. Jean I', *Orientalia Christiana Periodica* 24 (1958), 339-352.

M. T. Gibson (ed.), *Boethius: his life, thought and influence* (Oxford, 1981).

H. Chadwick, *Boethius: the Consolations of Music, Logic, Theology, and Philosophy* (Oxford, 1981; reprint 1998).

L. Duchesne, 'La succession du pape Félix IV', *Mélanges d'Archéologie et d'Histoire de l'école française de Rome* 3 (1883), 239-266.

A. Harnack, 'Der erste deutsche Papst, Bonifatius II, 530-532 und die beiden letzten Dekrete des römischen Senats', *Sitzungsberichte der Preussischen Akademie der Wissenschaften zu Berlin* 5 (1924), 24-42.

O. Bertolini, 'La fine del pontificato di papa Silverio', *Archivo della Reale società romana di storia patria* 47 (1924), 325-340.

L. Duchesne, 'Vigile et Pélage', *Revue des questions historiques* 36 (1884), 369-440; 37 (1885), 529-593.

E. Stein, 'La disparition du sénat de Rome à la fin du VIe siècle', in his *Opera minora selecta*, 359-384 (Amsterdam, 1968).

J. Richards, *Consul of God. The Life and Times of Gregory the Great* (London, 1980).

R. A. Markus, *Gregory the Great and his World* (Cambridge, 1997).

R. E. McNally, 'Gregory the Great (590-604) and his declining World', *Archivum Historiae Pontificiae* 16 (1978), 7-26.

P. A. B. Llewellyn, 'The Roman Church in the Seventh Century: the Legacy of Gregory I', *Journal of Ecclesiastical History* 25 (1974), 363-380.

B. Bavant, 'Le duché byzantin de Rome. Origine, durée et extension géographique', *Mélanges de l'école française de Rome, moyen âge* 91 (1979), 41-88.

T. S. Brown, 'The Church of Ravenna and the imperial administration in the seventh century', *English Historical Review* 94 (1979), 1-28.

P. A. B. Llewellyn, 'Constans II and the Roman Church: a possible instance of imperial pressure', *Byzantion* 46 (1976), 120-126.

J. Breckenridge, 'Evidence for the nature of relations between Pope John VII and the Byzantine Emperor Justinian II', *Byzantinische Zeitschrift* 65 (1972), 364-374.

S. Kuttner, 'Cardinalis; the history of a canonical concept', *Traditio* 3 (1945), 129-214.

C. G. Fürst, *Cardinalis: Prolegomena zu eine Rechtsgeschichte des römischen Kardinalskollegiums* (Munich, 1967).

MODERN WORKS—LEGENDARY AND FORGED MATERIAL

G. Fowden, 'The Last Days of Constantine: Oppositional Versions and their Influence', *Journal of Roman Studies* 84 (1994), 146-170 (for the legend of Constantine's baptism by Silvester).

H. Fuhrmann, 'Konstantinische Schenkung und Silvesterlegende in neuer Sicht', *Deutsches Archiv für Erforschung des Mittelalters* 15 (1959), 523-540.

R. J. Loenertz, 'Constitutum Constantini. Destination, destinataires, auteur, date', *Aevum* 48 (1974), 199-245.

E. Ewig, 'Das Bild Constantins des Grossen im abendländischen Mittelalter', *Historisches Jahrbuch* 75 (1956), 10-46.

W. T. Townsend, 'The so-called Symmachian Forgeries', *Journal of Religion* 13 (1933), 165-174.

W. Polnitz, 'Synodes apocryphes du pape Symmaque', *Revue d'histoire ecclésiastique* (1936), 81-88.

H. Fuhrmann, 'False Decretals', *New Catholic Encyclopedia* 5 (1967), 820-824.

MODERN WORKS—LITURGY AND RELATED MATTERS

J. A. Jungmann, *Missarum Sollemnia. The Mass of the Roman Rite: its origins and development* (English translation, new edition, London, 1959).

A. Chavasse, 'Les grands cadres de la célébration à Rome 'in urbe' et 'extra muros' jusqu'au VIIIe siècle', *Revue Bénédictine* 96 (1986), 7-26.

B. Capelle, 'Innocent I et le canon de la messe', *Recherches de théologie ancienne et médiévale* 19 (1952), 5-16.

E. Dekkers, 'Autour de l'oeuvre liturgique de S. Léon le Grand', *Sacris Erudiri* 10 (1958), 363-398.

B. Capelle, 'L'oeuvre liturgique de S. Gélase', *Journal of Theological Studies* n.s. 2 (1951), 129-144.

S. J. P. Van Dijk, 'Gregory the Great, founder of the urban *Schola Cantorum*', *Ephemerides Liturgicae* 77 (1963), 345-356.

MODERN WORKS—TOPOGRAPHY AND HISTORY

R. Thomsen, *The Italic Regions from Augustus to the Lombard Invasions* (Copenhagen, 1947).

F. Lanzoni, *Le diocesi d'Italia dalle origini al principio del secolo VII*, 2 volumes (2nd edition, Faenza, 1927).

G. and F. Tomassetti, *La Campagna romana antica, medioevale e moderna*, 4 volumes (Rome, 1913, revised edition by L. Chiumenti and F. Bilancia, Rome, 1975-1976).

A. Claridge, *Rome, an Oxford Archaeological Guide* (Oxford, 1998).

E. M. Steinby (ed.), *Lexicon Topographicum Urbis Romae* (Rome, 1993-1999; 4 volumes, covering A to S, have so far appeared).

S. B. Platner and T. Ashby, *A Topographical Dictionary of Ancient Rome* (Oxford, 1929).

R. Valentini, G. Zucchetti, *Codice topografico della città di Roma*, 4 volumes, R. Istituto storico italiano per il medio evo (Rome, 1940-1953).

R. Krautheimer, *Rome, Profile of a City, 312-1308* (Princeton, 1980).

R. Krautheimer, *Three Christian Capitals* (California, 1983).

L. Duchesne, *Scripta Minora, études de topographie romaine et de géographie ecclésiastique* (Rome, École française de Rome, 1973).

C. Pietri, 'Duchesne et la topographie romaine', *Monseigneur Duchesne et son temps, Actes du Colloque organisé par l'école française de Rome (23-25 mai 1973)*, Collection de l'école française de Rome 23 (1975), 23-48.

Robert Coates-Stephens, 'The Walls and Aqueducts of Rome in the Early Middle Ages, A.D. 500-1000', *Journal of Roman Studies* **88** (1998), 166-178.

MODERN WORKS—CHURCH FOUNDATIONS

R. Krautheimer, S. Corbett, W. Frankl, *Corpus Basilicarum Christianarum Romae. The Early Christian Basilicas of Rome (IV-IX Centuries)*, 5 volumes (Vatican City, 1937-1977). This work is fundamental on the early churches in Rome from the archaeological and literary points of view; volumes 1 to 4 cover most of the buildings in the alphabetical order of their Italian names, volume 5 deals with the Lateran (but not the Baptistery), St Paul's and St Peter's. The volumes contain very full bibliographies to the date of publication, which may be partly updated from the following:

R. Krautheimer, *Early Christian and Byzantine Architecture* (4th edition, London, 1986).

C. L. Striker (ed.), *Architectural Studies in memory of Richard Krautheimer* (Mainz, 1996).

M. Armellini (ed. 3 by C. Cecchelli), *Le Chiese di Roma dal secolo IV al XIX*, 2 volumes (Rome, 1942; there is also a 1982 reprint of Armellini's 2nd edition, 1891).

C. Hülsen, *Le Chiese di Roma nel medio evo* (Florence, 1927).

F. Mancinelli, *Catacombs and Basilicas. The Early Christians in Rome* (Florence, 1984).

F. W. Deichmann, 'Märtyrerbasilika, Martyrion, Memoria und Altargrab', *Römische Mitteilungen* 77 (1970), 144-169.

G. Ferrari, *Early Roman Monasteries. Notes for the history of the monasteries and convents at Rome from the V through the X century*, Studi di antichità cristiana 23 (Vatican, 1957).

E. Ferguson with D. M. Scholer and P. C. Finney (edd.), *Studies in Early Christianity, a collection of scholarly essays*, vol. XVIII (ed. P. C. Finney), *Art, Archeology, and Architecture of Early Christianity* (New York, 1993), reprints a number of interesting pieces.

H. Geertman, *More Veterum, Il Liber Pontificalis e gli edifici ecclesiastici di Roma nella tarda antichità e nell'alto medioevo*, Archaeologia Traiectina 10 (Groningen, 1975; also published in Dutch).

S. S. Alexander, 'Studies in Constantinian Church Architecture', *Rivista di archeologia cristiana* 47 (1971), 281-330.

M. T. Smith, 'The Lateran Fastigium: a gift of Constantine the Great', *Rivista di archeologia cristiana* 46 (1970), 149-175.

P. Liverani, 'Le colonne e il capitello in bronzo d'età romana dell'altare del SS. Sacramento in Laterano, analisi archeologica e problematica storica', *Atti della pontificia accademia romana di archeologia, Rendiconti* 65 (1992-1993 [ed. 1995]), 75-99.

T. F. Mathews, 'An early Roman chancel arrangement and its liturgical uses', *Rivista di archeologia cristiana* 38 (1962), 71-95.

G. Pelliccioni, *Le nuove scoperte sulle origini del Battistero Lateranense*, Atti della pontificia accademia romana di archeologia, serie 3, memorie XII.1 (Rome, 1973).

J. Toynbee and J. Ward Perkins, *The Shrine of St Peter* (London and New York, 1956).

E. Kirschbaum, *The Tombs of St Peter and St Paul* (London, 1959).

J. B. Ward Perkins, 'The Shrine of St Peter and its Twelve Spiral Columns', *Journal of Roman Studies* 42 (1952), 21-33.

R. Krautheimer, 'A note on the inscription in the apse of Old St Peter's', *Dumbarton Oaks Papers* 41 (1987), 317-320.

J.-C. Picard, 'Le quadriportique de Saint-Pierre-du-Vatican', *Mélanges de l'école française de Rome, antiquité* 86 (1974), 851-890.

J.-C. Picard, 'Le quadriportique de Saint-Paul-hors-les-murs à Rome', *ibid.* 87 (1975), 377-395.

A. P. Frutaz, *Il complesso monumentale di Sant'Agnese* (5th edition, Rome, 1992).

H. Stern, 'Les mosaiques de Sainte-Constance', *Dumbarton Oaks Papers* 12 (1958), 159-218.

F. W. Deichmann and A. Tschira, 'Das Mausoleum des Kaierin Helena und die Basilika der Heiligen Marcellinus und Petrus an der Via Labicana vor Rom', *Jahrbuch des Deutschen Archäologischen Instituts* 72 (1957), 44-110.

J. Guyon, L. Strüber and D. Manacorda, 'Recherches autour de la basilique constantinienne des saints Pierre et Marcellin sur la via Labicana à Rome: le mausolée et l'enclos au nord de la basilique', *Mélanges de l'école française de Rome, antiquité* 93 (1981), 999-1056.

G. N. Verrando 'L'attività edilizia di papa Giulio I e la basilica al III miglio della via Aurelia ad Callistum', *Mélanges de l'école française de Rome, antiquité* 97 (1985), 1021-1061.

C. Ceschi, *S. Stefano Rotondo*, Atti della pontificia accademia romana di archeologia, serie 3, memorie 15 (Rome, 1982).

G. McN. Rushforth, 'S. Maria Antiqua', *Papers of the British School at Rome* 1 (1902), 1-123.

P. J. Nordhagen, *The Frescoes of John VII in S Maria Antiqua* (Rome, 1968).

U. Broccoli, 'Ostia Antica, S. Aurea, Gregoriopoli: spigolature sulle vicende di Ostia dalla tarda antichità all'alto medio evo', *Lunario Romano XII: Il Lazio nell'antichità romana*, ed. R. Lefevre (Rome, 1982).

E. Champlin, 'St Gallicanus (consul 317)', *Phoenix* 36 (1982), 71-76.

M. Pagano et J. Rougetet, 'Il Battistero della basilica costantiniana di Capua (cosidetto *Catabulum*)', *Mélanges de l'école française de Rome, antiquité* 96 (1984), 987-1016.

R. di Stephano, *La cattedrale di Napoli. Storia, Restauro, Scoperti, Ritrovamenti* (2nd edition, Naples, 1975).

Akten des XII internationalen Kongresses für christliche Archäologie, Bonn 22-28 Sept. 1991, edd. E. Dassmann, J. Engemann, 3 volumes (Jahrbuch für Antike und Christentum, Ergänzungsband 20; Studi di antichità cristiana 52; Münster/Vatican, 1995-1997), contains valuable contributions. Note particularly:

A. Bonanni, 'La basilica di S. Susanna a Roma: indagini topografiche e nuove scoperte archeologiche', 586-589; É. Ó Carragáin, 'Rome

Pilgrimage, Roman Liturgy, and the Ruthwell Cross', 630-639; M. Cecchelli, 'La basilica di San Marco a Piazza Venezia (Roma), Nuove scoperte e indagini', 640-644; L. Cuppo Csaki, 'La catacomba di S. Domitilla come centro di culto e pellegrinaggio nel sesto secolo ed alto medioevo', 658-662; S. Episcopo, 'La basilica di S. Marcello al Corso a Roma: nuove scoperte', 734-740; V. Fiocchi Nicolai, "Itinera ad sanctos', Testimonianze monumentali dal passaggio dei pellegrini nei santuari del suburbio romano', 763-775; idem, 'Una nuova basilica a deambulatorio nel comprensorio della catacomba di S. Callisto a Roma', 776-786 (for the basilica of pope Mark located in 1991); P. Pensabene, 'Reimpiego e nuove mode architettoniche nelle basiliche cristiane di Roma tra IV e VI secolo', 1076-1096.

THE BOOK OF PONTIFFS

(*Liber Pontificalis*)

From Jerome to the most blessed pope Damasus.

I humbly beg your glorious holiness to [assist me] with the [authority] of the apostolic see which I know your holiness rules. My respectful prayer is that you oblige me with an orderly account of the history enacted in your see from the reign of the apostle St Peter down to your own time, so that in humility I may learn which of the bishops of your see deserved the crown of martyrdom and which of them is reckoned to have transgressed against the canons of the apostles. Pray for me, most blessed pope.

From Damasus bishop of Rome to <the priest> Jerome.

The church is pleased that it is already fully supplied with what you have produced, and the interest which *sacerdotes* show in the past causes an even deeper thirst to learn what is worthwhile and reject what is not. It is with pleasure and devotion to my see that I send you, dear friend, what I have been able to find out about its history. Pray for me that I may share the holy resurrection, my brother and fellow priest. Farewell in Christ our Lord God.

Dated 23 May. Received 26 September. Sent from Rome to Jerusalem.

1. **1.** ST PETER [- 64/67], the apostle and prince of apostles, an Antiochene, the son of John, from the village of Bethsaida in the province of Galilee, the brother of Andrew, first occupied the episcopal *cathedra* at Antioch for seven years. Peter went to Rome when Nero was Caesar and there he occupied the episcopal *cathedra* 25 years 2 months 3 days. He was bishop in the time of Tiberius Caesar, Gaius, Tiberius Claudius, and Nero. **2.** He wrote two epistles called catholic, and Mark's gospel— because Mark was his hearer, and his son by baptism; later he was the complete source of the four gospels—when he was questioned, Peter confirmed them by his testimony. Whether in Greek, Hebrew or Latin, they are in agreement, and it was by his testimony they were confirmed. **3.** He ordained two bishops, Linus and Cletus, to be present in Rome to

provide the entire sacerdotal ministry for the people and for visitors; while Peter himself was free to pray and preach, to teach the people. **4.** He held many debates with Simon Magus, both before the emperor Nero and before the people, because Simon was using magical tricks and deceptions to scatter those whom Peter had gathered into Christ's faith. When their disputes had lasted a long time, Simon was struck down by God's will. **5.** He consecrated St Clement as bishop and entrusted the *cathedra* and the whole management of the church to him, saying: 'As the power of government, that of binding and loosing, was handed to me by my Lord Jesus Christ, so I entrust it to you; ordain those who are to deal with various cases and execute the church's affairs; do not be caught up in the cares of the world but ensure you are completely free for prayer and preaching to the people'.

6. After making this arrangement he was crowned with martyrdom along with Paul in the 38th year after the Lord suffered. He was buried on the Via Aurelia at the temple of Apollo, close to the place where he was crucified, and to Nero's palace on the Vatican, and to the Triumphal territory, on 29 June. He performed December ordinations, 3 bishops, 10 priests, 7 deacons. <He was the first to lay down that mass be celebrated to commemorate the Lord's passion in bread and wine mixed with water, using only the Lord's prayer and hallowing with the holy cross; this the other holy apostles copied when celebrating it.>

2. **1.** LINUS [c. 70], born in Italy, from the region of Etruria, son of Herculanus, held the see 11 years 3 months 12 days. He was bishop in the time of Nero from the consulship of Saturninus and Scipio [56] to that of Capito and Rufus [67]. He was crowned with martyrdom. **2.** On St Peter's instruction he decreed that a woman should have her head covered when entering church. He performed two ordinations, 15 bishops, 18 priests. He was buried close to St Peter's body on the Vatican on 23 September.

3. **1.** CLETUS [Anencletus, c. 85], born in Rome, from the region Vicus Patricius, son of Aemilianus, held the see 12 years 1 month 11 days. He was bishop in the time of Vespasian and Titus from the 7th consulship of Vespasian [76] and the 5th of Domitian [77] to the 9th of Domitian and that of Rufus [83]. He was crowned with martyrdom. **2.** On St Peter's instruction he ordained 25 priests in Rome <in December>. He was buried close to St Peter's body on the Vatican on 26 April. The bishopric was vacant 20 days.

4. **1.** CLEMENT [c. 95], born in Rome, from the region of the Caelian Hill, son of Faustinus, held the see 9 years 2 months 10 days. He was bishop in the time of Galba and Vespasian from the consulship of Trachalus and Italicus [68] to the 9th of Vespasian and that of Titus [79]. After writing many books in his devotion to the faith of Christianity, he was crowned with martyrdom. **2.** He created the seven regions, dividing them among notaries faithful to the church so that each of them in his own region could concern himself with careful and diligent investigation into the acts of the martyrs. He produced two epistles called catholic. **3.** On St Peter's instruction he undertook the pontificate for governing the church, as the *cathedra* had been handed down and entrusted to him by the Lord Jesus Christ; you will find in the letter written to James how the church was entrusted to him by Peter. Hence Linus and Cletus are recorded before him because they were ordained bishops to provide the sacerdotal ministry by the prince of the apostles himself. **4.** He performed two December ordinations, 10 priests, 2 deacons; for various places 15 bishops. He died a martyr in the third of Trajan [100]. He was buried in Greece on 24 November. The bishopric was vacant 21 days.

5. **1.** ANECLITUS [same as no. 3], born in Greece, from Athens, son of Antiochus, held the see 9 years 2 months 10 days. He was bishop in the time of Domitian from the 10th consulship of Domitian and Sabinus [84] to the 17th of Domitian and that of Clemens [95]. **2.** He constructed and arranged the memorial of St Peter, as it was by St Peter he had been made a priest, and also other burial places where the bishops could be laid; there he too was buried close to St Peter's body on 13 July. **3.** He performed two December ordinations, 5 priests, 3 deacons; for various places 6 bishops. The bishopric was vacant 13 days.

6. **1.** EVARISTUS [c. 100], born in Greece, son of a Jew named Judas from the city of Bethlehem, held the see 9 years 10 months 2 days. He was bishop in the time of Domitian and Nerva Trajan from the consulship of Valens and Vetus [96] to that of Gallus and Bradua [108]. He was crowned with martyrdom. **2.** He divided the *tituli* in Rome among the priests and ordained 7 deacons to watch over the bishop when reciting [mass] and safeguard the expression of the truth. **3.** He performed three December ordinations, 17 priests, 2 deacons; for various places 15 bishops. He was buried close to St Peter's body on the Vatican on 27

October. The bishopric was vacant 19 days.

7. **1.** ALEXANDER [c. 110], born in Rome, son of Alexander, from the region of Caput Tauri, held the see 10 years 7 months 2 days. He was bishop in the time of Trajan to the consulship of Aelianus and Vetus [116]. **2.** He inserted the Lord's Passion into what *sacerdotes* recite when mass is celebrated. He was crowned with martyrdom; with him were the priest Eventius and the deacon Theodulus. He decreed that water should be blessed with salt for sprinkling in the dwellings of the people. **3.** He performed three December ordinations, 6 priests, 2 deacons; for various places 5 bishops. He was buried on the Via Nomentana where he was beheaded, not far from Rome, at the 7th mile, on 3 May. The bishopric was vacant 35 days.

8. **1.** XYSTUS [I; c. 120], born in Rome, son of Pastor, from the region Via Lata, held the see 10 years 2 months 1 day. He was bishop in the time of Hadrian to the consulship of Verus and Anniculus [Ambibulus, 126]. He was crowned with martyrdom. **2.** He decreed that objects consecrated for the ministry should be touched by ministers only. He decreed that any bishop summoned to the apostolic see should not be received on his return to his own *paroecia* unless he had the letter called a *formata* from the apostolic see to greet the people. <He decreed that within the performance [of mass], with the priest beginning it, the people should sing the hymn 'Holy, holy, holy Lord God Sabaoth et cetera'.> **3.** He performed three December ordinations, 11 priests, 4 deacons; for various places 4 bishops. He was buried close to St Peter's body on the Vatican on 3 April. The bishopric was vacant 2 months.

9. **1.** TELESPHORUS [c. 130], born in Greece, a former anchorite, held the see 11 years 3 months 21 days. He was bishop in the time of Antoninus and Marcus. **2.** He decreed that a fast of seven weeks should be observed before Easter and that mass should be celebrated at night on the Lord's birthday <and the angelic hymn be sung>—for normally no one would presume to celebrate mass before the office of the third hour, the time that our Lord went up on the cross; and that the angels' hymn (that is, Glory be to God on high) should be sung before the sacrifice. He was crowned with martyrdom. He was buried close to St Peter's body on the Vatican on 2 January. **3.** He performed four December ordinations, 12

priests, 8 deacons; for various places 13 bishops. The bishopric was vacant 7 days.

10. **1.** HYGINUS [c. 140], born in Greece, a former philosopher, from Athens, whose ancestry I have not traced, held the see 4 years 3 months 4 days. He was bishop in the time of Verus and Marcus from the consulship of Magnus [Niger] and Camerinus [138] to that of Orfitus and Priscus [149]. **2.** He organized the clergy and allotted the ranks. He performed three December ordinations, 15 priests, 5 deacons; for various places 6 bishops. He was buried close to St Peter's body on the Vatican on 11 January. The bishopric was vacant 3 days.

11. **1.** PIUS [c. 145], born in Italy, son of Rufinus, brother of Pastor, from the city of Aquileia, held the see 19 years 4 months 3 days. He was bishop in the time of Antoninus Pius, from the consulship of Clarus and Severus [146]. **2.** In his episcopacy, Hermas wrote a book in which he includes the order that an angel of the Lord imposed on him when he came to him in shepherd's apparel, and instructed him that <holy> Easter be celebrated on a Lord's day. **3.** He decreed that a heretic coming from the heresy of the Jews should be received and baptized. He issued a decree about the church. <**4.** At the request of blessed Praxedes he dedicated a church at the baths of Novatus on the Vicus Patricius in honour of her sister St Pudentiana; there he presented many gifts and often used to minister, offering sacrifice to the Lord. In addition he had a font constructed for baptism and blessed and consecrated it with his own hand; many who came to the faith he baptized in the name of the Trinity.> **5.** He performed five December ordinations, 19 priests, 21 deacons; for various places 12 bishops. He was buried close to St Peter's body on the Vatican on 11 July. The bishopric was vacant 14 days.

12. **1.** ANICETUS [c. 160], born in Syria, son of John, from the village of Umisa [Emesa?], held the see 11 years 4 months 3 days. He was bishop in the time of Severus [Verus] and Marcus from the consulship of Gallicanus and Vetus [150] to that of Praesens and Rufinus [153]. **2.** He decreed that, as the apostle had instructed, a cleric should not groom his hair. He performed five December ordinations, 19 priests, 4 deacons; for various places 9 bishops. He died a martyr and was buried in the cemetery of Callistus on 20 April. The bishopric was vacant 17 days.

13. **1.** SOTER [c. 170], born in Campania, son of Concordius, from the city of Fundi, held the see 9 years 6 months 21 days. He was bishop in the time of Severus [Verus] from the consulship of Rusticus and Aquilinus [162] to that of Cethegus and Clarus [170]. **2.** He decreed that no monk should touch the consecrated pall or place the incense in the holy church. **3.** He performed three December ordinations, 18 priests, 9 deacons; for various places 11 bishops. He was buried in the cemetery of Callistus on the Via Appia on 22 April. The bishopric was vacant 21 days.

14. **1.** ELEUTHER [c. 180], born in Greece, son of Abundius, from the town of Nicopolis, held the see 15 years 3 months 2 days. He was bishop in the time of Antoninus and Commodus to the [consulship] of Paternus [Maternus] and Bradua [185]. **2.** He received a letter from Lucius, a British king, who wanted to become a Christian at his order. He confirmed again that no <common> food that God had created should be shunned by even the most faithful Christians, which is reasonable and merciful. **3.** He performed three December ordinations, 12 priests, 8 deacons; for various places 15 bishops. He was buried close to St Peter's body on the Vatican on 24 May. The bishopric was vacant 15 days.

15. **1.** VICTOR [c. 195], born in Africa, son of Felix, held the see 10 years 2 months 10 days. He was bishop in the time of Caesar Augustus from the 5th consulship of Commodus and that of Gravio [Glabrio, 186] to that of Lateranus and Rufinus [197]. **2.** He decreed like Eleuther that the holy Easter should be celebrated on a Lord's Day. He made the acolytes clerics. He was crowned with martyrdom. He decreed that in case of necessity anyone coming from paganism might be baptized wherever he happened to be, whether in a river or in the sea or in springs, provided only that his confession of faith as a Christian was delivered clearly. **4ª.** He performed two December ordinations, 4 priests, 7 deacons; for various places 12 bishops. **3.** When *sacerdotes* had questioned him on the cycle of Easter, he issued a decree that the Lord's day of Easter...after a discussion with priests and bishops and after holding an assembly to which Theophilus bishop of Alexandria had been invited, that the holy Easter should be kept on the Lord's day from the 14th to the 21st day of the first lunar month. **4ᵇ.** He was buried close to the body of the apostle St Peter on the Vatican on 28 July. The bishopric was vacant 12 days.

16. **1.** ZEPHYRINUS [198/199 - 217], born in Rome, son of Abundius, held the see 8 years 7 months 10 days. He was bishop in the time of Antoninus and Severus from the consulship of Saturninus and Gallicanus [Gallus, 198] to that of Praesens and Extricatus [217]. **2.** He decreed that the ordination of a cleric, deacon or *sacerdos* should take place in the presence of all the clerics and the faithful laity. He issued a decree about the church, and that glass patens <should be held> in front of the *sacerdotes* in church, and that ministers <should hold them while the bishop> celebrates <mass> with the *sacerdotes* standing in front of him; that mass should be celebrated in this way, and that the clergy should remain present for the whole of it, subject only to the bishop having the right [to dispense them]; and that from what is consecrated a priest should receive from the bishop's hand an already consecrated ring to give to the people. **3.** He performed four December ordinations, 14 priests, 7 deacons; for various places 13 bishops. He was buried in his own cemetery close to the cemetery of Callistus on the Via Appia on 25 August. The bishopric was vacant 6 days.

17. **1.** CALLISTUS [217 - 14. 10. 222], born in Rome, son of Domitius, from the region Urbs Ravennatium, held the see 6 years 2 months 10 days. He was bishop in the time of Macrinus and Theodoliobollus from the consulship of Antoninus [218] and of Alexander [222]. He was crowned with martyrdom. **2.** He decreed that on Saturdays three times a year <in the fourth, seventh and tenth months> there should be a fast from corn, wine and oil according to the prophecy. **3.** He built the basilica across the Tiber. **4.** He performed five December ordinations, 16 priests, 4 deacons; for various places 8 bishops. He was buried in the cemetery of Calepodius on the Via Aurelia at the 3rd mile on 14 October. He built another cemetery on the Via Appia, where many *sacerdotes* and martyrs lie at rest; even to this day it is called the cemetery of Callistus. The bishopric was vacant 16 days.

18. **1.** URBAN [222 - 19. 5. 230], born in Rome, son of Pontian, held the see 4 years 10 months 12 days. **2.** He caused all the objects consecrated for the ministry to be of silver and provided 25 silver patens. He was a distinguished confessor in the time of Diocletian. **3.** By the teaching he passed on he converted many to baptism and the faith, including the most noble Valerian, husband of St Caecilia, and he also led them to the palm

of martyrdom; and through his encouragement many were crowned with martyrdom. **4.** He performed five December ordinations, 19 priests, 7 deacons; for various places 8 bishops. He was buried in the cemetery of Praetextatus on the Via Appia—St Tiburtius buried him—on 19 May. The bishopric was vacant 30 days.

19. 1. PONTIAN [230 - 28. 9. 235], born in Rome, son of Calpurnius, held the see 9 years 5 months 2 days. He was crowned with martyrdom. He was bishop in the time of Alexander from the consulship of Pompeianus and Paelignianus [231]. **2.** Then Pontian the bishop and Hippolytus the priest were carried off into exile by Alexander to Sardinia, the island Bucina, in the consulship of Severus and Quintianus [235]. In that island he suffered, was beaten with clubs and died on 30 October; in his place Anteros was ordained on 21 November. **3.** He performed two December ordinations, 6 priests, 5 deacons; for various places 6 bishops. St Fabian and the clergy brought him by ship and buried him in the cemetery of Callistus on the Via Appia. The bishopric was vacant 10 days <from the day of his burial>.

20. 1. ANTEROS [22. 11. 235 - 3. 1. 236], born in Greece, son of Romulus, held the see 12 years 1 month 12 days. He was crowned with martyrdom in the time of the consuls Maximinus and Africanus [236]. **2.** He carefully sought out the acts of the martyrs from the notaries and deposited them in the church, because of a certain priest Maximinus, who was crowned with martyrdom. **3.** He made one bishop in the Campanian city of Fundi in December. He was buried in the cemetery of Callistus on the Via Appia on 3 January. The bishopric was vacant 13 days.

21. 1. FABIAN [10. 1. 236 - 20. 1. 250], born in Rome, son of Fabius, held the see 14 years 11 months 11 days. He was crowned with martyrdom. He was bishop in the time of Maximus [Maximinus] and Africanus [236] to the 2nd of Decius and that of Quadratus [Gratus, 250]; **3[a].** he suffered on 19 January. **2.** He divided the regions among the deacons and created 7 subdeacons who were to watch over the 7 notaries so they would faithfully collect the complete acts of the martyrs. He ordered many works to be carried out in the cemeteries. **3[b].** After his passion the priests Moyses and Maximus and the deacon Nicostratus were arrested and put in prison. **4.** Then Novatus came over from Africa and separated Novatian and some of the confessors from the church after Moyses had died in prison—he was there 11 months; so it was that many Christians fled <to various places>. **5.** He performed five December ordinations, 22 priests, 7 deacons; for various places 11 bishops. He was buried in the cemetery of Callistus on the Via Appia on 20 January. The bishopric was vacant 7 days.

22. 1. CORNELIUS [251 - 253], born in Rome, son of Castinus, held the see 2 years 2 months 3 days. He was crowned with martyrdom. **2.** In his episcopacy Novatus ordained Novatian outside the church, and also Nicostratus in Africa. When this happened the confessors who had separated from Cornelius with the priest Maximus—the one who was with Moyses—returned to the church and became faithful confessors. **3.** After this, bishop Cornelius was expelled to Centumcellae where he received a letter sent by Cyprian; Cyprian wrote it in prison to strengthen him <for martyrdom> and tell him about the reader Celerinus.

4. In his time, at the request of a certain lady Lucina, he took up the bodies of the apostles Saints Peter and Paul from the Catacombs at night; in fact first of all the blessed Lucina took the body of St Paul and put it on her estate on the Via Ostiensis close to the place where he was beheaded; the blessed bishop Cornelius took the body of St Peter and put it close to the place where he was crucified, among the bodies of the holy bishops at the temple of Apollo on the Mons Aureus, on the Vatican at Nero's palace, on 29 June.

After this he travelled by night to Centumcellae. **5.** Decius then heard that he had received a letter from St Cyprian bishop of Carthage. He sent to Centumcellae and brought out the blessed bishop Cornelius, and ordered him to be brought before him and the prefect of the city by night at Tellus in front of the temple of Pallas. He went up to him and said: 'Have you decided to pay no heed to the gods, and not to fear the instructions of our ancestors or our threats, that you receive and send letters against the state?' Bishop Cornelius replied: 'I have received letters about the Lord's crown, not against the state, but rather with spiritual advice for redeeming souls'. **6.** Then Decius filled with anger ordered that St Cornelius' mouth be beaten with lead-weighted lashes, and that he be taken to the temple of Mars to adore there, saying that if he did not do it he would be beheaded. And so it happened: he was beheaded in that place and became a martyr. The blessed Lucina along with the clergy collected his body at night and buried him in the crypt close to the cemetery of

Callistus on the Via Appia on her estate, on 14 September. **7.** The bishopric was vacant 66 days.

23. 1. LUCIUS [26. 6. 253 - 5. 3. 254], born in Rome, son of Porphyrius, held the see 3 years 3 months 3 days. He was crowned with martyrdom. He was bishop in the time of Gallus and Volusian [252] to the 3rd of Valerian and that of Gallicanus [Gallienus, 255]. **2.** He was exiled. Later by God's will he returned safe to the church. **3.** He laid down that 2 priests and 3 deacons should not leave the bishop, wherever he was, to be witnesses on the church's behalf. He was beheaded by Valerian on 5 March. **4.** He gave power over the whole church to his archdeacon Stephen while on the way to his passion. **5.** He performed two December ordinations, 4 priests, 4 deacons; for various places 7 bishops. He was buried in the cemetery of Callistus <in the *arenaria*> on the Via Appia on 25 August. The bishopric was vacant 35 days.

24. 1. STEPHEN [I; May 254 - 2. 8. 257], born in Rome, son of Jovius, held the see 6 years 5 months 2 days. He was crowned with martyrdom. He was bishop in the time of Valerian and Gallicanus [Gallienus], and Maximus [253], to the 3rd of Valerian and 2nd of Gallicanus [Gallienus, 255]. <**2.** In his time he was sent into exile; later by God's will he returned safe to the church. After 34 days he was arrested by Maximian and put in prison with 9 priests, 2 bishops, Honorius and Castus, and 3 deacons, Xystus, Dionysius, and Gaius. There in prison at the Arcus Stillans he held a synod and placed all the church vessels and the money chest in the control of his archdeacon Xystus. After 6 days he came out under guard and was beheaded.> **3.** He decreed that *sacerdotes* and deacons should not use the consecrated vestments for everyday purposes but only in church. **4.** He performed two December ordinations, 6 priests, 5 deacons; for various places 3 bishops. He was buried in the cemetery of Callistus on the Via Appia on 2 August. The bishopric was vacant 22 days.

25. 1. XYSTUS [II; 30. 8. 257 - 6. 8. 258], born in Greece, formerly a philosopher, held the see 1 year 10 months 23 days. He was crowned with martyrdom. He was bishop in the time of Valerian and Decius, when there was a very great persecution. **2.** Then he was arrested by Valerian and taken to sacrifice to demons. He spurned Valerian's instructions. He was beheaded, and with him six others, the deacons Felicissimus and Agapitus, Januarius, Magnus, Vincent, and Stephen, on 6 August. The priests were in charge from the 2nd consulship of Maximus and Gravio [Glabrio, 256] to that of Tuscus and Bassus [258], from the consulship of Tuscus and Bassus to 20 July, **3.** while there was a great persecution under Decius. After the passion of blessed Xystus, three days later his archdeacon St Laurence suffered on 10 August, with Claudius the subdeacon, Severus the priest, Crescentius the reader, and Romanus the doorkeeper. **4.** He performed two December ordinations, 4 priests, 7 deacons; for various places 2 bishops. He was buried in the cemetery of Callistus on the Via Appia, while the six above-named deacons were buried in the cemetery of Praetextatus on the Via Appia <on 6 August>; whereas St Laurence was buried <on the Via Tiburtina> in the cemetery of Cyriaces on the Ager Veranus in the crypt with many other martyrs <on 10 August>. The bishopric was vacant 35 days.

26. 1. DIONYSIUS [22. 7. 260 - 26. 12. 267], a former monk, whose ancestry we have been unable to trace, held the see 6 years 2 months 4 days. He was bishop in the time of Gallienus from 22 July in the consulship of Aemilianus and Bassus [259] to 26 December in the consulship of Claudius and Paternus [269]. **2.** He gave the churches to the priests and organized the cemeteries and parishes as dioceses. **3.** He performed two December ordinations, 12 priests, 6 deacons; for various places 8 bishops. He was buried in the cemetery of Callistus on the Via Appia on 27 December. The bishopric was vacant 5 days.

27. 1. FELIX [I; 5. 1. 268 - 30. 12. 273], born in Rome, son of Constantius, held the see 4 years 3 months 25 days. He was crowned with martyrdom. He was bishop in the time of Claudius and Aurelian, from the consulship of Claudius and Paternus [269] to that of Aurelian and Capitolinus [274]. **2ª.** He decreed that mass be celebrated over the memorials of martyrs. **3ª.** He performed two December ordinations, 9 priests, 5 deacons; for various places 5 bishops. **2ᵇ.** He built a basilica on the Via Aurelia, where he was buried on 30 May, at the 2nd mile from Rome. **3ᵇ.** The bishopric was vacant 5 days.

28. 1. EUTYCHIAN [4. 1. 274 - 7. 12. 282], born in Tuscia, son of Marinus, from the city of Luna, held the see 1 year 1 month 1 day. He was bishop in the time of Aurelian, from the 3rd consulship of Aurelian and that of Marcellinus [275] to 13 December in the 2nd of Carus and that of

Carinus [283]. **2.** He decreed that the only produce to be blessed on the altar should be beans and grapes. In his time he buried 342 martyrs in various places with his own hands. He also decreed that any of the faithful who buried a martyr should never do so without wearing a dalmatic or a purple cloak—it had been brought to his notice that this was happening. **3.** He performed five December ordinations, 14 priests, 5 deacons; for various places 9 bishops. He was crowned with martyrdom. He was buried in the cemetery of Callistus on the Via Appia on 25 July. The bishopric was vacant 8 days.

29. 1. GAIUS [17. 12. 282 - 22. 4. 295], born in Dalmatia of the family of the emperor Diocletian, son of Gaius, held the see 11 years 4 months 12 days. He was bishop in the time of <Carus and> Carinus, from 17 December in the 2nd consulship of Carus and that of Carinus [283] to 22 April in the 4th [6th] of Diocletian and 2nd of Constantius [296]. **2.** He decreed that advancement through the orders in the church should be as follows: anyone who might deserve to be a bishop should be doorkeeper, reader, exorcist, acolyte, subdeacon, deacon, priest, and then be ordained bishop. **3.** He divided the regions among the deacons. Fleeing from the persecution of Diocletian he lived in the crypts and was crowned with martyrdom 8 years later. **4.** He performed four December ordinations, 25 priests, 8 deacons; for various places 5 bishops. After 11 years he was crowned with martyrdom, with his brother Gabinius the priest, on account of Gabinius' daughter named Susanna. He was buried in the cemetery of Callistus on the Via Appia on 22 April. The bishopric was vacant 11 days.

30. 1. MARCELLINUS [30. 6. 295 - autumn 303], born in Rome, son of Projectus, held the see 9 years 4 months 16 days. He was bishop in the time of Diocletian and Maximian, from 1 July in the 6th consulship of Diocletian and 2nd of Constantius [296] to the 9th of Diocletian and 8th of Maximian [304], **2.** when there was so great a persecution that within 30 days 17,000 persons of both sexes were crowned with martyrdom as Christians in various provinces. This was why Marcellinus also was taken to sacrifice, to offer incense, which he did. **3.** After a few days <when a synod was held in the province of Campania at the city of Suessa [Sinuessa], he repented out of his own mouth before 180 bishops, being clothed in a hairshirt and with ash on his head, and did penance saying he had sinned. Then Dioletian in anger arrested him and forced him to sacrifice to idols. But he cried out tearfully saying: 'I greatly repent of my former ignorance'. And he began to

blaspheme Diocletian and the idols of demons that were made by hand. So>
overcome with repentance, along with Claudius, Cyrinus, and Antoninus,
he was beheaded and crowned with martyrdom by Diocletian. While he
was proceeding to his passion, blessed Marcellinus made the priest
Marcellus swear not to fulfil Diocletian's orders. **4.** After this the holy
bodies lay in the street for 25 days at Diocletian's command as an
example to the Christians. Then the priest Marcellus with priests and
deacons brought the bodies together at night with hymns, and buried them
on the Via Salaria in the cemetery of Priscilla in the chamber which is still
open today, as he had ordered when he repented and was being taken to
his death, in the crypt close to the body of St Crescentio, on 25 April. **5.**
He performed two December ordinations, 4 priests, 2 deacons; for various
places 5 bishops. From that day the bishopric was vacant 7 years 6 months
25 days while Diocletian was persecuting Christians.

31. MARCELLUS [305/306; exiled 306/307], born in Rome, son of
Benedict, from the region Via Lata, held the see 5 years 7 months 21 days.
He was bishop in the time of Maxentius from the 4th consulship of
Maxentius and that of Maximus until the post-consulship [309]. **2.** He
<requested a certain lady named Priscilla and> built the cemetery <of Novella>
on the Via Salaria, and organized the 25 *tituli* within Rome as dioceses for
the baptism and repentance of many converts from paganism, and for the
burial of martyrs. **6ᵃ.** He ordained 25 priests in Rome and 2 deacons, in
December; for various places 21 bishops. **3.** He was caught and held
because he made arrangements for the church, and arrested by Maxentius
to deny he was a bishop and be brought low by sacrificing to demons. He
kept despising and spurning the pronouncements and instructions of
Maxentius, and was condemned to the Catabulum. While he was a slave
for many days in the Catabulum, he did not fail to serve the Lord with
prayers and fasting. But in the ninth month his entire clergy came and
rescued him from the Catabulum at night. **4.** A certain lady named Lucina,
a widow, who had lived with her husband Marcus 15 years and had been
19 years in her widowhood, received the blessed man; she dedicated her
house as a *titulus* in the name of blessed Marcellus and there she
confessed the Lord Jesus Christ by day and night with hymns and prayers.
5. Hearing this, Maxentius sent and rearrested the blessed Marcellus, and
ordered boards to be relaid in that church, the animals of the Catabulum to
be gathered there, and blessed Marcellus to be at their service. Naked but
for a hairshirt, he died in servitude to animals. The blessed Lucina

collected his body and buried it in the cemetery of Priscilla on the Via Salaria on 16 January. **6**[b]. The bishopric was vacant 20 days. As for Lucina, she was condemned by a writ.

32. 1. EUSEBIUS [18. 4. 308; exiled Sept. 308], born in Greece, formerly a doctor, held the see 6 years 1 month 3 days. He was bishop in the time of Constans. **2.** In his time the cross of our Lord Jesus Christ was discovered on 3 May, and Judas, known also as Cyriac, was baptized. He found heretics in Rome and reconciled them by the laying on of hands. **3.** He performed one December ordination, 13 priests, 3 deacons; for various places 14 bishops. He was buried <in the crypt> in the cemetery of Callistus on the Via Appia on 2 October. The bishopric was vacant 7 days.

33. 1. MILTIADES [2. 7. 310 - 10. 1. 314], born in Africa, held the see 4 years 7 months 8 days from 7 July in the 9th [8th] consulship of Maxentius [Maximian] to the 2nd of Maximus [Maximinus] which from September was the consulship of Volusianus and Rufinus [311]. **2.** He decreed that none of the faithful should on any account fast on Sunday or Thursday, because the pagans observed those days as a holy fast. Manichaeans were discovered in the city. From that day he brought it about that consecrated offerings from what the bishop consecrated should be sent around the churches; this is called the *fermentum*. **3.** He performed one December ordination, 7 priests, 5 deacons; for various places 11 bishops. He was buried <in the crypt> in the cemetery of Callistus on the Via Appia on 10 December. The bishopric was vacant 16 days.

34. 1. SILVESTER [31. 1. 314 - 31. 12. 335], born in Rome, son of Rufinus, held the see 23 years 10 months 11 days. He was bishop in the time of Constantine and Volusianus from 1 February to 1 January in the consulship of Constantius and Volusianus. **2.** He was in exile on Mount Syraptim <troubled by Constantine's persecution>; afterwards he returned in glory and baptized the emperor Constantine, whom the Lord cured from leprosy <by baptism>, and from whose persecution he is known to have previously fled into exile.

3. He built a church in Rome on the estate of one of his priests named Equitius close to Domitian's baths and established it as a Roman *titulus*; even today it is still called the *titulus* of Equitius.

There he also assigned these gifts:

a silver paten weighing 20 lb, from the gift of the emperor
Constantine;

and he provided:

2 silver scyphi each weighing 10 lb;

a gold chalice weighing 2 lb;

5 service chalices each weighing 2 lb;

2 silver amae each weighing 10 lb;

a silver chrism-paten, inlaid with gold, weighing 5 lb;

10 crown lights each weighing 8 lb;

20 bronze lights each weighing 10 lb;

12 bronze candlestick chandeliers each weighing 30 lb;

the farm Valerianus, Sabine territory, revenue 80 solidi;

the farm Statianus, Sabine territory, revenue 55 solidi;

the farm Duae Casae, Sabine territory, revenue 40 solidi;

the farm Percilianus, Sabine territory, revenue 20 solidi;

the farm Corbianus, territory of Cora, revenue 60 solidi;

a house with bath in the city, in the region of Sicininum,
revenue 85 solidi;

a garden inside Rome in the region Ad Duo Amantes,
revenue 15 solidi;

a house in the region Orpheus inside the city, revenue 58
solidi, 1 tremiss.

4. He issued a decree about the whole church. In his time a council was held at his instruction at Nicaea in Bithynia, and 318 catholic bishops gathered <and 208 others whose signatures were circulated were indisposed>. They expounded the entire <holy> catholic unsullied faith and condemned Arius, Photinus, Sabellius, and their followers. 5. On the emperor's advice he gathered in Rome 277 <bishops> and repeated the condemnation of Callistus, Arius, Photinus, and Sabellius; and he decreed that a priest should not reconcile an Arian who had a change of mind but only the bishop of the designated place should do so; 6. and that chrism should be consecrated by the bishop; and as a privilege for bishops, that he should confirm one already baptized at the urging of heretics. He also decreed that a priest should mark the chrism on one baptized, when he is lifted up from the water, because of the risk of death occurring. He decreed that no layman should presume to indict a cleric for a crime. 7. He decreed that deacons should wear dalmatics in church, and that their left arms should be covered with *pallia* half wool, half linen. He decreed

that no cleric should enter a court for any case, nor should he plead a cause before a robed judge except in church. He decreed that the sacrifice of the altar should not be celebrated on silk or on dyed cloth, but only on naturally produced linen, just as the body of our Lord Jesus Christ was buried in a fine linen shroud; <in this way mass should be celebrated. **8.** He decreed> that if anyone wished to undertake service in the church or be given preferment, he should be a reader 30 years, an exorcist 30 days, an acolyte 5 years, a subdeacon 5 years, a guardian of the martyrs 5 years, a deacon 7 years, a priest 3 years; in this way, being shown to have good testimony borne to him on all sides, even from outsiders, and being the husband of one wife and the wife blessed by a *sacerdos*, he should reach the order of the episcopate; none should intrude into a higher place or the place of his senior, except by acquaintance with these times in order and with modesty, by the expressed consent of all the clerics, and with no cleric <and none of the faithful> making any objection. He performed ordinations of priests and deacons 6 times in December, 42 priests, 27 deacons on various occasions in Rome; for various places 65 bishops.

9. In his time the emperor Constantine built these churches and adorned them:

the Constantinian Basilica, where he placed these gifts:

a hammered silver fastigium—on the front it has the Saviour seated on a chair, 5 ft in size, weighing 120 lb, and 12 apostles each 5 ft and weighing 90 lb with crowns of finest silver; **10.** for someone in the apse looking at it from behind, it has the Saviour sitting on a throne, 5 ft in size, of finest silver weighing 140 lb, and 4 spear-carrying silver angels, each 5 ft and weighing 105 lb, with jewels of Alabanda in their eyes; the fastigium itself <where the angels and apostles stand> weighing 2025 lb of burnished silver; the vault of finest gold;

and hanging beneath the fastigium, a light of finest gold with 50 dolphins, of finest gold weighing 50 lb, with chains weighing 25 lb.

4 crowns of finest gold with 20 dolphins, each weighing 15 lb;

the apse-vault of the basilica, of gold-foil in both directions, 500 lb;

7 altars of finest silver each weighing 200 lb;

7 gold patens each weighing 30 lb;

16 silver patens each weighing 30 lb;

7 scyphi of finest gold each weighing 10 lb;

a special scyphus of hard coral, adorned on all sides with prase and jacinth jewels, inlaid with gold, weighing in all its parts 20 lb 3 oz;

20 silver scyphi each weighing 15 lb;

2 amae of finest gold each weighing 50 lb, capacity 3 medimni each;

20 silver amae each weighing 10 lb, capacity 1 medimnus each;

40 smaller chalices of finest gold each weighing 1 lb;

50 smaller service chalices each weighing 2 lb.

11. Adornment in the basilica:

a chandelier of finest gold in front of the altar, in which pure nard-oil is burnt, with 80 dolphins, weighing 30 lb <where candles of pure nard-oil burn in the body of the church>;

a silver chandelier with 20 dolphins, weighing 50 lb, in which pure nard-oil is burnt;

45 silver chandeliers in the body of the basilica, each weighing 30 lb, in which the same oil is burnt;

40 silver lights on the right of the basilica, each weighing 20 lb;

25 silver chandeliers on the left of the basilica, each weighing 20 lb;

50 silver candlestick chandeliers in the body of the basilica, each weighing 20 lb;

3 metretae of finest silver each weighing 300 lb, capacity 10 medimni <each>;

7 brass candelabra in front of the altars, 10 ft in size, adorned with medallions of the prophets inlaid with silver, each weighing 300 lb.

12. For these he assigned to provide for the lights:

the estate Gargiliana, territory of Suessa, <annual> revenue 400 solidi;

the estate Bauronica, territory of Suessa, revenue 360 solidi;

the estate Auriana, territory of Laurentum, revenue 500 solidi;

the estate Urbana, territory of Antium, revenue 240 solidi;

<the estate Sentiliana, territory of Ardea, revenue 240 solidi;>

the estate Castis, territory of Catina, revenue 1000 solidi;

the estate Trapeas, territory of Catina, revenue 1650 solidi;

2 censers of finest gold weighing 30 lb;

a gift of spices in front of the altars, 150 lb annually.

13. The holy Font where the emperor Constantine was baptized <by the same bishop Silvester, the holy font itself> of porphyry stone, covered with finest silver on every side, inside and out, on top and as much as holds the water, 3008 lb;

in the middle of the Font, a porphyry column which supports a golden basin in which there is a candle, finest gold, weighing 52 lb, where at Eastertide 200 lb of balsam is burnt, while the wick is of coarse earth-flax;

at the edge of the Font of the Baptistery a lamb in finest gold, pouring water, weighing 30 lb;

on the right of the lamb, the Saviour in finest silver, 5 ft in size, weighing 170 lb;

on the left of the lamb, a silver St John the Baptist, 5 ft in size, bearing the inscription BEHOLD THE LAMB OF GOD, BEHOLD HIM WHO TAKES AWAY THE SIN OF THE WORLD, weighing 100 lb;

7 silver stags pouring water, each weighing 80 lb;

a censer of finest gold with 42 prase and jacinth jewels, weighing 15 lb;

14. Presented to the holy Font <of the Baptistery>:

the estate of Festus <chief of the imperial bedchamber, given by the emperor Constantine>, territory of Praeneste, revenue 300 solidi;

the estate Gaba, territory of Gabii, revenue 202 solidi;

the estate Pictas, same territory, revenue 205 solidi;

the estate Statiliana, territory of Cora, revenue 300 solidi;

the estate Taurana, in Sicily, territory Paramnense [of Tauromenium?], revenue 500 solidi;

inside Rome, houses and gardens, revenue 2300 solidi;

the farm of Bassus, revenue 120 solidi;

the estate Laninas, territory of Carseoli, revenue 200 solidi;

the farm Caculas, territory of Nomentum, revenue 50 solidi;

the estate Statiana, Sabine territory, revenue 350 solidi;

the estate Murinas, territory of Albanum on the Via Appia, revenue 300 solidi;

the estate Virginis, territory of Cora, revenue 200 solidi;

15. Overseas: in the districts of Africa:

the estate Iuncis, Mucarian territory, revenue 800 solidi;

the estate Capsis, territory of Capsis, revenue 600 solidi;

the estate Varia Sardana, Mimnensian territory, revenue 500 solidi;

the estate Camaras, territory Cryptalupi, revenue 405 solidi;

the estate Numas, territory of Numidia, revenue 650 solidi;

the estate Sulphorata, territory of Numidia, revenue 720 solidi;

the estate of Walzarus, an oil plantation, territory of Numidia, revenue 810 solidi;

in Greece, <territory of Crete,> the estate Cefalina <in Crete>, revenue 500 solidi;

in Mengaulus, the estate Amazon, revenue 222 solidi.

16. Then the emperor Constantine built <at bishop Silvester's request> a basilica to St Peter the Apostle, at the temple of Apollo, where he buried the tomb with St Peter's body in this way: the actual tomb he sealed on all sides with copper to make it immovable, 5 ft each at the head, the feet, the right and left sides, the bottom and the top; thus he enclosed St Peter's body and buried it. Above he decorated it with porphyry columns and other vine-scroll columns which he brought from Greece. **17.** He also built the basilica's apse-vault shining with gold-foil; and over St Peter's body, above the bronze in which he had sealed it, he provided a cross of finest gold weighing 150 lb, made to measure; on the cross itself is written in <fine> nielloed letters CONSTANTINE AUGUSTUS AND HELENA AUGUSTA. HE SURROUNDS THIS HOUSE WITH A ROYAL HALL GLEAMING WITH EQUAL SPLENDOUR.

18. He also provided 4 brass candelabra, 10 ft in size, finished in silver with silver medallions of the acts of the apostles, each weighing 300 lb;

3 gold chalices, <each> with 45 prase and jacinth jewels, each weighing 12 lb;

2 silver metretae weighing 200 lb;

20 silver chalices each weighing 10 lb;

2 gold amae each weighing 10 lb;

5 silver amae each weighing 20 lb;

a gold paten with a tower of finest gold and a dove, adorned with prase and jacinth jewels and with pearls, 215 in number, weighing 30 lb;

5 silver patens each weighing 15 lb;

a gold crown in front of the body, which is a chandelier, with 50 dolphins, weighing 35 lb;

32 silver lights in the centre of the basilica, with dolphins,

each weighing 10 lb;

on the right of the basilica, 30 silver lights each weighing 8 lb;

the altar itself, of silver chased with gold, weighing 350 lb,
decorated on all sides with prase and jacinth jewels and
pearls, the jewels 210 in number;

a censer of finest gold, decorated on all sides with jewels,
60 in number, weighing 15 lb;

19. Also, for revenue, the presentation made by the emperor Constantine
to the apostle St Peter:

in the diocese of the East: in the city of Antioch:

the house of Datianus, revenue 240 solidi;

a small house in Caene, revenue 20 solidi, 1 tremiss;

rooms in Aphrodisia, revenue 20 solidi;

a bath in Cerataea, revenue 42 solidi;

a bakery in the same place, revenue 23 solidi;

a tavern in the same place, revenue 10 solidi;

the garden of Maro, revenue 10 solidi;

a garden in the same place, revenue 11 solidi;

in the suburbs of Antioch:

the property Sybilles, presented to the emperor, revenue 322 solidi,
150 decads of paper, 200 lb spices, 200 lb nard-oil, 35 lb balsam;

in the suburbs of Alexandria:

the property Timialica, given to the emperor Constantine by
Ambronius, revenue 620 solidi, 300 decads of paper, 300 lb nard-
oil, 60 lb balsam, 150 lb spices, 50 lb Isaurian storax;

the escheated property of Euthymius, revenue 500 solidi, 70 decads
of paper;

20. in Egypt, in the suburbs of Armenia [Hermonthis?]:

the property of Agapius, which he gave to the emperor Constantine;

the property Passinopolimse, revenue 800 solidi, 400 decads of
paper, 50 medimni of pepper, 100 lb saffron, 150 lb storax, 200 lb
cassia spices, 300 lb nard-oil, 100 lb balsam, 100 sacks of linen, 150
lb cloves, 100 lb cyprus-oil, 1000 clean papyrus stalks;

the property which Hybromius gave to the emperor Constantine,
revenue 450 solidi, 200 decads of paper, 50 lb cassia spices, 200 lb
nard-oil, 50 lb balsam;

in the province of Euphratensis, in the suburbs of Cyrrhus:

the property Armanazon, revenue 380 solidi;

the property Obariae, revenue 260 solidi.

21. Then the emperor Constantine <and the lord emperor Constantius> built a basilica to St Paul the apostle at the petition of bishop Silvester; and he buried and sealed his body in bronze just like St Peter's. To this basilica he presented the following gift:

in Cilicia, in the suburbs of Tarsus, the island Cordionon, revenue 800 solidi.

He placed and arranged all the sacred vessels of gold, silver and bronze at St Paul's basilica just as at St Peter's basilica. He also put a gold cross over the burial place of the apostle St Paul, weighing 150 lb;

in the suburbs of Tyre:

the property Comitum, revenue 550 solidi;

the property Timia, revenue 250 solidi;

the property Fronimusa, revenue 700 solidi, 70 lb nard-oil, 50 lb spices, 50 lb cassia;

in the suburbs of Aegyptia[?]:

the property Cyrios, revenue 710 solidi, 70 lb nard-oil, 30 lb balsam, 70 lb spices, 30 lb storax, 150 lb stacte;

the property Basilea, revenue 550 solidi, 50 lb spices, 60 lb nard-oil, 20 lb balsam, 60 lb saffron;

the property of the island Maccabes, revenue 510 solidi, 500 clean papyrus stalks, 300 sacks of linen.

22. Then the emperor Constantine built a basilica in the Sessorian Palace; there he placed some of the wood of our Lord Jesus Christ's holy Cross and sealed it with gold and jewels; and from this he chose the name for the dedication of the church, which today is still called Jerusalem. In this place he assigned the following gift:

4 silver candelabra shining in front of the holy wood, to match the number of the 4 gospels, each weighing 80 lb;

50 silver chandeliers each weighing 15 lb;

a scyphus of finest gold weighing 10 lb;

5 gold service chalices each weighing 1 lb;

3 silver scyphi each weighing 8 lb;

10 silver service chalices each weighing 2 lb;

<a gold paten weighing 10 lb;>

a silver paten chased with gold, and with jewels, weighing 50 lb;

a silver altar weighing 250 lb;

3 silver amae each weighing 20 lb;

and he presented to the church all the lands around the
    Palace;

also the property Sponsas, Via Labicana, revenue 263 solidi;

in the suburbs of Laurentum, the property Patras, revenue
    120 solidi;

in the suburbs of Nepet, the property Anglesis, revenue 150
    solidi;

in the suburbs of the same city, the property Terega,
    revenue 160 solidi;

in the suburbs of Falerii, the property Nymphas, revenue
    115 solidi;

also in the suburbs of Falerii, the property of Herculius,
    which he gave to the emperor and the emperor
    presented to the Jerusalem church, revenue 140 solidi;

in the suburbs of Tuder, the property Angulas, revenue 153
    solidi.

23. Then he built a basilica to the martyr St Agnes at the request of his
daughter <Constantia>, and a baptistery in the same place, where his sister
Constantia was baptized along with the emperor's daughter by bishop
Silvester. And there he assigned the following gift:

a paten of finest gold weighing 20 lb;

a gold chalice weighing 10 lb;

a crown chandelier of finest gold, with 30 dolphins,
    weighing 15 lb;

2 silver patens each weighing 20 lb;

5 silver chalices each weighing 10 lb;

30 silver chandeliers each weighing 8 lb;

40 brass chandeliers;

40 brass candlesticks, chased with silver, with medallions;

a gold lantern with 12 wicks, above the font, weighing 15 lb;

and the gift for revenue:

all the land around the city of Fidenae, revenue 160 solidi;

on the Via Salaria all the land beneath the old walls as far
    as St Agnes', revenue 105 solidi;

the land of Mucius, revenue 80 solidi;

the property Vicus Pisonis, revenue 250 solidi;

the land Casulas, revenue 100 solidi.

24. Then the emperor Constantine built a basilica to the martyr St
Laurence on the Via Tiburtina at the Ager Veranus, above the *arenarium*

of the crypt; to reach the body of the martyr St Laurence he built steps for going up and down. In that place he built an apse and decorated it with purple marble, and above the burial place he sealed it with silver, and decorated it with railings of finest silver weighing 1000 lb; and in front of the actual burial place in the crypt he placed a lantern of finest gold with 10 wicks, weighing 20 lb, a crown of finest silver, with 50 dolphins, weighing 30 lb, 2 bronze candelabra 10 ft in size, each weighing 300 lb; in front of the body of the martyr St Laurence, his *passio* in medallions chased with silver, with 6-wick silver lanterns each weighing 15 lb. <The gift he presented: >

25. In the same place, the property of one Cyriaces, a religious woman, of which the fisc had taken possession in the time of the persecution, the farm Veranus, revenue 160 solidi;

the property Aqua Tuscia alongside, revenue 153 solidi;

the property of Augustus, Sabine territory, revenue to the account of the Christians, 120 solidi;

<the property Sulfuratarum, revenue 62 solidi;>

the property Micinas of Augustus, revenue 110 solidi;

the property Termulas, revenue 60 solidi;

the property Aranas, revenue 70 solidi;

<the property Septimiti, revenue 130 solidi;>

a gold paten weighing 20 lb;

2 silver patens each weighing 30 lb;

a scyphus of finest gold weighing 15 lb;

2 silver scyphi each weighing 10 lb;

10 silver service chalices each weighing 2 lb;

2 silver amae each weighing 10 lb;

30 silver lights each weighing 20 lb;

a metreta of silver weighing 150 lb, capacity 2 medimni.

26. Then the emperor Constantine built a basilica to the martyrs Saints Marcellinus the priest and Peter the exorcist on the land between the Two Laurels, and a mausoleum where his own <blessed> mother the empress Helena was buried <in a porphyry sarcophagus>, on the Via Labicana at the 3rd mile. There, both for love of his mother and to honour the saints, he placed his votive gifts:

a paten of finest gold weighing 35 lb;

4 silver candelabra chased with gold, 12 ft in size, each weighing 200 lb;

a gold crown, which is a chandelier, with 120 dolphins,
weighing 30 lb;

3 gold chalices each weighing 10 lb, with prase and jacinth jewels;

2 gold amae each weighing 40 lb;

an altar of finest silver weighing 200 lb in front of the tomb
of the blessed empress Helena—the tomb itself is of
hard porphyry, carved with medallions;

20 silver chandeliers each weighing 20 lb.

27. Also in the basilica of Saints Peter and Marcellinus, the gift he gave:

an altar of finest silver weighing 200 lb;

2 patens of finest gold each weighing 15 lb;

2 silver patens each weighing 15 lb;

a larger gold scyphus, with the imperial name represented
on it, weighing 20 lb;

a smaller gold scyphus weighing 10 lb;

5 silver scyphi each weighing 12 lb;

20 silver service chalices each weighing 3 lb;

4 silver amae each weighing 15 lb;

every year 900 lb pure nard-oil, 100 lb balsam, 100 lb
spices for incense for the above martyrs Saints
Marcellinus and Peter;

the farm Laurentum close to the aqueduct, with a bath and
all the land from the Porta Sessoriana as far as the Via
Praenestina, by the route of the Via Latina as far as
Mons Gabus, <Mons Gabus itself,> the property of the
empress Helena, revenue 1120 solidi;

the island of Sardinia, with all the properties pertaining to
that island, revenue 1024 solidi;

the island of Misenum, with the properties pertaining to
that island, revenue 810 solidi;

the island of Matidia, which is Mons Argentarius, revenue
600 solidi;

the property called Duae Casae, Sabine territory, under
Mons Lucretilis, revenue 200 solidi.

28. Then the emperor Constantine <at the petition of bishop Silvester>
built in the city of Ostia close to Portus Romanus the basilica of the
blessed apostles Peter and Paul and of John the Baptist, where he
presented the following gifts:

a silver paten weighing 30 lb;

10 silver chalices each weighing 2 lb;

2 silver amae each weighing 10 lb;

30 silver chandeliers each weighing 5 lb;

2 silver scyphi each weighing 8 lb;

a single silver chrism-paten weighing 10 lb;

a silver basin for baptism, weighing 20 lb;

the island called Assis between Portus and Ostia, all the coastal properties as far as Digitus Solis, revenue 300 solidi;

the property of the Greeks, territory of Ardea, revenue 80 solidi;

the property Quiriti, territory of Ostia, revenue 311 solidi;

the property Balneolum, territory of Ostia, revenue 42 solidi;

the property Nymfulas, revenue 30 solidi.

29. Also what Gallicanus presented to the above basilica of the holy apostles Peter and Paul and of John the Baptist; he presented the following:

a silver crown with dolphins, weighing 20 lb;

a silver chalice decorated in relief, weighing 15 lb;

a silver ama weighing 18 lb;

the estate Mallianum, Sabine territory, revenue 115 solidi, 1 tremiss;

the farm Picturas, territory of Velitrae, revenue 43 solidi;

the farm of the Suri on the Via Claudia, territory of Veii, revenue 56 solidi;

the estate Gargiliana, territory of Suessa, revenue 655 solidi.

30. Then the emperor Constantine built in the city of Albanum the basilica of St John the Baptist, where he placed the following:

a silver paten weighing 30 lb;

a silver-gilt scyphus weighing 12 lb;

10 silver service chalices each weighing 3 lb;

2 silver amae each weighing 20 lb;

the property Lacus Turni with the adjacent plains, revenue 60 solidi;

the farm Molas, revenue 50 solidi;

the property Albanensis with Lacus Albanensis, revenue 250 solidi;

the estate of Mucius, revenue 170 solidi;

all the city's abandoned barracks and houses, in the city of Albanum, the emperor presented as a gift to the holy Constantinian church;

the property Horti, revenue 20 solidi;

the property of Tiberius Caesar, revenue 280 solidi;

the property Marinas, revenue 50 solidi;

<the estate Nemus, revenue 280 solidi>;

the property Amartianas, territory of Cora, revenue 150 solidi;

the property Statiliana, revenue 70 solidi;

the property Mediana, revenue 30 solidi.

31. Then the emperor Constantine built in the city of Capua the basilica of the Apostles, which he styled Constantinian, where he presented the following gifts:

2 silver patens each weighing 20 lb;

3 silver scyphi each weighing 8 lb;

15 service chalices each weighing 2 lb;

2 silver amae each weighing 10 lb;

4 bronze candelabra, 10 ft in size, each weighing 180 lb;

30 silver chandeliers each weighing 5 lb;

30 bronze chandeliers;

and he presented properties:

the estate Statiliana, territory of Minturnae, revenue 315 solidi;

the property [...], territory of Caieta, revenue 85 solidi;

the property Paternum, territory of Suessa, revenue 150 solidi;

the property Ad Centum, territory of Capua, revenue 60 solidi;

the property Gauronica, territory of Suessa, revenue 40 solidi;

the property of Leo, revenue 60 solidi.

32. Then the emperor Constantine built the basilica in the city of Naples, to which he presented the following:

2 silver patens each weighing 25 lb;

2 silver scyphi each weighing 10 lb;

15 service chalices each weighing 2 lb;

2 silver amae each weighing 15 lb;

20 silver lights each weighing 8 lb;

20 bronze lights each weighing 10 lb;

and he built an aqueduct 8 miles long; he also built a forum in the same city; and presented the following gift:

the property Macari, revenue 150 solidi;
the property Cimbriana, revenue 105 solidi;
the property Sclina, revenue 108 solidi;
the property Afilas, revenue 140 solidi;
the property Nymfulas, revenue 90 solidi;
the property 'the Island' with the fort, revenue 80 solidi.

33. Then the blessed Silvester established his *titulus* in Rome in the 3rd region next to Domitian's baths, called those of Trajan—the *titulus* of Silvester where the emperor Constantine gave:
a silver paten weighing 20 lb;
a silver ama weighing 10 lb;
2 silver scyphi each weighing 8 lb;
10 silver chandeliers each weighing 5 lb;
16 bronze candlestick chandeliers each weighing 40 lb;
5 silver service chalices each weighing 2 lb;
the farm Percilianus, Sabine territory, revenue 50 solidi;
the farm Barbatianus, territory of Ferentinum, revenue 35 solidi, 1 tremiss;
the farm Statianus, territory of Trebula, revenue 66 solidi, 1 tremiss;
the farm Beruclas, territory of Cora, revenue 40 solidi;
the farm Sulpicianus, territory of Cora, revenue 70 solidi;
the farm of Taurus, territory of Veii, revenue 42 solidi;
the farm Sentianus, territory of Tibur, revenue 30 solidi;
the farm Ceianus, territory of Praeneste, revenue 50 solidi;
the farm Termulas, territory of Praeneste, revenue 35 solidi;
the property of Cylo, territory of Praeneste, revenue 58 solidi.
He also presented everything necessary to the *titulus* of Equitius.

34. Silvester performed 6 December ordinations, 42 priests, 26 deacons; for various places 65 bishops. He was buried in the cemetery of Priscilla on the Via Salaria at the 3rd mile from Rome on 31 December. Truly it was as a catholic and a confessor that he went to his rest. The bishopric was vacant 15 days.

35. **1.** MARK [18. 1. 336 - 7. 10. 336], born in Rome, son of Priscus, held the see 2 years 8 months 20 days. He was bishop in the time of Constantine and in the consulship of Nepotianus and Facundus [336] from 1 February to 1 October. **2.** He decreed that the bishop of Ostia, who consecrates the bishop, should use the *pallium*, and that the bishop of

Rome should be consecrated by him. He laid down a decree about the
whole church. **3.** He built two basilicas, one on the Via Ardeatina where
he is buried, the other in Rome close to the Pallacinae.

At his petition the emperor Constantine presented to the basilica which
he established as a cemetery on the Via Ardeatina:

the farm Rosarius with all the land of the plains, revenue 40 solidi.

4. At the basilica in Rome he presented the following:

a silver paten weighing 30 lb;

2 silver amae each weighing 20 lb;

1 silver scyphus weighing 10 lb;

3 silver service chalices each weighing 2 lb;

a silver crown weighing 10 lb;

the farm Antonianus on the Via Claudia, revenue 30 solidi;

the farm Vaccanas on the Via Appia, revenue 40 solidi, 2
tremisses;

the farm Orrea on the Via Ardeatina, revenue 55 solidi, 1
tremiss.

5. He performed two December ordinations in Rome, 25 priests, 6
deacons; for various places 27 bishops. He was buried on the Via
Ardeatina in the cemetery of Balbina to whose building he applied
himself, on 6 October. The bishopric was vacant 20 days.

36. 1. JULIUS [6. 2. 337 - 12. 4. 352], born in Rome, son of Rusticus,
held the see 15 years 2 months 6 days. He was bishop in the time of
Constantine son of Constantine, the heretic, from the consulship of
Felicianus and Maximinus [Titianus, 337]. He endured many troubles and
was in exile for 10 months; after the death of this Constantine he returned
in glory to the see of St Peter the apostle. **2.** He built two basilicas, one in
Rome close to the Forum, the other across the Tiber; and three cemeteries,
one on the Via Flaminia, one on the Via Aurelia, and one on the Via
Portuensis. **3.** He issued a decree that no cleric should take part in any
lawsuit in a public court, but only in a church; that the document which
everyone has vouching for his holding the church's faith should be
gathered in by the notaries; and that the drawing up of all documents in
the church should be carried out by the *primicerius notariorum*—whether
they be bonds, deeds, donations, exchanges, transfers, wills, declarations
or manumissions, the clerics in the church should carry them out through
the church office. **4.** He performed three December ordinations in Rome,
18 priests, 4 deacons; for various places 9 bishops. He was buried on the

Via Aurelia in the cemetery of Calepodius at the 3rd mile <from Rome> on 12 April. The bishopric was vacant 25 days.

37. 1. LIBERIUS [17. 5. 352 - 24. 9. 366], born in Rome, son of Augustus, held the see 6 years 3 months 4 days. He was bishop in the time of Constantine son of Constantine until the 3rd [5th] of the emperor Constantius [352]. **2.** He was carried off into exile by Constantius for refusing to agree to the Arian heresy, and spent 3 years in exile. Gathering *sacerdotes* together, with their consent Liberius ordained the priest Felix, a revered man, as bishop in his place. Felix held a council and found that two priests named Ursacius and Valens were in agreement with the Arian emperor Constantius, and he condemned them in a council of 48 bishops. **3.** But a few days later Ursacius and Valens were driven by jealousy to request Constantius to recall Liberius from exile, so he could share in a single communion—apart from rebaptism. Then a warrant was sent through Catulinus the *agens in rebus*, and Ursacius and Valens both came to Liberius. Liberius agreed with the emperor's instructions that he should share in a single communion with the heretics, provided they did not rebaptize. **4.** Then they recalled Liberius from exile. On his return from exile Liberius lived at the cemetery of St Agnes with the emperor Constantius' sister, in the hope that her intervention or request might gain him admittance to the city. Then Constantina Augusta, who was faithful to the Lord Jesus Christ, refused to request her brother the emperor Constantius, as she had realized what his scheme was. **5.** Then Constantius along with Ursacius and Valens summoned some of those from the Arian dung-hill, and just as if a council had been held he sent and recalled Liberius from St Agnes' cemetery. Immediately on his entry into Rome the emperor Constantius held a council with the heretics including Ursacius and Valens; he ejected the catholic Felix from the bishopric and recalled Liberius. From that day the clergy suffered a persecution which caused the deaths and martyrdom in church of priests and clerics. Deprived of the bishopric, Felix lived on his small estate on the Via Portuensis, where he died in peace on 29 July. **6.** On 2 August Liberius entered Rome and gave his assent to the heretic Constantius. Liberius was not actually rebaptized, but he did give his assent, and for 7 years he held the basilicas of St Peter and St Paul and the Constantinian basilica; there was a great persecution in Rome, which meant that the clergy and *sacerdotes* could gain no entry into church or baths.
   7. Liberius decorated the tomb of the martyr St Agnes with marble

tablets. So all of Felix's years are included in his reckoning. He built the basilica which bears his name close to the market of Livia; **8.** and performed two December ordinations in Rome, 18 priests, 5 deacons; for various places 19 bishops. He was buried on the Via Salaria in the cemetery of Priscilla on 9 September. The bishopric was vacant 6 days.

38. 1. FELIX [II; 355 - 22. 11. 365], born in Rome, son of Anastasius, held the see 1 year 3 months 2 days. He proclaimed Constantius son of Constantine to be a heretic and to have undergone a second baptism by Eusebius bishop of Nicomedia near Nicomedia at the villa called Aquilone. For making this proclamation he was crowned with martyrdom by beheading on the instruction of the emperor Constantius son of the emperor Constantine. **2.** He built a basilica on the Via Aurelia while he still discharged the office of the priesthood, and at the same church he purchased the land around the place, which he presented to the church he built <at the 2nd mile from Rome>. **3.** He performed one December ordination in Rome, 21 priests, 5 deacons; in various places 19 bishops. He was beheaded with many of the clerics and faithful in secret close to the city walls, alongside the aqueduct of Trajan, on 11 November. Straightaway the Christians with the priest Damasus got hold of his body <at night> and buried it in peace in that same basilica of his <which he had built> on the Via Aurelia, on 15 November. The bishopric was vacant 38 days.

39. 1. DAMASUS [1. 10. 366 - 11. 12. 384], born in Spain, son of Antonius, held the see 18 years 3 months 11 days. Ursinus was ordained in rivalry with him. A council of *sacerdotes* was held, and they confirmed Damasus because he was the stronger and had the greater number of supporters; that was how Damasus was confirmed. They ejected Ursinus from the city and set him up as bishop of Naples; Damasus stayed at Rome as prelate in the apostolic see. He was bishop in the time of Julian. **2.** He built two basilicas: one to St Laurence close to the Theatre, and the other on the Via Ardeatina where he is buried. At the Catacombs, the place where lay the bodies of the apostles St Peter and St Paul, he <dedicated and> adorned with verses the actual tablet at the place where the holy bodies lay. He searched for and discovered many bodies of holy martyrs, and also proclaimed their [acts] in verses. **3.** He issued a decree about the church. He was maliciously accused on a charge of adultery; when a synod was held he was cleared by 44 bishops, who also condemned his accusers, the deacons Concordius and Callistus, and expelled them from the church.

4. He established as a *titulus* in Rome the basilica he constructed, where he presented:

a silver paten weighing 20 lb;

a silver ama weighing 15 lb;

a scyphus decorated in relief weighing 10 lb;

5 silver service chalices each weighing 3 lb;

5 silver crowns each weighing 8 lb;

16 bronze candlestick chandeliers;

houses around the basilica, revenue 155 solidi;

the property Papirana, territory of Ferentinum, with contiguous adjoining properties, revenue 120 solidi, 1 tremiss;

the property Antoniana, territory of Casinum, revenue 103 solidi;

a bath close to the *titulus*, revenue 27 solidi.

6ª. He performed five December ordinations in the city, 31 priests, 11 deacons; for various places 62 bishops. **5.** He decreed that in all the churches the psalms should be sung by day and night, a requirement he placed on priests, bishops, and monasteries. **6ᵇ.** He was buried on the Via Ardeatina in his own basilica on 11 December, close to his mother and sister. The bishopric was vacant 31 days.

40. **1.** SIRICIUS [384 - 26. 11. 399], born in Rome, son of Tiburtius, held the see 15 years. He issued a decree about the whole church and against every heresy, and he broadcast it through the whole world, to be kept in the archive of every church for rebutting every heresy. **2.** He decreed that no priest should celebrate mass every week without receiving the guaranteed consecrated element from the designated bishop of the place—this is called the *fermentum*. He discovered Manichaeans in the city and sent them into exile, and he decreed that they should not share communion with the faithful, since it would be wrong to abuse the Lord's holy body with a defiled mouth; **3.** he decreed that any convert from the Manichaeans who returned to the church should on no account be given communion but should be removed to a monastery and held in subjection throughout his life, so that tortured by fasting and prayer and tested by every trial till the final day of his death, through the church's mercy the *viaticum* should be given them. He decreed that a heretic should be reconciled by the laying on of hands in the presence of the whole church.

4. He performed five December ordinations in Rome, 31 priests, 16 deacons; for various places 32 bishops. He was buried in the cemetery of Priscilla on the Via Salaria on 22 February. The bishopric was vacant 20 days.

41. **1.** ANASTASIUS [I; 27. 11. 399 - 19. 12. 401/402], born in Rome, son of Maximus, held the see 3 years 10 days. He decreed that whenever the holy gospels are recited, *sacerdotes* should not be seated but should stand bowing. He issued a decree about the church. **2.** He also built a basilica called Crescentiana in the 2nd region of Rome on the Via Mamurtini. He decreed that no cleric from overseas should be received unless he had a certificate signed by five bishops, because at that time Manichaeans were discovered in Rome. **3.** He performed two December ordinations <in Rome>, 9 priests, 5 deacons; for various places 11 bishops. He was buried in his own cemetery Ad Ursum Pileatum on 27 April. The bishopric was vacant 21 days.

42. **1.** INNOCENTIUS [401/402 - 12. 3. 417], born in Albanum, son of Innocentius, held the see 15 years 2 months 21 days. He issued a decree about the whole church, about the rules of monasteries and about Jews and pagans; he discovered many Cataphrygians <in the city> and removed them to exile in a monastery. **2.** He found that Pelagius and Caelestius were heretics and condemned them. He decreed that one born of a Christian mother must be born again by baptism, that is, must be baptized, which Pelagius was condemning.

3. Then he dedicated the basilica of Saints Gervasius and Protasius, from a bequest in the will of a certain illustrious woman Vestina, through the activity of the priests Ursicinus and Leopardus and the deacon Livianus. This woman had directed in the text of her will that a basilica of the holy martyrs should be constructed from her ornaments and pearls by selling what was reckoned to be enough. When the basilica was completely finished blessed Innocentius established in it a Roman *titulus*, from the assignment of the illustrious woman Vestina, **4.** and in the same Lord's house he presented:

　　2 silver patens each weighing 20 lb;
　　2 silver amae each weighing 20 lb;
　　12 silver crowns each weighing 15 lb;
　　1 <silver> chandelier weighing 22 lb;
　　4 silver candlesticks each weighing 25 lb;

a silver tower with a paten and a gilt dove, weighing 30 lb;
5. Ornament for baptism:
a silver stag pouring water, weighing 25 lb;
a silver vessel for the oil of chrism, weighing 5 lb;
another vessel for the oil of exorcism, weighing 5 lb;
2 patens for chrism, each weighing 3 lb;
a silver scyphus decorated in relief, weighing 10 lb;
a silver scyphus weighing 10 lb;
5 silver chalices weighing 3 lb;
3 silver chalices for baptism, each weighing 2 lb;
<and he presented many other gifts: >
a silver handbasin weighing 16 lb;
16 bronze chandeliers each weighing 10 lb;
20 bronze candlestick chandeliers in the body of the
   basilica, each weighing 40 lb;
6. a house close to the basilica Liviana, revenue 85 solidi, 1
   tremiss;
a bath in the same place close to the temple of Mamurus,
   revenue 32 solidi;
a house with a bath on the Clivus Salutis, revenue 77 solidi,
   1 tremiss;
the property Sorras, territory of Clusium, revenue 71 solidi,
   1 tremiss;
the property Corbianus, territory of Clusium, revenue 79
   solidi;
the property Fundanensis, territory of Fundi, with 15
   contiguous adjoining properties, revenue 181 solidi, 1
   tremiss;
the property Figlinas, territory of Casinum, revenue 58
   solidi, 1 tremiss;
the property of Amandinus, which he gave to his cousin the
   illustrious woman Vestina, territory of Veii, revenue 46
   solidi, 1 tremiss;
the property Antonianus, territory of [Forum] Clodii,
   revenue 62 solidi;
the house of Emeritus on the Clivus Mamuri within Rome,
   close to the basilica, revenue 62 solidi;
the house on the Clivus Patricius, in dispute;
the house close to the basilica, on the Vicus Longus, called

Ad Lacum, revenue 82 solidi;
the house Floriana, at the Stone Seats, revenue 58 solidi;
the bakery called Castoriani on the Vicus Longus, revenue
    61 solidi;
the bath on the Vicus Longus, called the Temple, revenue
    40 solidi, 3 siliquae;
3 unciae of the Porta Nomentana, revenue 22 solidi, 1
    tremiss.

He decreed that a fast should be observed on Saturdays, since it was during a Saturday that the Lord had lain in the tomb and the disciples fasted. **7.** He decreed that the basilica of the martyr St Agnes should be run by the care of the priests Leopardus and Paulinus, and be roofed and decorated; on their assignment the authority was yielded to the priests of the above *titulus* of Vestina. **8.** He performed four December ordinations in Rome, 30 priests, 12 deacons; for various places 54 bishops. He was buried in the cemetery Ad Ursum Pileatum on 28 July. The bishopric was vacant 22 days.

43. **1.** ZOSIMUS [18. 3. 417 - 26. 12. 418], born in Greece, son of Abramius, held the see 1 year 3 months 11 days. He decreed many things for the church, including that deacons should have their left arms covered with *pallia* half wool, half linen; and permission was granted for the blessing of the [Easter] candle throughout the parishes. He ordered that no cleric should drink in a public tavern but only in cellars owned by the faithful, particularly by clerics. **2.** He performed <one> December ordinations in Rome, 10 priests, 3 deacons; for various places 8 bishops. He was buried on the Via Tiburtina close to the body of St Laurence the martyr on 26 December. The bishopric was vacant 11 days.

44. **1.** BONIFACE [I; 29. 12. 418 - 4. 9. 422], born in Rome, son of the priest Jocundus, held the see 3 years 8 months 7 days. He and Eulalius were ordained in rivalry on the same day and the clergy were divided 7 months 15 days. Now Eulalius was ordained in the Constantinian basilica, whereas Boniface was ordained in that of Julius. **2.** On hearing this the empress Placidia, with her son the emperor Valentinian [III], then residing at Ravenna, reported it to the emperor Honorius in residence at Milan. The two emperors sent a warrant ordering that both men should leave the city. When they had been forced out, Boniface stayed at the cemetery of the martyr St Felicity on the Via Salaria, while Eulalius stayed at St

Hermes' in the city of Antium. **3.** But when the following Easter was coming Eulalius, relying on the fact he had been ordained in the Constantinian basilica, dared to enter the city and perform baptisms and celebrate Easter in the Constantinian basilica, while Boniface celebrated the Easter baptism in the normal way at the basilica of the martyr St Agnes. **4.** When the emperors heard of this they sent to both of them, ejected Eulalius by means of 52 bishops, and sent a warrant recalling Boniface into Rome and appointing him as bishop, while they despatched Eulalius out into Campania. After 3 years 8 months Boniface died. The clergy and people asked for the recall of Eulalius, but Eulalius would not agree to return to Rome. A year after Boniface's death, Eulalius died at the same place in Campania.

5. Boniface decreed that no woman or nun should touch the consecrated pall or wash it, or should place the incense—this should be done only by a minister; nor should a slave become a cleric, nor anyone under obligation to a *curia* or anything else.

6. He built an oratory in the cemetery of St Felicity, close to her body, and decorated the tomb of the martyr St Felicity and of St Silvanus, where he placed the following:

a silver paten weighing 20 lb;
a silver scyphus weighing 10 lb;
a silver ama weighing 13 lb;
2 smaller <silver> chalices each weighing 4 lb;
3 silver crowns each weighing 15 lb.

7. He performed one December ordination <in Rome>, 13 priests, 3 deacons; for various places 36 bishops. He was buried on the Via Salaria <in the cemetery> close to the body of the martyr St Felicity on 25 October. The bishopric was vacant 9 days.

45. **1.** CELESTINE [10. 9. 422 - 27. 7. 432], born in Campania, son of Priscus, held the see 8 years 10 months 17 days. He issued many decrees, including one that before the sacrifice the 150 psalms of David should be performed antiphonally by everyone; this used not to be done, but only St Paul's epistle and the holy gospel were recited <in this way mass should be celebrated>. He issued a decree about the whole church and especially about religious life, which is kept safe today in the church archive.

2. He dedicated the basilica of Julius, in which he presented after the Gothic conflagration:

a silver paten weighing 25 lb;
2 silver scyphi each weighing 8 lb;
2 silver amae each weighing 10 lb;
5 smaller silver chalices each weighing 3 lb;
5 silver handbasins weighing 10 lb;
2 silver candelabra each weighing 30 lb;
24 bronze candlestick chandeliers each weighing 30 lb;
also 10 silver crowns each weighing 10 lb;
at St Peter's:
a chandelier weighing 25 lb of finest silver;
24 silver candlestick chandeliers in the body of the basilica,
   each weighing 20 lb;
at St Paul's:
a silver chandelier weighing 25 lb;
24 candlestick chandeliers each weighing 20 lb.

3. He performed three December ordinations <in Rome>, 32 priests, 12 deacons; for various places 46 bishops. He was buried in the cemetery of Priscilla on the Via Salaria on 6 April. The bishopric was vacant 21 days.

46. 1. XYSTUS [III; 31. 7. 432 - 19. 8. 440], born in Rome, son of Xystus, held the see 8 years 19 days. After 1 year 8 months he was arraigned on a charge by one Bassus. On hearing this the emperor Valentinian ordered the gathering of a council, a holy synod; and when the assembly met, after much investigation he was cleared by the 56 bishops in their synodical judgment; Bassus was condemned by the synod, but so that through the merciful piety of the church he should not be denied the *viaticum* on his last day. **2.** On hearing this the emperor Valentinian and his mother the empress Placidia were moved with holy indignation and sent a writ condemning Bassus and merging all his estates and goods with the catholic church. Within 3 months, by the will of the Deity, Bassus died. Bishop Xystus saw to the wrapping of his body with linens and spices with his own hands and buried it at St Peter's in his parents' tomb-chamber.

3. He built the basilica of St Mary, which the ancients called that of Liberius, close to the market of Livia, where he presented the following:
an altar of finest silver weighing 300 lb;
3 silver patens weighing 60 lb;
4 silver amae weighing 60 lb;
a scyphus of finest gold weighing 12 lb;

5 silver scyphi weighing 50 lb;

2 gold service chalices each weighing 1 lb;

10 silver service chalices each weighing 3 lb;

a silver handbasin weighing 8 lb;

a silver crown light in front of the altar, weighing 30 lb;

34 silver crown lights each weighing 10 lb;

4 silver candelabra each weighing 20 lb;

a silver censer weighing 5 lb;

24 brass candlestick chandeliers each weighing 15 lb;

the property Scauriana, territory of Caieta, revenue of everything therein with the contiguous adjoining properties, 312 solidi, 1 tremiss;

the property Marmorata, territory of Praeneste, revenue 92 solidi;

the property of Celer, territory of Afile, revenue 111 solidi, 1 tremiss;

the house of Palmatus in Rome, almost next to the basilica, with bath and bakery, revenue 154 solidi, 3 siliquae;

the house of Claudius in Sicininum, revenue 104 solidi;

a silver stag at the font, pouring water, weighing 20 lb;

all the sacred silver vessels for baptism, weighing 15 lb;

the garrets adjoining the steps to the main door of the basilica, and everything reckoned as included therein.

4. He decorated the confessio of St Peter with silver: it weighs 400 lb. At his entreaty the emperor Valentinian presented a gold image with 12 portals, 12 apostles, and the Saviour, decorated with very precious jewels; as an offering for prayers answered he placed this over the confessio of St Peter.

At bishop Xystus' request the emperor Valentinian constructed a silver fastigium in the Constantinian basilica—it had been removed by the barbarians—weighing 1610 lb.

5. In his time the emperor Valentinian built a confessio for St Paul's of silver weighing 200 lb.

Also bishop Xystus built a confessio for the martyr St Laurence with porphyry columns, and decorated the passageway with tablets, and the altar and confessio for the martyr St Laurence of finest silver, the altar he provided weighing 50 lb; silver railings over the porphyry tablets, weighing 300 lb; a niche over the railings, with a silver statue of the martyr St Laurence, weighing 200 lb.

6. He built a basilica to St Laurence, with the agreement of the emperor Valentinian, where he presented:

3 silver patens each weighing 20 lb;
3 silver amae each weighing 15 lb;
4 silver scyphi each weighing 8 lb;
a special gold scyphus adorned with pearls, weighing 10 lb;
a gold lantern with 10 wicks, weighing 10 lb;
12 silver service chalices each weighing 2 lb;
a silver handbasin weighing 8 lb;
a service for baptism or penance, of silver, weighing 5 lb;
a brass shell weighing 20 lb;
30 silver crown lights each weighing 6 lb;
3 chandeliers each weighing 15 lb;
2 silver candelabra each weighing 30 lb;
24 bronze candlestick chandeliers in the body of the basilica;
60 bronze lights.

7. He built a monastery at the Catacombs; and he built the font of the Baptistery at St Mary's and adorned it with porphyry columns.

<At the Constantinian basilica he provided adornment over the font, which had not been there before, that is> in the Baptistery of the Constantinian basilica he set up the hard porphyry columns, 8 in number; these had been gathered <and left> from the time of the emperor Constantine, and he erected them with their <marble> entablatures and adorned them with verses.

And <he provided> a tablet in the cemetery of Callistus <on the Via Appia> on which he recorded the names of the bishops <and martyrs in writing>.

He provided 3 gold scyphi, one for St Peter's weighing 6 lb, one for St Paul's weighing 6 lb, one for St Laurence's weighing 3 lb; and 15 gold service chalices each weighing 1 lb.

9[a]. He performed three December ordinations in Rome, 28 priests, 12 deacons; for various places 52 bishops. **8.** In his time the bishop Peter built in Rome the basilica of St Sabina, where he also built a font. **9[b].** He was buried on the Via Tiburtina in the crypt close to the body of St Laurence. The bishopric was vacant 22 days. <From Silvester's death to Leo I are 99 years 5 months 26 days.>

47. **1.** LEO <the first> [I; 29. 9. 440 - 10. 11. 461], born in Tuscia, son of Quintianus, held the see 21 years 1 month 13 days. In his time God's

handmaid Demetrias built a basilica to St Stephen on her estate at the 3rd mile of the Via Latina.

2. Through certain bishops he discovered two heresies, the Eutychian and the Nestorian. He listed his instructions in a warrant which he sent to the emperor Marcian, an orthodox catholic prince, and after a discussion with the prince the bishops were brought together and a holy council of bishops was held in Chalcedon at the martyr-shrine of St Euphemia. There were gathered 256 *sacerdotes*, and the signatures of 406 other bishops were circulated; and they were gathered with the Tome, that is, the faith of the apostolic Roman church which came with the signature of the holy bishop Leo and of the catholic prince Marcian. 3. In the emperor's presence the council was gathered, of 1200 bishops together with the emperor Marcian. They expounded the catholic faith that in one Christ there are two natures, God and Man. There the pious emperor Marcian and his wife the empress Pulcheria laid the royal majesty aside and expounded their faith in the sight of the holy bishops, and there they also condemned Eutyches and Nestorius <and Dioscorus>. 4. Again expounding their faith with their own signatures the emperor Marcian with his wife the empress Pulcheria craved the holy council to send it to the blessed pope Leo <requesting him to expound the catholic faith; and blessed Leo sent the Tome of the catholic faith and expounded it> in condemnation of all heresies. 5. Again the blessed archbishop Leo despatched many letters on the faith, which are kept safe today in the archive. He frequently confirmed the synod of Chalcedon in his letters—12 letters to Marcian, 13 to the emperor Leo, 9 to bishop Flavian, 18 to the bishops throughout the East; in these letters he confirmed the synod's faith.

6. After the Vandal disaster he replaced all the consecrated silver services throughout all the *tituli*, by melting down 6 water-jars, two at the Constantinian basilica, two at the basilica of St Peter, two at St Paul's, which the emperor Constantine had presented, each weighing 100 lb; from these he replaced all the consecrated vessels.

He renewed St Peter's basilica and the apse-vault; and he renewed St Paul's after the divine fire. He also constructed an apse-vault in the Constantinian basilica.

He built a basilica to the bishop and martyr St Cornelius near the cemetery of Callistus on the Via Appia.

7. For the sake of the Roman name he undertook an embassy and travelled to the king of the Huns, Attila by name, and he delivered the whole of Italy from the peril of the enemy. He established a monastery at

St Peter's <which is called that of Saints John and Paul>. **8.** He decreed that in the performance of the sacrifice should be said: 'a holy sacrifice' etc. He decreed that a nun should not receive the blessing of a head-veil unless she had been tested in her virginity for 60 years. He established the wardens called *cubicularii* from among the Roman clergy, over the tombs of the apostles. **9.** He performed four December ordinations in Rome, 81 priests, 31 deacons; for various places 185 bishops. He was buried in St Peter's on 11 April. The bishopric was vacant 7 days.

48. 1. HILARUS [19. 11. 461 - 29. 2. 468], born in Sardinia, son of Crispinus, held the see 6 years 3 months 10 days. He issued a decretal and broadcast it through the whole of the East, and letters on the catholic <and apostolic> faith, confirming the three synods of Nicaea, Ephesus, and Chalcedon, and the Tome of the holy archbishop Leo; and he condemned Eutyches and Nestorius and all their followers, and all heresies, and confirmed the dominion and preeminence of the holy catholic and apostolic see. He issued a decree about the church in the basilica of St Mary <the mother of God>, on 16 November in the consulship of Basiliscus and Hermenericus [465].

2. He built 3 oratories in the baptistery of the Constantinian basilica, of St John the Baptist, St John the Evangelist, and the Holy Cross, all of silver and precious stones:

the confessio of St John the Baptist, of silver, weighing 100 lb, and a gold cross;

the confessio of St John the Evangelist of silver, weighing 100 lb, and a gold cross;

in both oratories bronze doors chased with silver;

3. the oratory of the Holy Cross:

the confessio, in which he placed the Lord's wood;

a gold cross with jewels, weighing 20 lb;

silver doors into the confessio, weighing 50 lb;

above the confessio, a gold arch weighing 4 lb, supported on onyx columns, on which stands a golden lamb weighing 2 lb;

in front of the confessio, a gold crown, a light with dolphins, weighing 5 lb;

4 gold lamps each weighing 2 lb.

4. In front of the oratory of the Holy Cross, a fountain and a triple porch, where there are the columns of marvellous size called *hecatonpentaic*, and 2 striated shells, with striped porphyry columns, pouring water; and in the middle a porphyry basin with a striped shell pouring water in the middle, surrounded right, left, and centre by bronze railings and columns with pediments and entablatures, decorated on all sides with mosaics and with Aquitanian, Tripolitan, and porphyry columns.

5. In front of the confessio of St John:

a silver crown weighing 20 lb;

a chandelier weighing 25 lb;

Also at St John's ...

Within the holy Font:

a gold lantern with 10 wicks for lighting, weighing 5 lb;

3 silver stags pouring water, each weighing 30 lb;

a silver tower with dolphins, weighing 60 lb;

a gold dove weighing 2 lb.

6. In the Constantinian basilica:

10 silver chandeliers, which hang in front of the altar, each weighing 20 lb;

a gold scyphus weighing 6 lb;

another gold scyphus weighing 5 lb;

5 gold chalices each weighing 1 lb;

5 silver scyphi each weighing 10 lb;

20 silver service chalices each weighing 2 lb;

5 silver amae each weighing 10 lb.

7. At St Peter's:

a gold scyphus weighing 5 lb;

another gold scyphus with prase and jacinth jewels, weighing 4 lb;

10 silver service chalices each weighing 2 lb;

2 silver amae each weighing 8 lb;

24 silver chandeliers each weighing 5 lb.

8. At St Paul's:

a gold scyphus weighing 5 lb;

another gold scyphus with jewels, weighing 5 lb;

4 silver scyphi each weighing 6 lb;

10 <silver> service chalices each weighing 2 lb;

2 silver amae each weighing 10 lb.

9. At St Laurence the martyr's:

a gold scyphus with prase and jacinth jewels, weighing 4 lb;

a lantern of finest gold with 10 wicks, weighing 5 lb;

a scyphus of finest gold weighing 5 lb;

2 gold lamps each weighing 1 lb;

a gold chandelier weighing 2 lb;

a silver tower with dolphins, weighing 25 lb;

3 silver scyphi each weighing 8 lb;

12 <silver> service chalices each weighing 2 lb;

a silver altar weighing 40 lb;

10 silver lamps weighing 20 lb;

2 silver amae each weighing 10 lb.

10. In the basilica of St Laurence the martyr:

10 silver chandeliers weighing 60 lb;

26 bronze chandeliers;

silver services for baptism and for penance, weighing 10 lb;

50 bronze lights.

11. In Rome he arranged services to circulate around the established *stationes*:

a gold scyphus for stational use, weighing 8 lb;

25 silver scyphi for the *tituli*, each weighing 10 lb;

25 silver amae each weighing 10 lb;

50 <silver> service chalices each weighing 2 lb.

He had all these kept in safety at the Constantinian basilica and at St Mary's.

12. He built a monastery at St Laurence's, and a bath, and another in the open air, and a *praetorium* to St Stephen (he also built the oratory of St Stephen in the Lateran Baptistery). In the same place he also built two libraries; and in Rome a monastery, Ad Lunam.

13. He performed one December ordination in Rome, 25 priests, 6 deacons; for various places 22 bishops. He was buried at St Laurence's in the crypt, close to the body of the holy bishop Xystus. The bishopric was vacant 10 days.

49. 1. SIMPLICIUS [3. 3. 468 - 10. 3. 483], born in Tibur, son of Castinus, held the see 15 years 1 month 7 days.

He dedicated the basilica of St Stephen on the Caelian Hill in Rome; and the basilica of St Andrew the apostle close to the basilica of St Mary; and another basilica of St Stephen close to the basilica of St Laurence; and in Rome close to the Licinian palace another basilica, of St Bibiana the martyr, where her body rests.

2. He fixed the weekly turns at St Peter's, St Paul's, and St Laurence's, so that priests should remain there for penitents and for baptism—from region 3 at St Laurence's, region 1 at St Paul's, regions 6 and 7 at St Peter's.

3. In his episcopacy a report came from Greece from Acacius bishop of Constantinople. It asserted that Peter of Alexandria was a Eutychian heretic; the memorial had been produced by bishop Acacius and bore his own signature. Then the church, that is the first apostolic see, took official action. The prelate bishop Simplicius heard the case and condemned Peter of Alexandria, against whom Acacius brought innumerable charges, but so as to grant him a time for repentance. **4.** Then Timothy, the catholic, and Acacius wrote back saying that Peter had even been mixed up in the death of the catholic Proterius. Archbishop Simplicius then dissembled and never sent Acacius a reply; but he condemned Peter, awaiting the time of his repentance.

5. In the Roman church he provided a gold scyphus weighing 5 lb; 16 silver chandeliers at St Peter's each weighing 12 lb.

He performed three December and February ordinations in Rome, 58 priests, 11 deacons; for various places 88 bishops. He was buried in St Peter's on 2 March. The bishopric was vacant 6 days.

50. 1. FELIX [III; 13. 3. 483 - 1. 3. 492], born in Rome, son of Felix, priest of the *titulus* of Fasciola, held the see 8 years 11 months 17 days. He was bishop in the time of king Odovacer until the time of king Theoderic. He built the basilica of St Agapitus close to the basilica of St Laurence the martyr.

2. In his episcopacy there came another report from Greece, that Peter of Alexandria had been reinstated by Acacius bishop of Constantinople. Then the revered Felix, archbishop of the apostolic see of Rome, sent a *defensor* with the advice of his see—a council had been held—and condemned Acacius as well as Peter. **3.** Three years later there came another report from the emperor Zeno, that Acacius had repented and should be readmitted. Then pope Felix sent two bishops, Misenus and Vitalis: if they found Acacius still in league with Peter they should condemn them again, but if not they should present them with a document of repentance. When they entered Constantinople the above-mentioned bishops were corrupted by a bribe and failed to fulfil the instruction of the apostolic see. **4.** But when they returned to the apostolic see at Rome, pope Felix held a council and after an inquiry he found that the two bishops on trial, Misenus and Vitalis, were guilty of accepting a bribe, and he excommunicated bishops Misenus and Vitalis. Then bishop Misenus admitted he had been corrupted by a bribe; and the council granted him a time for repentance. This happened when Odovacer was king.

5. He performed two December ordinations in Rome, 28 priests, 5 deacons; for various places 31 bishops. He was buried in St Paul's. The bishopric was vacant 5 days. After his death a decree about the whole church was issued by the priests and deacons <that no one should ever presume to take precipitate action about a matter which should at some time come up for legal restitution>.

51. 1. GELASIUS [1. 3. 492 - 21. 11. 496], born in Africa, son of Valerius, held the see 4 years 8 months 18 days. He was bishop in the time of king Theoderic and the emperor Zeno. <In his time was discovered the church of the holy angel on Mount Garganus.> In his time Manichaeans were discovered in Rome; these he ordered to be deported into exile, and their books he burnt with fire before the doors of St Mary's basilica. **2.** In pursuance of the acts of a synod he tearfully recalled bishop Misenus who had been purged to the satisfaction of a document [of repentance]; he restored to his church the man who had sinned in the matter of Acacius and Peter. He was a lover of the clergy and the poor and he augmented the clergy. He delivered the city of Rome from danger of famine. He issued a decree about the whole church. **3.** In his time there again came a report from Greece, that Peter and Acacius were causing many evils and murders at Constantinople. At that time John, the catholic bishop of Alexandria, came in flight to the apostolic see in Rome; blessed Gelasius received him gloriously and even provided a second bishopric for him. **4.** Then he held a synod and sent a despatch throughout the district of the East; he sent a second despatch and condemned Acacius and Peter for all time if they did not repent and crave a penance to satisfy the document <—he would wait for the apostolic see to be satisfied according to the humanity of the church's first see>.

5. He dedicated the basilica of St Euphemia the martyr in the city of Tibur 20 miles from the city; and other basilicas: those of Saints Nicander, Eleutherius, and Andrew on the Via Labicana at the Villa Pertusa; and he built another basilica of St Mary on the Via Laurentina on the farm Crispinis <20 miles from the city>.

6. He produced five books against Nestorius and Eutyches <which are kept safe today in the archive of the church library>; and he produced <tracts,

and> hymns in the metre of St Ambrose; and two books against Arius; he also produced with careful wording prefaces and prayers for the sacraments; and many letters on the faith with polished vocabulary. The clergy increased while he was bishop. **7.** He performed two February and December ordinations in Rome, 32 priests, 2 deacons; for various places 67 bishops. He was buried in St Peter's on 21 November. After his death the bishopric was vacant 7 days.

52. 1. ANASTASIUS [II; 24. 11. 496 - 19. 11. 498], born in Rome, son of Peter, from the 5th region, Caput Tauri, held the see 1 year 11 months 24 days. He was bishop in the time of king Theoderic. He built the confessio of St Laurence the martyr, of silver weighing 100 lb. **2.** At that time many clerics and priests removed themselves from communion with him because, without taking advice from the priests, bishops and clerics of the whole catholic church, he had entered into communion with a deacon of Thessalonica named Photinus who was in league with Acacius, and because he wanted to reinstate Acacius secretly, though in this he failed. He was struck down by God's will. **3.** He performed one December ordination in Rome, 12 priests; for various places 16 bishops. He was buried in St Peter's on 19 November. The bishopric was vacant 4 days.

53. 1. SYMMACHUS [22. 11. 498 - 19. 7. 514], born in Sardinia, son of Fortunatus, held the see 15 years 7 months 27 days. He was bishop in the time of king Theoderic and the emperor Anastasius, from 22 November to 19 July. **2.** He and Laurence were ordained in rivalry on the same day, Symmachus in the Constantinian basilica, Laurence in St Mary's. That was why the clergy were split and the senate were also divided, some with Symmachus, others with Laurence. Once the dispute had begun, both sides agreed to go to Ravenna for king Theoderic to arbitrate. When both reached Ravenna, he made the fair decision that the one who was ordained first and whose faction was found to be the largest should hold the apostolic see. In applying this principle, an investigation into the facts found in favour of Symmachus, and he was made prelate. Then pope Symmachus gathered a synod and, guided by sympathy for Laurence, set him up as bishop of the city of Nuceria.

3. But four years later some of the clergy and some of the senate, particularly Festus and Probinus, were driven by jealousy to bring a charge against Symmachus; they suborned false witnesses whom they sent to king Theoderic at Ravenna with their accusation against blessed

Symmachus; and they privately recalled Laurence after drawing up the written charge at Rome. They created a schism and the clergy were again divided, some in communion with Symmachus, others with Laurentius. Then the senators Festus and Probinus sent the king a report and began to negotiate with the king to send a visitor to the apostolic see; and the king, contrary to the canons, gave them Peter, bishop of the city of Altinum. **4.** Then blessed Symmachus gathered 115 bishops, and a synod was held in which he was acquitted of the false charge, while Peter of Altinum was condemned as an intruder into the apostolic see as was Laurence of Nuceria for invading bishop Symmachus' see while he was still alive. Then blessed Symmachus was gloriously reinstated to sit in St Peter's as prelate of the apostolic see by all the bishops, priests, and deacons, the whole clergy and the people. **5.** Then Festus the leader of the senate and exconsul and Probinus the exconsul began to battle with other senators in Rome, particularly with Faustus the exconsul. Their malice caused slaughter and murder among the clergy. Those who were rightly in communion with blessed Symmachus and chanced to be at large in the city were killed by the sword; they even displaced dedicated women and virgins from their monasteries or houses; they stripped women, injured them with cuts, and wounded them with blows. In the midst of the city they fought battles every day against the church. He [Festus] even killed many *sacerdotes*, including Dignissimus and Gordian the priests of St Peter *ad vincula* and Saints John and Paul; these they killed with clubs and sword. They killed many Christians, so that it was unsafe for any of the clergy to travel in the city by day or night. On the church's side there fought only the exconsul Faustus.

After all this, blessed Symmachus found Manichaeans in Rome; all their images and books he destroyed by fire outside the doors of the Constantinian basilica, and he sent the actual persons into exile. He was bishop from the consulship of Paulinus [498] to that of Senator [514].

6. He built the basilica of St Andrew the apostle at St Peter's, where he provided:

> a canopy of finest silver and a confessio weighing 120 lb;
> 3 silver arches weighing 60 lb;
> the oratory of St Thomas the apostle:
>> silver weighing <300 lb>, for the confessio, 20 lb;
>> a silver arch weighing 16 lb;
> the confessio of St Cassian and of Saints Protus and
>> Hyacinth, of silver weighing 20 lb;

a silver arch weighing 12 lb;
the oratory of St Apollinaris:
31 lb weight of silver for the confessio with the arch;
the oratory of St Sossus:
a confessio of silver weighing 20lb.

7. Also, at the font in St Peter's basilica:
the oratory of the Holy Cross: the confessio of silver, and the cross of gold with jewels in which he enclosed the Lord's wood—the gold cross itself weighing 10 lb;
and he built 2 oratories, of St John the Evangelist and St John the Baptist—30 lb weight of silver for their confessiones and arches; all these chambers he contructed complete from the ground up.

He decorated St Peter's basilica with marble: at St Peter's fountain with the square colonnade he provided marble adornments, including mosaic lambs, crosses, and palms. He completely enclosed the actual atrium; outside the doors of St Peter's he widened the steps, he built other steps under the awning on right and left, and there he also built episcopal rooms on right and left. He also set up by the steps to the atrium another fountain outside in the open, and he built a convenience for people to use when needed; he built other steps for the climb to St Andrew's, and set up a fountain.

8. He built the basilica of St Agatha the martyr on the Via Aurelia at the farm Lardarius; he constructed it from the ground up, with a font, where he placed 2 silver arches.

Then he built the basilica of St Pancras; he provided a silver arch weighing 15 lb and there he also built a bath.

Also, at St Paul's: in the basilica he renewed the apse which was liable to collapse; he provided a picture as decoration behind the confessio, and built an apse-vault and a *matroneum*. Over the confessio he placed a silver image of the Saviour and the 12 apostles, weighing 120 lb. He built steps in front of the basilica's doors into the atrium, and a fountain. Behind the apse he had water laid on, and he also built a bath there from the ground up.

9. Inside Rome he constructed the basilica of Saints Silvester and Martin from the ground up, close to the <baths of> Trajan, where he also built a silver canopy over the altar, weighing 120 lb;
12 silver arches each weighing 10 lb;
a silver confessio weighing 15 lb.

At Saints John and Paul he built steps behind the apse.

Also, at St Michael the Archangel's he enlarged the basilica, built steps, and laid on water.

Also, at St Mary's he constructed the oratory of Saints Cosmas and Damian from the ground up.

10. Also, on the Via Trebana at the 27th mile from Rome, at the request of the illustrious praetorian prefect Albinus and of Glaphyra who did the building from the ground up at their own expense, he dedicated a basilica to St Peter, on the farm Pacinianus.

Also, at St Peter's, St Paul's, and St Laurence's he constructed accommodation for the poor.

Also at St Peter's he provided:

> 20 silver chandeliers each weighing 15 lb;
> 22 silver arches each weighing 20 lb.

He repaired the basilica of St Felicity, which was liable to collapse.

He renewed the apse of St Agnes' which was liable to collapse, and the whole basilica.

11. He decreed that on every Lord's day and on the feasts of martyrs the <angelic> hymn 'Glory be to God on high' should be sung. For the sake of St Alexander's body, he improved the cemetery of the Jordani. Every year he provided cash and clothing throughout Africa and Sardinia for bishops who had been forced into exile. He ransomed for cash prisoners throughout the Ligurias, Milan, and various provinces; he gave them many gifts and let them go their way. **12.** He performed four December and February ordinations in Rome, 92 priests, 16 deacons; for various places 117 bishops. He was buried in St Peter's on 19 July. The bishopric was vacant 7 days. As a confessor he rested in peace. <Buried 19th day of July.>

54. 1. HORMISDAS [20. 7. 514 - 6. 8. 523], born in Campania, son of Justus, from the city of Frusino, held the see 9 years 17 days. He was bishop in the time of king Theoderic and the emperor Anastasius from the consulship of Senator [514] to that of Symmachus and Boethius [522]. He settled the clergy, and taught them the psalms. He built a basilica in the territory of Albanum on the property Mefontis.

2. Then, pursuant to the decree of a synod, he sent to Greece a display of the apostolic see's humanity, since the Greeks were held under the bond of an anathema because of Peter bishop of Alexandria and Acacius bishop of Constantinople, John being now bishop of Constantinople. On the advice of king Theoderic he despatched Ennodius bishop of Ticinum,

Fortunatus bishop of Catina, Venantius priest of the city of Rome, Vitalis deacon of the apostolic see, and Hilarus notary of the same see. They reached the emperor Anastasius but achieved nothing. **3.** A second time he sent the same Ennodius and Peregrinus bishop of Misenum carrying 19 letters to confirm the faith and secret admonishments, with the text of a document [of repentance]. The emperor Anastasius refused to agree to the document, since he too was implicated in the Eutychian heresy. So he wanted to corrupt these envoys of the apostolic see with a bribe. But they spurned Anastasius and absolutely refused to take the cash if he would not do what would satisfy the apostolic see. In fury the emperor threw them out by a postern gate and put them on a dangerous ship, along with soldiers, and the *magistriani* and *praefectiani* Heliodorus and Demetrius. Their orders from Anastasius included a prohibition on going to any city; **4.** yet the apostolic see's envoys stealthily used the services of orthodox monks to publish the 19 letters on the faith throughout all the cities. But the bishops of the cities who were in league with the emperor were afraid and sent all these letters on the faith to Constantinople as incriminating. Anastasius was enraged against pope Hormisdas and included in the imperial mandates he wrote: 'It is our wish to give orders, not to take them'. Then by the will of the Deity the emperor was struck by a divine thunderbolt and died.

5. And so the orthodox Justin assumed the *imperium*; and he sent his warrant by Gratus of illustrious name to Hormisdas pope of the apostolic see, in the hope the peace of the churches might be reinstated by the apostolic see. Then on the advice of king Theoderic bishop Hormisdas despatched from the apostolic see Germanus bishop of Capua, John, Blandus the priest, Felix and Dioscorus, deacons of the apostolic see, and Peter the notary (these he instructed on every aspect of the faith), with the text of the document of repentance. As they approached Constantinople the great grace of faith shone so brightly that a crowd of orthodox monks and an enormous crowd of illustrious men, including the emperor Justin and the consul Vitalianus, met them at the place called Castellum Rotundum and accompanied them into Constantinople. In glory and praise they entered the city, along with the illustrious Gratus; and gloriously were they received by the orthodox emperor Justin. **6.** So all the clergy, along with John bishop of Constantinople, aware that they had had such a welcome and conscious that they were the ones who had been in league with Anastasius, locked themselves in the great church called St Sophia, and after discussion sent this message to the emperor: 'Unless we get an account of why our bishop Acacius has been condemned, there is no way we will come to agree with the apostolic see'... *[for the lacuna see p. 112]*

8. Pope Hormisdas betook himself to king Theoderic at Ravenna, and on his advice sent his warrant to Justin; with his seal and signature and the text of the document he reinstated those who condemned Peter and Acacius and all the heretics into unity with the apostolic see.

9. He discovered Manichaeans whom he tried with an investigation under blows and sent into exile, and he burnt their books before the doors of the Constantinian basilica. In his time the episcopate was restored to Africa after 74 years—it had been wiped out by the heretics.

10. At that time a diadem with precious jewels came from Clovis the Christian king of the Franks as a gift to St Peter the apostle.

In his episcopacy there came from Greece many gold and silver vessels, and:

> gospels with gold covers and precious jewels, weighing 15 lb;
> a gold paten with jacinths, weighing 20 lb;
> 2 silver patens each weighing 25 lb;
> a gold scyphus with jewels, weighing 8 lb;
> a gold scyphus surrounded with a diadem, weighing 8 lb;
> 3 silver-gilt scyphi each weighing 5 lb;
> an electrum bowl weighing 2 lb;
> 2 gold wax-chests weighing 6 lb;
> purple-dyed pallia with gold-work patches of cloth and of
>   imperial vesture;
> an incense-burner over the confessio of St Peter the apostle.

All these were presented by the orthodox emperor Justin as an offering for prayers answered.

Then king Theoderic presented to St Peter the apostle 2 silver candlesticks weighing 70 lb.

11. Then pope Hormisdas constructed at St Peter's a beam which he covered with silver, weighing 1040 lb.

He provided in the Constantinian basilica:

> a silver arch before the altar, weighing 20 lb;
> 16 silver chandeliers each weighing 12 lb.

Also at St Paul's he provided:

> 2 silver arches each weighing 20 lb;
> 16 silver chandeliers <each> weighing 15 lb;
> 3 silver amae each weighing 10 lb;
> 6 silver scyphi for stational use, with stoppers, each weighing 6 lb.

12. He performed December ordinations in Rome, 21 priests; for various places 55 bishops. He was buried in St Peter's on 6 August in the consulship of Maximus [523]. The bishopric was vacant 6 days.

55. 1. JOHN [I; 13. 8. 523 - 18. 5. 526], born in Tuscia, son of Constantius, held the see 2 years 9 months 17 days. He was bishop from the consulship of Maximus [523] to that of Olybrius [526] in the time of Theoderic and the Christian emperor Justin. He was summoned to Ravenna by king Theoderic; at the king's request he agreed to be sent to Constantinople on an embassy to the orthodox emperor Justin, because at that time the devout Justin, in the burning depths of his love for the Christian faith, wanted to drive heretics out: in the deep fervour of his Christianity he adopted a plan to consecrate the churches of the Arians as catholic ones. **2.** That was why when the heretic king Theoderic heard of it he was incensed and wanted to put the whole of Italy to the sword. Then pope John, weak from illness, travelled in tears, and along with him went senators and exconsuls—Theodore, Importunus, and Agapitus the exconsuls, and another Agapitus, a patrician. The orders they were given to take on their embassy were that the churches in the areas of the east were to be restored to the heretics and if this was not done he would destroy the whole of Italy with the sword. **3.** While they were travelling with pope John, the whole city came out to meet blessed John at the 15th mile with torches and crosses in honour of the blessed apostles Peter and Paul. Those among the Greeks who were old men testified that from the time of the emperor Constantine and blessed Silvester bishop of the apostolic see [such an event had never occurred, but now] in the time of the emperor Justin the area of Greece had deserved to receive in glory the vicar of St Peter the apostle. Then the emperor Justin gave honour to God, abased himself on the ground and prostrated himself before the blessed pope John. **4.** Then pope and senators implored the emperor with much weeping that their embassy might be acceptable in his sight. Pope John and those devout senators deserved their complete success, and Italy was delivered from the heretic king Theoderic. Justin was filled with joy because he had deserved as emperor to see the vicar of St Peter the apostle in his own realm; and at his hands the emperor Justin was gloriously crowned.

5. Meanwhile, when the above-mentioned men—namely pope John and the senators Theodore, Importunus, and Agapitus the exconsuls, and Agapitus the patrician (who died at Thessalonica)—when they were still at Constantinople, the heretic king Theoderic arrested two distinguished senators and exconsuls, Symmachus and Boethius, and slew them with the sword. **6.** Then the venerable pope John and the senators came home in glory after obtaining everything from the emperor Justin; king Theoderic the heretic received them with great treachery and hatred—namely pope John and the senators—and he wanted to put them too to the sword, but in fear of the emperor Justin's wrath he destroyed them all by maltreatment in prison, so that blessed pope John, bishop of the principal see, maltreated in prison, grew weak and died. He died in prison at Ravenna on 18 May—a martyr. After this deed, it was almighty God's will that the heretic king Theoderic suddenly collapsed and died on the 98th day after the blessed John's death in prison.

7. Pope John rebuilt the cemetery of the martyrs Saints Nereus and Achilleus on the Via Ardeatina. He also renewed the cemetery of Saints Felix and Adauctus. He also renewed the cemetery of Priscilla <on the Via Salaria>.

At that time an adornment was placed above the confessio of St Peter the apostle, of prase and jacinth jewels.

Also in his time the emperor Justin presented:

a gold paten with jewels, weighing 20 lb;

a gold chalice with jewels, weighing 5 lb;

5 silver scyphi;

15 gold-worked pallia;

John himself brought these to St Peter's, St Paul's, St Mary's, and St Laurence's.

8. He ordained 15 bishops for various places. His body was transported from Ravenna and buried in St Peter's on 27 May in the consulship of Olybrius [526]. The bishopric was vacant 58 days.

56. **1.** FELIX [IV; 12. 7. 526 - 22. 9. 530], born in Samnium, son of Castorius, held the see 4 years 2 months 13 days. He was bishop in the time of king Theoderic and of the emperor Justin from 12 July in the consulship of Maburtius [527] to 12 October in that of Lampadius and Orestes [530]. **2.** He built the basilica of Saints Cosmas and Damian in Rome, in the area called the Via Sacra, close to the temple of the City of Rome. In his time the basilica of St Saturninus the martyr on the Via Salaria was destroyed by fire; he rebuilt it from the ground up. He was ordained peacefully, and lived through to the time of Athalaric. **3.** He performed two February and March ordinations in Rome, 55 priests, 4

deacons; for various places 29 bishops. He was buried in St Peter's basilica on 12 October. The bishopric was vacant 3 days.

57. **1.** BONIFACE [II; 22 9. 530 - 17. 10. 532], born in Rome, son of Sigibuld, held the see 2 years 26 days. He was bishop in the time of the heretic king Athalaric and of the <catholic> emperor Justin. He and Dioscorus were ordained in rivalry. Dioscorus was ordained in the Constantinian basilica, Boniface in the basilica of Julius; and the strife among the clergy and senate lasted 28 days. Then Dioscorus died on 14 October. **2.** In that same period Boniface, driven by jealousy and malice, caused great bitterness by reconciling the clergy under the bond of an anathema made out with their signatures—as if in condemnation of Dioscorus, he hid the manuscript in the church archive; he gathered the clergy together, yet no one assented to his episcopacy since the great majority had been on Dioscorus' side.

3. He presented the priests, deacons, subdeacons, and notaries with plates of metal from legacies he had received, and when there was a risk of famine he came to the clergy's assistance with much giving of alms. He gathered a synod in St Peter's basilica, and issued a decree that he should ordain his own successor. He reinforced this decree, in favour of the deacon Vigilius, with the signatures of the *sacerdotes* and with an oath before the confessio of St Peter. **4.** Then a second synod was held, and the *sacerdotes* all decided, thanks to their reverence for the holy see, that this had been done against the canons, and that his fault in appointing his own successor was glaring. Pope Boniface himself acknowledged he had acted unconstitutionally in putting his own signature to the document in favour of the deacon Vigilius. In front of the confessio of St Peter in the presence of all the *sacerdotes*, clergy, and senate, he destroyed the actual decree by fire.

5. Then a report arrived from the African bishops dealing with their government—that the bishop of Carthage was to act in every matter on the advice of the apostolic see. He was buried in St Peter's <on the 17th day of October in the consulship of Lampadius <and Orestes> [530]>. The bishopric was vacant 2 months 15 days <in the 11th indiction [532-533]>.

58. **1.** JOHN [II; 2. 1. 533 - 8. 5. 535], also known as Mercurius, born in Rome, son of Projectus, from the Caelian Hill, held the see 2 years 4 months 6 days. He was bishop in the time of king Athalaric and the <catholic> emperor Justinian. Then the devout emperor, in the depths of

his love for the Christian religion, sent to the apostolic see by the hands of the bishops Hypatius and Demetrius a statement of his faith, written in his own hand. **2.** At the same time the Christian emperor Justinian Augustus presented to St Peter the apostle:

a gold scyphus surrounded with prases and pearls;
and 2 other silver chalices;
silver scyphi weighing 5 lb;
2 silver chalices each weighing 5 lb;
4 purple-dyed gold-worked pallia.

3. He performed a December ordination in Rome, 15 priests; for various places 21 bishops. He was buried in St Peter's <on 27 May in the second year after Lampadius' consulship [532]>. The bishopric was vacant 6 days.

59. **1.** AGAPITUS [13. 5. 535 - 22. 4. 536], born in Rome, son of the priest Gordian, was a cleric from Saints John and Paul; he held the see 11 months 18 days. At the beginning of his episcopate in the midst of the church when everyone was gathered he destroyed by fire the documents of anathema which Boniface had uncanonically and maliciously extorted from the priests and bishops against Dioscorus, and he released the entire church from the malice of faithless men.

2. He was sent by Theodahad king of the Goths to the lord Justinian Augustus on an embassy, because the emperor was at that time infuriated with king Theodahad for killing king Theoderic's daughter queen Amalasuintha; she had entrusted herself to Justinian and he had made Theodahad king. Agapitus travelled to Constantinople, 22 April. On entering Constantinople bishop Agapitus was gloriously received. First he began to discuss religion with the pious prince Justinian. The blessed bishop Agapitus consistently gave him a response about the Lord Jesus Christ as God and Man which accorded with the apostolic faith, namely that there are two natures in one Christ. Once the dispute started, the Lord's presence enabled him to detect that the bishop of Constantinople, Anthimus by name, was a heretic. **3.** When the dispute occurred between the emperor and pope Agapitus, Justinian told him: 'Either you will agree with us or I will have you sent into exile'. Then the blessed pope Agapitus made this reply joyfully to the emperor: 'Sinner that I am, I have long wanted to come to the most Christian emperor Justinian—but now I have encountered Diocletian; yet I am not in the least afraid of your threats'. And the venerable pope Agapitus spoke to him again: 'Just to show you how inadequate you are in the Christian religion, try getting your bishop to admit that there are two natures in Christ'. **4.** Then on the emperor's instruction the bishop of Constantinople, Anthimus by name, was summoned and a debate was opened. Under the questioning of pope Agapitus he always refused to give a catholic reply which would admit the doctrine that there are two natures in one Lord Jesus Christ. The holy pope Agapitus convicted him of error and was honoured by all Christians. **5.** Then the pious emperor Justinian was filled with joy and abased himself before the apostolic see, prostrating himself before the blessed pope Agapitus. Straightaway he excommunicated Anthimus and sent him into exile. Then the emperor requested the pope to consecrate in Anthimus' place a catholic bishop, Menas by name.

So Agapitus achieved everything for which he had been sent. **6.** But a number of days later he was struck ill and died at Constantinople on 22 April. His body was transported in a lead coffin to St Peter's <at Rome> and buried there on 20 September. He performed an ordination in Rome, 4 deacons; for various places 11 bishops. The bishopric was vacant 1 month 28 days.

60. **1.** SILVERIUS [1. 6. 536 - deposed 11. 3, abdicated 11. 11, died 2. 12. 537], born in Campania, son of Hormisdas bishop of Rome, held the see 1 year 5 months 11 days. The tyrant Theodahad put him up without any consultation about the decree. Theodahad was corrupted by a cash gift, and instilled in the clergy the fear that anyone not consenting to this man's ordination would suffer by the sword. So the *sacerdotes* did not subscribe to him in accordance with the ancient method, nor did they confirm a decree before his ordination. Though he had been ordained through force and fear, in order to safeguard the unity of the church and religion the priests subscribed to Silverius after his ordination.

But two months later the tyrant Theodahad was snuffed out by God's will, and Vitiges was raised up as king. **2.** He immediately travelled to Ravenna and forcibly took queen Amalasuintha's daughter as his wife. The lord emperor Justinian Augustus was infuriated <when he heard> that Theodahad had killed a queen who had entrusted herself to him, and sent the patrician Belisarius with an army to free all of Italy from occupation by the Goths. When the patrician arrived he spent some time in the district of Sicily. **3.** But hearing that the Goths had made themselves a king against Justinian's wish, he came to the district of Campania close to Naples and with his army embarked on a siege of that city, since its citizens refused to open up to him. Then the patrician gained entry to the

city by fighting. Driven by fury he killed both the Goths and all the
Neapolitan citizens, and embarked on a sack from which he did not even
spare the churches, such a sack that he killed husbands by the sword in
their wives' presence and eliminated the captured sons and wives of
nobles. No one was spared, not *sacerdotes*, not God's servants, not virgin
nuns.

4. Then a great war took place—Vitiges came against Belisarius and
the city of Rome. The patrician entered Rome on 10 December; he
surrounded and fortified the city with garrisons and defences, by work on
the walls and repairs to the earthworks. On the very night of his entry, the
Goths who had been inside the city or outside its walls fled and left all the
gates open in their haste to get to Ravenna. Then king Vitiges collected an
enormous army of Goths and returned to attack Rome on 21 February. He
pitched camp by the Milvian Bridge and laid siege to the city. Then
Belisarius, fighting for the name of Rome, shut himself inside <and
garrisoned> it. **5.** During those days the city was under such a siege as
totally to prevent anyone leaving or entering it. All private, state, and
church property was destroyed by fire, while men were cut down by the
sword. The sword killed those it killed, famine killed those it killed,
pestilence killed those it killed. Even churches and bodies of the holy
martyrs were destroyed by the Goths. So great was the hunger within the
city that even water would have had to be paid for had not springs
provided relief. Great battles took place against the city. During that time
it was the patrician Belisarius whose resistance to king Vitiges and the
horde of Goths gave protection to the Romans and delivered the city and
name of Rome through his garrison. The siege of the city and of Portus
Romanus by the Goths lasted one year. But Belisarius won the fight
against the Goths, and one year later they fled to Ravenna.

Meanwhile so great was the famine throughout the world that Datius,
bishop of the city of Milan, in his report recounted openly that in the
district of Liguria women had eaten their own children from poverty and
hunger: some of these women, he reported, were members of his own
church...

* * *

6. Meanwhile Belisarius travelled to Naples and arranged its affairs.
Later he came to Rome and was given a courteous reception by the lord

Silverius; Belisarius moved to the Pincian Palace. On 11 May [March] in the 15th indiction [537]. ... The deacon Vigilius was then *apocrisiarius* at Constantinople. The empress was sympathetic to the patriarch Anthimus who had been deposed by holy pope Agapitus; he had found him to be a heretic and had set God's servant Menas in his place. Then the emperor after discussing the matter with the deacon Vigilius sent a letter to pope Silverius in Rome with the request and demand: 'Do not hesitate to come and visit us, or be sure to restore Anthimus to his place'. When blessed Silverius read this letter he groaned and said: 'Now I know that this affair has brought my life to an end'. But with his confidence placed in God and St Peter the apostle, the most blessed Silverius wrote back to the empress: 'Lady empress, to restore a heretic who has been condemned in his wickedness is something I can never bring myself to do'. 7. Then the empress was infuriated and sent mandates by the deacon Vigilius to the patrician Belisarius: 'Look for some pretexts to deal with pope Silverius and depose him from the bishopric, or be sure to send him quickly over to us. Look, you have present with you the archdeacon Vigilius our dearly beloved *apocrisiarius*, who has given us his word he will restore the patriarch Anthimus'.

When Belisarius received this mandate he said: 'For my part I will carry out the mandate, but if anyone gets involved in killing pope Silverius he will have to account for his actions to our Lord Jesus Christ'. Certain false witnesses, prompted by the mandate, came forward and said: 'We caught pope Silverius corresponding with the king of the Goths: 'Come to the Gate called Asinaria near the Lateran and I will hand the city and the patrician Belisarius over to you''. When Belisarius heard this he did not believe it since he knew that it was through malice that stories of this kind were told against the pope. But as many persisted with the same accusation, he grew afraid. 8. He had the blessed pope Silverius come to him at the Pincian Palace, and he made all the clergy wait at the first and second curtains. On Silverius' entry with Vigilius alone into the inner chamber, the patrician Antonina was lying on a couch with the patrician Belisarius sitting at her feet. When Antonina saw him she said to him: 'Tell us, lord pope Silverius, what have we done to you and the Romans to make you want to betray us into the hands of the Goths?' While she was still speaking, John, regionary subdeacon of the first region, came in, took the *pallium* from his neck and led him into a side room. He stripped him, dressed him in a monk's habit and hid him away. 9. Then Xystus, regionary subdeacon of the sixth region, seeing him now as a monk, came out and announced to the clergy that the lord pope had been deposed and had become a monk. On hearing this they all fled.

The archdeacon Vigilius took him into his own charge, so to speak, sent him into exile at Pontiae, and fed him on the Bread of Affliction and the Water of Distress. He grew weak, died, and became a confessor. He was buried in the same place on 20 June; and the sick come there in great numbers and are cured. He performed one December ordination, 14 priests <5 deacons>; for various places 18 bishops. The bishopric was vacant.

61. **1.** VIGILIUS [29. 3. 537 - 7. 6. 555], born in Rome, son of the consul John, held the see 17 years 6 months 26 days. At that time the patrician Belisarius began war against Vitiges king of the Goths. When the king fled by night, the master of the soldiers, John surnamed the Bloody, went in pursuit, caught him, and brought him to Belisarius and Vigilius at Rome. Then they swore him oaths in the basilica of Julius to take him safe to the emperor Justinian. When they had brought him to Constantinople, the emperor was pleased and made him a patrician and a count, and sent him over to the border with the Persians, where his life came to an end. The emperor questioned Belisarius about his dealings with the Romans, and how he had appointed Vigilius in Silverius' place. Emperor and empress then thanked him and giving him another post they sent him to Africa <against Wintarith king of the Vandals, so that he could do in Africa what he had done in Italy>. When he reached Africa, though pretending peace, he murdered Wintarith king of the Vandals, and Africa was brought back into the State. **2.** Then Belisarius came to Rome, and from the spoils of the Vandals presented to St Peter by the hands of pope Vigilius a gold cross with jewels, weighing 100 lb, with an inscription about his victories, and the two great silver-gilt candlesticks which still stand today before St Peter's body. Belisarius also presented many other gifts and alms for the poor; he built a hostel for strangers on the Via Lata, and the monastery of St Juvenal on the Via Flaminia close to the city of Horta, where he presented many properties and gifts.

3. Then the empress Theodora wrote to pope Vigilius: 'Come now, keep the promise you made us of your own free will about our father Anthimus, and restore him to his office'. To this Vigilius wrote back: 'Far be this from me, Lady empress. Once I spoke badly and unwisely, but now there is no way I can agree with you to restore a man who is a heretic and under an anathema. Unworthy I may be, but I am the vicar of St Peter the apostle just as were my holy predecessors Agapitus and Silverius who condemned him.'

Then the Romans sent their petitions against Vigilius—that it had been on his advice that the holy pope Silverius was deposed, pointing out 'to your Piety <Lady empress> that he is dealing harshly with your servants the Romans, his very own people: we accuse him of murder; he fell into such a rage that he struck his notary, who immediately fell dead at his feet. Also he gave his niece Vigilia to the consul Asterius, the son of a widow, and then took an opportunity to have him arrested at night and beaten to death.' **4.** Hearing this the empress sent the *scribo* Anthemus to Rome with her mandates and with greater authority, saying: 'Leave him be if he is in St Peter's basilica—otherwise if you find Vigilius in the Lateran or in the palace or in any church, put him on a ship immediately and bring him to us—or by Him that Lives for ever I will have you flayed'. Anthemus came to Rome and found him on 22 November in St Caecilia's church—it was her feast day. He was arrested as he distributed the gifts to the people, and they took him down to the Tiber and put him on a ship. The plebs and populace followed him, shouting to have a prayer from him. When he had given them a prayer the whole people replied 'Amen' and the ship cast off. When the Roman people saw that the ship in which Vigilius was sitting was on the move, they started to throw stones, branches, and cooking-pots after him, and to say: 'Take your famine with you! Take your deaths with you! You treated the Romans badly, may you meet evil where you are going.' His supporters also followed him away from the church.

5. When he reached the city of Catina in Sicily he was allowed to perform the December ordination, priests and deacons; from them he sent back over to Rome Ampliatus the priest as his *vicedominus*, and Valentine bishop of Saints Rufina and Secunda to guard the Lateran and govern the clergy. He bade farewell to all and entered Constantinople on Christmas Eve. The emperor came to meet him, they kissed each other and began to weep; the people went ahead of him till they got to the church of St Sophia, chanting: 'Behold the Lord and Master comes,' etc. During two years there were disputes about the patriarch Anthimus, how he had promised to give him his place back; and he was shown a bond in his own handwriting that he would recall him to his rank. But Vigilius completely refused to agree with them; he had enough courage to prefer death to life. **6.** Then pope Vigilius said: 'As I see it, it is not the most pious princes Justinian and Theodora who have made me come to them; instead I know today I have encountered Diocletian and Eleutheria. Do what you want; for I am getting my just deserts'. Then someone struck him on the face saying: 'Murderer! Don't you know those you are speaking to? Don't you know that you killed pope Silverius and murdered a widow's son with kicks and cudgels?' Then he fled into St Euphemia's basilica and clutched a column of the altar. He was pulled away from it, thrown outside the church, and <the empress Theodora> had a rope put round his neck; they dragged him through the whole city until nightfall, then cast him into prison, giving him small amounts of bread and water. The Roman clergy who were with him were sent into exile to work in various mines.

7. Then the Goths made Badua, called Totila, their king. He came down on Rome and besieged it. Such a famine occurred in Rome that they even wanted to eat their own children. One day in the 13th indiction [549-550] he entered Rome by St Paul's Gate. To prevent the Romans dying by the sword he had a war-trumpet sounded all night till the whole people fled or hid themselves in the churches. The king <after his entry> stayed with the Romans like a father with his children. Then some of the senators—the patricians and exconsuls Cethegus, Albinus, and Basilius—escaped, reached Constantinople and were presented before the emperor Justinian in their affliction and desolation. The emperor consoled them and enriched them as befitted Roman consuls.

8. Then he sent his eunuch and chamberlain Narses to Italy. He gave battle to the Goths; God gave him victory, the king was slain, and a large number of Goths were killed. Then the clergy came together and requested Narses to petition the emperor with them that if pope Vigilius and the priests, deacons, and clergy who had been sent into exile with him were still alive, they should be allowed to return. The emperor and all the senate received the report of Narses and the whole Roman clergy, and rejoiced that God had given peace to the Romans. Next the emperor sent his mandates to the various places where they had been sent into exile, Gypsus and Proconnesus, had them brought before him and said to them: 'Do you want to have your former pope Vigilius back? You have my pleasure. But if not you have here your archdeacon Pelagius, and my hand will go with you.' They all replied: 'May God rebuke your Piety; give us back Vigilius now, and when God <the creator of all> wishes him to pass from this world, then on your order we can be given our archdeacon Pelagius'. 9. Then he sent them all away with Vigilius. They came to the city of Syracuse in Sicily. In agony from his affliction with gallstones, Vigilius died. His body was taken to Rome and buried at St Marcellus' on

the Via Salaria <in the cemetery of Priscilla>. He performed two December ordinations, 46 priests, 16 deacons; for various places 81 bishops. The bishopric was vacant 3 months 5 days.

62. **1.** PELAGIUS [I; 16. 4. 556 - 4. 3. 561], born in Rome, son of the *vicarianus* John, held the see 11 years 10 months 18 days. Since there were no bishops who would ordain him, two bishops were found, John of Perusia and Bonus of Ferentinum, and Andrew a priest from Ostia; these ordained him pontiff. Then there were no clergy who could be given preferment: monasteries and a large number of the devout, the prudent, and the nobility withdrew from communion with him saying he had implicated himself in the death of pope Vigilius and so had brought great punishments on himself. **2.** Then Narses <the patrician> and pope Pelagius adopted a plan: when the litany had been given out from St Pancras' they processed with hymns and spiritual chants to St Peter's. Pelagius held the gospels and the Lord's cross above his head and went up to the ambo; in this way he satisfied the entire populace and plebs that he had caused Vigilius no harm. Pope Pelagius also added this: 'I ask you to confirm this memorial of mine: if there is anyone to be given preferment in holy church <he must be proved worthy> from doorkeeper up to the ranks of the episcopate, he should not advance by offering gold or by making promises: you all know that is simoniacal. But if there is anyone learned in God's work and living a good life, we bid him to reach the top rank not through bribery but by his good lifestyle.' **3.** Then he made a god-fearing man Valentine his notary, and had all the gold and silver vessels and *pallia* restored in all the churches. Then was begun the basilica of the apostles Philip and James; when the building of it was starting, he died and was buried at St Peter's. **4.** He performed two December ordinations, 26 priests, 9 deacons; for various places 49 bishops. The bishopric was vacant 3 months 25 days. <Buried 2nd day of March.>

63. **1.** JOHN [III; 17. 7. 561 - 13. 7. 574], born in Rome, son of the illustrious Anastasius, held the see 12 years 11 months 26 days. He loved and restored the cemeteries of the holy martyrs. It was his institution that every Sunday in these cemeteries the offering, the vessels, and the lighting should be serviced from the Lateran. He completed the church of the apostles Philip and James and dedicated it.

2. Then the Heruli rebelled, appointed themselves a king, Sindual, and oppressed all Italy. Narses went out against him, the king was killed, and he brought the whole Heruli people under his yoke. Next came Amingus, duke of the Franks, and Buccellinus, who likewise oppressed Italy, but with the Lord's help they too were killed by Narses: the whole of Italy was glad. **3.** Then the Romans, driven by malice, petitioned Justinian [Justin II] and Sophia: 'it would be better for the Romans to serve the Goths than the Greeks when the eunuch Narses is a ruler who subjects us to slavery and our most pious prince does not know it. Either deliver us from his hand or we and the Roman citizenry will serve the barbarians.' Hearing this Narses said: 'If I have maltreated the Romans let me suffer evil'. Then he left Rome, came to Campania, and wrote to the Lombard nation to come and occupy Italy. **4.** When pope John realized they had sent their petition against Narses to the emperor, he quickly went to Naples and began to request him to come back to Rome. Narses said: 'Tell me, most holy pope, how have I maltreated the Romans? I shall go to the feet of him who sent me. Let all Italy know how I have laboured on its behalf with all my strength.' Pope John replied: 'I shall depart before you leave this land'. Narses returned with pope John. **5.** The holy pope kept himself back at the cemetery of Tiburtius and Valerian and stayed there a long time—he even consecrated bishops there. But Narses did enter Rome. A long time later he died; his body was put in a lead coffin and taken back with all his riches to Constantinople.

6. Then pope John also died and was buried in St Peter's. He performed two December ordinations, 38 priests, 13 deacons; for various places 61 bishops. The bishopric was vacant 10 months 3 days. <On 13th day of July.>

64. 1. BENEDICT [I; 2. 6. 575 - 30. 7. 579], born in Rome, son of Boniface, held the see 4 years 1 month 28 days. At that time the Lombard nation invaded the whole of Italy, and the famine then was so extreme that a large number of walled towns even surrendered to the Lombards to relieve their want and hunger. When the pious emperor Justinian [Justin II] realized that Rome was endangered by hunger and mortality he sent to Egypt and had ships laden with corn sent across to Rome; so it was that God showed mercy on the land of Italy. **2.** In the midst of these labours and afflictions the holy pope Benedict died. He was buried in St Peter's in the *secretarium*. He performed one December ordination, 15 priests, 3 deacons; for various places 21 bishops. The bishopric was vacant 3 months 10 days. <On the 30th day of July.>

65. 1. PELAGIUS [II; 26. 11. 579 - 7. 2. 590], born in Rome, son of Unigild, held the see 10 years 2 months 10 days. He was ordained without the emperor's mandate because the Lombards were besieging Rome and causing much devastation in Italy. At that time the rains were so great that everyone said the waters of the Flood had overflowed; so great was the disaster that no one could remember anything ever like it. **2.** He covered St Peter's body with silver-gilt panels. He made his own house into an almshouse for the aged poor. He built the cemetery of St Hermes the martyr. Over the body of St Laurence he built a basilica from the ground up and decorated the martyr's tomb with silver panels. **3.** He died and was buried at St Peter's. He performed two December ordinations, 28 priests, 8 deacons; for various places 48 bishops. The bishopric was vacant 6 months 25 days <on the 7th day of February> <in the 5th indiction [587]>. <From the death of St Silvester to Gregory I was 246 years>.

66. 1. GREGORY [I; 3. 9. 590 - 12. 3. 604], born in Rome, son of Gordian, held the see 13 years 6 months 10 days. He produced 40 homilies on the gospels, 35 on Job, 20 on Ezekiel, the Pastoral <Care>, 4 books of Dialogues, and many other <good> works we cannot enumerate. **2.** At that time the patrician and exarch Romanus came to Rome and on his return journey to Ravenna recaptured cities held by the Lombards— Sutrium, Polymartium, Horta, Tuder, Ameria, Perusia, Lucioli, and many others. **3.** Then the holy Gregory sent God's servants Mellitus, Augustine, John, and many other godfearing monks with them, to preach to the English nation and convert them to the Lord Jesus Christ. In the recital of the Canon he added: 'and dispose our days in thy peace' etc. **4.** For St Peter's <over the altar> he provided a fine-silver canopy with its four columns, provided a purple-dyed cloth to go above the apostle's body, and decorated it with the finest gold, weighing 100 lb; he brought it about that mass could be celebrated above St Peter's body. At St Paul's he made the same arrangements. Then he dedicated the church of the Goths in the Subura in the name of St Agatha the martyr. **5.** He established his own house as a monastery. He died and was buried in St Peter's in front of the *secretarium* <on the 12th day of March>. He performed two ordinations, one in Lent, the other in September, 39 priests, 5 deacons; for various places 62 bishops. The bishopric was vacant 5 months 18 days <in the 7th indiction [604]>.

67. **1.** SABINIAN [13. 9. 604 - 22. 2. 606], born in Tuscia, from the city of Blera, son of Bonus, held the see 1 year 5 months 9 days. At that time there was a serious famine in Rome. Then peace was made with the Lombard people and he ordered the church's granaries to be opened and corn to be put on sale at 30 *modii* of wheat a solidus. **2.** He added lights at St Peter's. On his death his funeral procession was taken out by St John's Gate and conducted outside the city walls to the Milvian Bridge; he was buried in St Peter's. He filled the church with clergy. He made 26 bishops for various places. The see was vacant 11 months 26 days. <Buried on 22nd day of February.>

68. **1.** BONIFACE [III; 19. 2. 607 - 12. 11. 607], born in Rome, son of the *cataadioces* John, held the see 8 months 22 days. Because the church of Constantinople was describing itself as the first of all churches, he obtained from the emperor Phocas that St Peter's apostolic see <the Roman church> should be head of all the churches. **2.** At St Peter's where 72 bishops, 33 Roman priests, the deacons, and all the clergy were in session, he issued a decree under an anathema that no one while the pontiff or bishop of his city was living <or dying> should presume to address <anyone> or acquire supporters for himself; but that on the third day from his burial, with the clergy and the church's sons then assembled, there should be an election and anyone should have licence to elect whomever he wanted to have as his *sacerdos*. On his death he was buried in St Peter's <on the 12th day of November>. He made 21 bishops for various places. The bishopric was vacant 10 months 6 days.

69. **1.** BONIFACE [IV; 25. 8. 608 - 8. 5. 615], born among the Marsi, from the city of Valeria, son of the doctor John, held the see 6 years 8 months 13 days. In his time there were a very serious famine, plagues, and floods. **2.** At that time he asked the emperor Phocas for the temple called the Pantheon, and in it he made the church of <the glorious mother of God> the ever-virgin St Mary and all <holy> martyrs; <he placed relics in it;> in this church the emperor <Phocas> presented many gifts. **3.** He made his own house into a monastery and enriched it. On his death he was buried in St Peter's. He performed two December ordinations, 8 deacons; for various places 36 bishops. The bishopric was vacant 6 months 25 days. <Buried on the 25th day of May.>

70. **1.** DEUSDEDIT [19. 10. 615 - 8. 11. 618], born in Rome, son of the

subdeacon Stephen, held the see 3 years 23 days. He greatly loved the clergy; he restored the *sacerdotes* and clergy to their original places. **2.** At that time the patrician and chamberlain Eleutherius came to Ravenna and killed all who had been implicated in the death of the exarch John and the judges of the State. He came to Rome and was excellently received by the holy pope Deusdedit. Leaving Rome he came to Naples which was held by the rebel John of Compsa. Eleutherius fought his way against him into Naples and killed that upstart <and many others with him>. He returned to Ravenna, gave the soldiers their stipend, and <great> peace was achieved throughout Italy. **3.** He established the second *missa* among the clergy. Then in August of the 6th indiction [618] there was a major earthquake. Afterwards ensued a disaster among the people, affliction with the scab, so no one could recognize his own deceased. **4.** On his death he was buried in St Peter's; for his funeral he left an entire stipend to all the clergy. He performed three ordinations, 14 priests, 5 deacons; for various places 29 bishops. The bishopric was vacant 1 month 16 days. <Buried on the 8th day of November.>

71. **1.** BONIFACE [V; 23. 12. 619 - 25. 10. 625], born in Campania, from the city of Naples, son of John, held the see 5 years <10 days>. He decreed that a will should be valid in accordance with the emperor's mandate; that no one should be dragged from a church; that an acolyte should not presume to take up the relics of the holy martyrs, only a priest should; that at the Lateran a deacon should not be assisted at baptism by an acolyte but by the attached subdeacons. He completed the cemetery of St Nicomedes and dedicated it. Blessed Boniface was the most mild and compassionate of all men. He loved his clergy and gave them an entire stipend.

2. Before the date of his ordination, the patrician and eunuch Eleutherius rebelled and assumed the kingship. On his way to Rome he was killed at the Castrum called Lucioli by soldiers from the army of Ravenna, and his head was taken to the pious emperor at Constantinople.

3. On his death he was buried in St Peter's; for his funeral he left an entire stipend to all the clergy. He performed two December ordinations, 26 priests, 4 deacons; for various places 29 bishops. The bishopric was vacant 13 days. <Buried on the 25th day of October.>

72. **1.** HONORIUS [27. 10. 625 - 12. 10. 638], born in Campania, son of the consul Petronius, held the see 12 years 11 months 17 days. In his time he did much good. He educated the clergy.

He renewed all the sacred equipment at St Peter's and covered the apostle's confessio with fine silver weighing 187 lb. **2.** He covered the great main doors into the church—the ones called *Mediana*—with silver weighing 975 lb. He provided two pairs of great silver candlesticks, which are in front of St Peter's body, each weighing 62 lb. In the same place at St Andrew's, in front of the confessio, he provided a silver panel weighing 73 lb. In his time 16 roofbeams were hoisted up at St Peter's; he roofed his whole church with bronze tiles which he removed from the temple called that of Rome, with the assent of the pious emperor Heraclius.

3. Then he built from the ground up the church of St Agnes the martyr at the 3rd mile from Rome on the Via Nomentana, where the body rests. He decorated it to perfection on every side, and there he put many gifts. He also decorated her tomb with silver weighing 252 lb; over it he placed a bronze-gilt canopy of marvellous size, and he provided 3 gold bowls each weighing 1 lb; the apse of the same basilica he made of mosaic, and there too he presented many gifts.

In Rome he also built from the ground up the basilica of St Apollinaris the martyr, in the portico of St Peter's which is called *ad Palmata*, and there he bestowed many gifts. **4.** In the church he issued a decree, that every week on Saturday a litany should come out from St Apollinaris' to St Peter's with hymns and chants, and the whole people should join in it.

He built from the ground up the church to St Cyriac the martyr at the 7th mile on the Via Ostiensis, and there he presented a gift.

Then he built a church to the holy martyrs the Quattuor Coronati; he dedicated it and presented a gift.

He built from the ground up a church to St Severinus close to the city of Tibur at the 20th mile from Rome; he dedicated it and presented many gifts.

He also renewed the cemetery of Saints Marcellinus and Peter the martyrs on the Via Labicana.

5. Then he built from the ground up a basilica to St Pancras the martyr at the 2nd mile <from Rome> on the Via Aurelia, and decorated his tomb with silver weighing 120 lb; <and there he established a mill on the wall at the place of Trajan close to the city wall and [repaired?] the channel which brings water into [from?] Lacus Sabbatinus, and under it a channel which brings the water of [to?] the Tiber;> and he built a silver canopy above the altar, weighing 187 lb. He provided 5 silver arches each weighing 15 lb, and 3 gold candelabra each weighing 1 lb; he also presented many good things there.

6. In Rome he built the church of St Lucy close to St Silvester's; he also dedicated it and presented many gifts.

He built the church of St Hadrian <the martyr> <on the Via Sacra> at the Three Fates; he also dedicated it and presented many gifts.

<He made in his own house close to the Lateran a monastery in honour of Saints Andrew and Bartholomew the apostles, which is called that of Honorius; there he also presented estates and gifts.>

He did much else which would take too long to recount. <He built many basilicas and monasteries for monks; he confirmed the decree of St Gregory on the Antiphonal and order of offices and psalms; and that the monks should leave off Alleluia in Septuagesima; and at Easter and Whitsun, as the people were displeased, they should recite only 3 lessons and 3 psalms like the Roman church, and should perform their office in the Roman manner during all of those two weeks.> **7.** He performed three <December> ordinations, 13 priests, 11 deacons; for various places 81 bishops. He <died and> was buried in the above place <at St Peter's> on 12 October. The bishopric was vacant 1 year 7 months 18 days.

73. **1.** SEVERINUS [28. 5. 640 - 2. 8 640], born in Rome, son of Avienus, held the see 2 months 4 days. In his time, while lord Severinus was still bishop-elect, the Lateran Episcopium was plundered by Maurice the *cartularius* and Isaac the patrician and exarch of Italy. But before Isaac arrived, it was Maurice who was driven by malice against God's church and adopted a plan with some perverse men: they incited the Roman army saying 'What use is it that so much money has been gathered into the Lateran Episcopium by pope Honorius while this army gets no support from it?—sometimes that man even stashed away the stipends the lord emperor periodically sent you'. **2.** On hearing this they were all incensed against God's church; in a state of excitement all the armed men who chanced to be in Rome, from youths to old men, came to the Lateran Episcopium. They could not get in by armed force as they met resistance from those who were with the holy lord Severinus. Seeing that they could achieve nothing, Maurice maliciously made the army take up occupation there inside the Lateran Episcopium where they stayed for three days. **3.** After the three days Maurice came in with the judges who were his accomplices in the plot. They sealed up the entire Vestry of the church and the sacred equipment of the Episcopium, which various Christian emperors, patricians, and consuls had bequeathed to St Peter for the redemption of their souls, for distribution as alms to the poor at particular

times, and for the redemption of captives. **4.** Afterwards Maurice sent a letter to Isaac the patrician at Ravenna about the action that had been taken, how he had used the army to seal up the entire Vestry of the Episcopium, and that they could plunder all its wealth without any trouble. When Isaac had realized how true this was, he came to Rome and sent all the dignitaries of the church into exile, each to a different city, so that there would be none of the clergy likely to resist. Some days later Isaac entered the Lateran Episcopium, and was there for eight days until they had plundered all the wealth. Then he sent a portion of the wealth to Heraclius at the imperial city. After this the holy Severinus was ordained; **5.** and Isaac returned to Ravenna.

He renewed the mosaic in the apse of St Peter's, which had been destroyed. He loved the clergy and increased the bounty for them all. He was holy, the kindliest of all men, a lover of the poor, generous, and most mild. For various places he made 4 bishops. He left an entire stipend to all the clergy. He was buried in St Peter's on 2 August. The bishopric was vacant 4 months 24 days.

74. **1.** JOHN [IV; 24. 12. 640 - 12. 10. 642], born in Dalmatia, son of the *scholasticus* Venantius, held the see 1 year 9 months 18 days. In his time he sent much money by the holy and trustworthy abbot Martin throughout Dalmatia and Histria to redeem captives who had been despoiled by the barbarians. **2.** He built a church for the martyrs Saints Venantius, Anastasius, Maurus, and many other martyrs whose relics he had ordered to be brought from the Dalmatias and Histrias; he deposited them in that church close to the Lateran Font and the oratory of St John the Evangelist; he decorated it and presented various gifts: in the same place, 2 silver arches each weighing 15 lb, and also many other silver vessels. **3.** He performed two December ordinations, 19 priests, 5 deacons; for various places 18 bishops. He left an entire stipend to all the clergy. He was buried in St Peter's on 12 October. The bishopric was vacant 1 month 13 days.

75. **1.** THEODORE [24. 11. 642 - 14. 5. 649], born in Greece, son of Theodore a bishop from Jerusalem, held the see 6 years 5 months 18 days. He was a lover of the poor, generous, the kindliest of all men, and very compassionate.

In his time Maurice the *cartularius* (through whom the patrician Isaac had done much evil), now that his sins against St Peter had so increased as to inherit unquenchable fire, was driven into a plot with those who had previously joined him in pillaging God's church to rebel against Isaac. He sent through all the walled towns around Rome, gathered them together, and had them bind themselves under oath to him that none of them would thenceforth obey Isaac or his men—he claimed that Isaac had wanted to crown himself king. **2.** On hearing that Maurice and the whole army of Italy had taken oaths, Isaac sent Donus, the master of the soldiers and his *sacellarius*, with an army to Rome. When he reached Rome, all the judges and Roman armies who had previously bound themselves under oath to Maurice the *cartularius* were terrified into abandoning Maurice and siding with Donus. Coming into Rome Maurice fled into St Mary's *ad praesepe*. They took him from the church, put a halter round his neck, and did the same to all who were in the plot with him. He sent them in irons to Ravenna in the charge of Marinus the *scribo* and Thomatius the *cartularius*. They took them as far as a place close to Ravenna called Ficuclae, at the 12th mile from that city; there they beheaded Maurice, because the orders they had received from Isaac said that he should not enter Ravenna alive. After Maurice had been beheaded they carried his head into Ravenna. At the sight of it Isaac was glad and had it placed on a pole in the circus at Ravenna as an example to many. As for those who had been sent with him, he ordered them all to be closely confined in irons in prison until he had thought of a punishment. But in the period that all this was happening, Isaac soon by <the judgment of> God's will received a divine stroke; he collapsed and died. As for those who had been locked up, they were brought out from prison and each returned home. When the emperor heard that Isaac was dead, he sent the patrician Theodore, surnamed Calliopas, as exarch to rule all Italy.

3. Then Pyrrhus, former <bishop and> patriarch of Constantinople, came from Africa to the homes of the apostles at Rome. On his arrival he presented a signed acknowledgment to our apostolic see, in the presence of the whole clergy and people; in it he condemned everything written or done by himself or his predecessors against our unsullied faith. When he had done this, Theodore had him distribute gifts to the people and had a *cathedra* placed for him close to the altar, honouring him as the *sacerdos* of the imperial city. Later on he went back again like a dog to the vomit of his own impiety. Then the holy pope Theodore summoned all the *sacerdotes* and clergy in the church of St Peter prince of the apostles, condemned him under the bond of an anathema, and assigned deposition as the canonical penalty, a suitable reward and retribution for his transgression. Pyrrhus returned to the districts of the East.

4. At that time the bodies of the martyrs Saints Primus and Felician, which were buried in the *arenarium* on the Via Nomentana, were lifted and brought into Rome; they were deposited in the church of St Stephen the first martyr, and there he presented gifts: 3 gold bowls, a silver panel in front of the confessio, 2 silver arches.

5. He also built from the ground up the church to St Valentine on the Via Flaminia near the Milvian Bridge; he dedicated it and presented many gifts.

He also built an oratory to St Sebastian inside the Lateran Episcopium, and there too he bestowed gifts.

He built an oratory to St Euplus the martyr outside St Paul's Gate, and this he also <dedicated and> decorated.

6. Then the holy pope Theodore wrote to Paul, patriarch of the imperial city, both requesting him and reproving him in accordance with the canons, and also through *apocrisiarii*, as has been mentioned, who were specially delegated for this purpose and being present in person admonished him and declared that he should correct his falsehood and return to the orthodox faith of the catholic <and apostolic> church. Yet neither by request nor by reproof were they at all able to bring him back from his endeavour. On this account he was struck by the apostolic see with the just penalty of deposition.

7. He performed one December ordination, 21 priests, 4 deacons; for various places 46 bishops. The bishopric was vacant 52 days. He was buried in St Peter's on 14 May.

76. 1. MARTIN [5. 7. 649 - arrested 17. 6. 653, died in exile 16. 9. 655 (or 13. 4. 656?)], from the city of Tuder in the province of Tuscia, held the see 6 years 1 month 26 days. In his time Paul bishop of Constantinople, puffed up with a spirit of pride against the correct dogma of God's holy church, boldly presumed to contravene the definitions of the Fathers; what was more, he took care to mask his error with deceptions such as to induce even the clement emperor to issue a *Typus* which would destroy catholic dogma. In it he crippled all the statements of the holy Fathers with the utterances of the wickedest heretics, to give no definition or acknowledgment of either one or two wills or operations in Christ our Lord. It was to protect this kind of iniquity of his that he did what even the earlier heretics had never dared: lawlessly and presumptuously **2.** he went so far as to have the altar of our holy See, which had been consecrated in the venerable oratory in the house of Placidia, overthrown and destroyed, thus stopping our *apocrisiarii* from offering to God there the adorable immaculate Victim and receiving the sacraments of communion. Now in warning him to pull back from such a heretical purpose and in censuring him these *apocrisiarii* were following orders in an apostolic warrant; for this he variously persecuted them and other orthodox men and venerable *sacerdotes*—some of them he confined in custody, some he sent into exile, others he subjected to the lash. These men were convulsing nearly the whole world. Very many of the orthodox from different places openly brought complaints against them to our apostolic see, beseeching that the entire fabric of evil and perversion should be eradicated through an apostolic warrant, so as to stop the pernicious sickness of their *Ecthesis* tearing the body of the whole catholic church apart.

3. Then the holy and blessed Martin sent and gathered 105 bishops in Rome; and following the teachings of the orthodox Fathers he held a synod in the church of the Saviour close to the Lateran Episcopium. In session were the bishops and priests, with the deacons and the whole clergy in attendance. They condemned Cyrus of Alexandria, Sergius, Pyrrhus, and Paul patriarchs of Constantinople, for daring to contrive novelties against the unsullied faith: in their haste to throttle it, they had concocted a confusion of heretical dogmas against God's catholic church, and so they were sentenced to the penalty of anathema. This synod is kept today in the church archive. He made copies and sent them through all the districts of East and West, broadcasting them by the hands of the orthodox faithful.

4. At the same period the emperor sent to Italy the chamberlain and exarch Olympius to rule all Italy, giving him his instructions: 'As Paul the patriarch of this City (which God preserve) has pointed out to us, it is essential that your Honour bring matters to a conclusion. On the one hand if you find that that province agrees with the *Typus* we have issued you must get all the bishops there, the church officials attached to proprietors and occupiers, and those who are away from home, to subscribe to it; if, as their Honours Plato the patrician and Eupraxius have pointed out to us, you find you can persuade the army stationed there, we order you to arrest Martin who used to be *apocrisiarius* here in the imperial city, and afterwards to read the orthodox *Typus* we have issued in all the churches, and have all the bishops of Italy subscribe to it. On the other hand, if you find the army opposed to this course, keep quiet about it until you have

taken control of the whole province and can gather the army both of Rome and Ravenna to yourself. In this way you will be able to carry out your instructions as quickly as possible.'

5. Olympius came to Rome and found the holy Roman church united with all the Italian bishops, *sacerdotes*, and clergy. He attempted to carry out his orders by using the army and tried to introduce a schism into holy church by force. This went on a very long time; almighty God did not allow him to complete his efforts. **6.** Once he saw he was defeated by God's holy catholic and apostolic church he was forced to veer a little in his evil scheme so as to achieve by stealth what he had failed to do by force of arms. His intention was to kill the holy pope during the ceremonies of mass in the church of the ever-virgin Mary mother of God *ad praesepe* while he was giving him communion, and for this he had given orders to his *spatharius*. But almighty God, who casts a shield around his orthodox servants and delivers them from every evil, blinded the exarch's *spatharius*, and he was not permitted to see the pontiff distributing communion to the exarch or giving him the Peace, as this would have caused his blood to be shed and God's catholic church to be subjected to heresy—this is what that same bodyguard afterwards avowed to different people on oath. **7.** So when Olympius saw that God's hand was shielding holy pope Martin, he was forced to reconcile himself to the pontiff and disclose all his orders to that holy man. Now that he had made peace with God's holy church he mustered the army and set out for Sicily against the Saracen people who were living there. The result of sin was that the destruction befalling the Roman army was all the greater. After this the exarch died of disease.

* * *

8. Then the emperor sent his mandates with the exarch Theodore, surnamed Calliopas, and the imperial chamberlain Theodore also called Pellurius. Taking the holy pope Martin from the church of the Saviour, also called the Constantinian, they brought him to Constantinople. Even so, they failed to get his agreement. Then this holy man was sent into exile to the place called Chersona, where, as it pleased God, the life of this confessor of Christ ended in peace <and he was buried in the basilica of the ever-virgin St Mary>; and he works many miracles even to the present day. He performed two December ordinations, 11 priests, 5 deacons; for various places 33 bishops. <Buried on 17th day of September.>

77. 1. EUGENE [I; 10. 8. 654 - 2. 6. 657], born in Rome, from the 1st—the Aventine—region, a cleric from his cradle, son of Rufinianus, held the see 2 years 9 months 24 days. He was kind, mild, meek, courteous to all, and of remarkable holiness. He gave the customary stipend to the clergy and supplied alms to the needy, so that he ordered the full priestly allowances to be distributed to the poor, the clergy, and the household even on the day he passed away. **2.** In his time Peter, patriarch of Constantintople, following custom, sent a synodic letter to the apostolic see; it was completely unintelligible and went beyond the canons, failing to be explicit about the operations and wills in our Lord Jesus Christ. The people and clergy were incensed that he had sent such a synodic letter and refused to accept it, but with a great outcry it was flung out of God's holy church—the people and clergy would not even let the pope finish celebrating mass in the basilica of the ever-virgin Mary mother of God, called *ad praesepe*, until the pontiff himself had promised them he would permanently reject it. **3.** He performed ordinations: for various places 21 bishops. He was buried in St Peter's on 2 June. The bishopric was vacant 1 month 28 days.

78. 1. VITALIAN [30. 7. 657 - 27. 1. 672], born in Signia, province of Campania, son of Anastasius, held the see 14 years 6 months. He sent his *apocrisiarii* with the usual synodic letter to the pious emperors in the imperial city, informing them of his ordination. When they had been received and had secured the renewal of the church's privileges they returned home. Their Clemency sent to St Peter by the same envoys gold gospels decorated around with pearls of wondrous size. In every way he maintained the customary ecclesiastical discipline and authority. **2.** In his time the emperor Constantine [Constans II] came from the imperial city along the coast to Athens, thence to Tarentum, and then to Beneventum and Naples in the 6th indiction [663]. Afterwards he came to Rome, on the 5th day of July, a Wednesday, in the same indiction. The Apostolicus went to meet him with his clergy at the 6th mile from Rome and welcomed him. On the same day the emperor travelled to St Peter's for prayer and there he presented a gift; <another day to St Paul's and there he presented a gift;> on Saturday to St Mary's and again he presented a gift. On Sunday he proceeded to St Peter's with his army, all with wax tapers, and on its altar he presented a gold-wrought *pallium*; and mass was celebrated. **3.** Again on Saturday the emperor came to the Lateran, and bathed and dined there in the basilica of Vigilius. Again on Sunday there was a *statio* at St Peter's, and after mass was celebrated the emperor and pontiff bade farewell to each other. He stayed in Rome twelve days; he dismantled all the city's bronze decorations; he removed the bronze tiles from the roof of the church of St Mary *ad martyres*, and sent them to the imperial city with various other things he had dismantled. Afterwards on Monday he left Rome, returned to Naples, and thence passed on by land to Rhegium. **4.** Entering Sicily in the 7th indiction he lived in Syracuse. He imposed such afflictions on the people, occupiers, and proprietors of the provinces of Calabria, Sicily, Africa, and Sardinia for years on end by registrations of land and persons and by imposts on shipping as had never before been seen, and such as even to separate wives from their husbands and sons from their parents; so much else unheard of did they suffer that no one expected to survive. They even took away all the sacred vessels and equipment from God's holy churches, leaving nothing behind. Afterwards, on the 15th day of July in the 12th indiction [669], the said emperor was murdered in his bath.

5. <Then pope Vitalian sent archbishop Theodore and abbot Hadrian to Britain; both were very learned men and they made very many of the churches of the English fruitful with the doctrine of the church; one of them, archbishop Theodore, with marvellous and accurate deliberation set down the judgments on sinners, that is to say how many years anyone has to do penance for each and every sin.> Not long after, the life of this holy man came to an end. **6.** He performed four ordinations, 22 priests, 1 deacon; for various places 97 bishops. He was buried in St Peter's on 27 January. The bishopric was vacant 2 months 13 days.

79. 1. ADEODATUS [11. 4. 672 - 17. 6. 676], born in Rome, one of the monks, son of Jovian, held the see 4 years 2 months 5 days. So great was he, so very mild and kind, that he freely welcomed any man, from the greatest to the least. To those away from home he showed compassion, so that no one doubted he would get what he craved. He increased the stipend for everyone.

2. In his time Mezezius, who was in Sicily with the eastern army, rebelled and seized the kingship. The army of Italy made their way, some through the districts of Histria, some through the districts of Campania; others, those of Africa, made their way through the districts of Sardinia. In this way they all came to Sicily and to Syracuse, and with God's help the unspeakable Mezezius was killed. Many of his judges were taken mutilated to Constantinople along with the rebel's head. **3.** Afterwards the

Saracens came to Sicily, occupied Syracuse and caused much slaughter among the people who had fled to the walled towns and the hills. They returned to Alexandria taking with them enormous booty and the bronze which had been brought there by sea from Rome.

4. He suitably restored and dedicated the church of St Peter on the Via Portuensis close to the Pons Meruli.

With many new buildings this holy man enlarged the monastery of St Erasmus on the Caelian Hill, in which he had grown up; he acquired farmsteads, and in his lifetime he established there an abbot and a community.

5. After he passed away there was rain and thunder such as no one however old could remember—even men and cattle were destroyed by lightning. It was only because the Lord was placated by the Litanies which took place every day that men were able to thresh the grain and store it in granaries—so much so that the rain itself caused the crops to revive and ripen, and on this account men were amazed. **6.** He performed one December ordination, 14 priests, 2 deacons; for various places 46 bishops. He was buried in St Peter's on 26 June. The bishopric was vacant 4 months 15 days. <From the time of pope St Gregory's ordination down to here is 95 years 5 months 14 days.>

80. 1. DONUS [2. 11. 676 - 11. 4. 678], born in Rome, son of Maurice, held the see 1 year 5 months 10 days.

He paved the upper atrium of St Peter's, in the square colonnade in front of the church, with marble slabs.

He suitably repaired and restored the church of the Apostles on the Via Ostiensis.

He also dedicated the church of St Euphemia on the Via Appia.

He honoured the clergy of various ranks with preferments. **2.** At Rome, in the monastery called the Boethian, he discovered that the Syriac monks were Nestorians; he divided them among different monasteries, and established Roman monks in that monastery. In his time the church of Ravenna, which had separated itself from the Roman church to achieve independence, brought itself back into subjection to the ancient apostolic see; as it pleased God, that church's prelate, named Reparatus, instantly died. **3.** In the August while he was bishop-elect there appeared from the east a star from cockcrow till morning for three months, and its rays pierced the skies; at the sight of it all the provinces were agitated and peoples amazed. After turning in its tracks it disappeared; on which count a very great mortality ensued from the east. He performed one ordination, 10 priests, 5 deacons; for various places 6 bishops. He was buried in St Peter's on 11 April. The bishopric was vacant 2 months 15 days.

81. 1. AGATHO [27. 6. 678 - 10. 1. 681], born in Sicily, <one of the monks,> held the see 2 years 6 months 4 days. So kind and gentle was he that everyone attested him to be cheerful and pleasant. In his time Theodore archbishop of Ravenna, after the passage of many years, presented himself to the apostolic see.

3. He received an imperial mandate from the pious princes the emperors Constantine, Heraclius, and Tiberius, sent by the honourable secretary Epiphanius to his predecessor pope Donus, requesting and urging him about the need to send his *sacerdotes* and envoys to the imperial city to achieve the unity of God's holy churches; this he had no hesitation in arranging. He sent bishops Abundantius of Paternum [Tempsa], John of Rhegium, and John of Portus, the priests Theodore and George, the deacon John, the subdeacon Constantine, the priest Theodore from Ravenna, and some of God's servants the professed monks.

17. He honoured the clergy of various ranks with preferments beyond what was appropriate. Contrary to custom he became *arcarius* of the Roman church, and he dealt with the affairs of this treasurership by himself, issuing receipts under his own hand through the *nomenclator*. When weakened by illness he appointed an *arcarius* in the customary way. **16.** In his time on the 18th day of June in the 8th indiction [680], the moon underwent an eclipse; also in that month, July, August, and September, there was a great mortality in Rome, more serious than is recalled in the time of any other pontiff; so that parents and their children, brothers and their sisters, were taken in pairs on biers to their graves. Afterwards it kept causing devastation out in the suburbs and walled towns all around.

4. The apostolic see's envoys named above, who had been sent to the imperial city, entered it on the 10th day of November in the 9th indiction [680]; the Lord comforted them and the prince of the apostles went with them. They were received by the emperor in St Peter's chapel in the palace and they also presented him with the pontiff's documents. When he had received these, he urged and advised them not to be stubborn or angry but peaceably disposed, to leave out philosophical declarations, and so satisfy the pure approved faith of the holy scriptures and the Fathers in their synodal decrees. He granted an adjournment for going over the documents and gave them everything necessary for their support and expenses, at the house called after Placidia. On the 18th day of the same month, **5.** a Sunday, they were summoned in procession to the church of the holy mother of God at Blachernae; to honour them the pious emperor even sent saddled horses with an escort from the palace. In this way he received them and repeated his advice that they should set out the testimonies of the venerable Fathers in a peaceable declaration.

6. On the 22nd day of November, in the basilica called Trullus inside the palace, he took his seat in royal state, and with him were George, patriarch of Constantinople, and Macarius of Antioch; the envoys of the apostolic see were received, then the metropolitans and bishops of the eastern parts, 150 in number. They stooped low to salute him and he bade them take their seats along with our men. After this came the patricians, the consuls, and the whole senate. His Piety inquired which side's evidence should be given first. The legates of the apostolic see said: 'It suits the interests of truth and reason that the side which claims there is one will and operation in the Lord Jesus Christ should put its case to the apostolic see.' **7.** They were pleased to hear this and said they were ready. When they were given permission, at that moment they brought in their books, various volumes and synods which they had falsified—for they reckoned they would not win with the truth, only with the lies and various fabrications they had added in their books. As they read them through one by one, they were found to be liars in stating there was one operation and will: in the fifth synod they had inserted fresh quires to falsify the letter of pope Vigilius to the patriarch Menas, and the document of Menas himself, so as to say one will and operation; this was evident to emperor and synod. On another day the pious emperor, defender of the catholic faith, took his seat in the council chamber, an inquiry into those codices was held, and thus he found that there were freshly inserted forgeries.

8. On the 12th day of November the synod was in session with his Piety; the envoys of the apostolic see were received and he bade them take their seats in the synod so that they represented the holy and blessed pope Agatho. They stated they would bring before the synod all the books they knew to deal with the matter of faith at issue; and this they did. George, deacon and archivist of the church of Constantinople, was summoned and instructed to bring the codices from the church's library out into the open for their inspection. When these were produced and read, both sets were found to agree in mentioning two natures and two wills and operations. Macarius was confounded before the synod and proved a liar. Then his imperial Piety laid a command on the patriarch George not to receive Macarius and his men into his church, and forbidding him to pursue the matter. This was his first downfall.

9. On the 14th day of February St Peter helped the light of truth appear: there were brought into the synod the statements of the venerable Fathers—John of Constantinople, Cyril, Athanasius, Basil, Gregory, Dionysius, Hilary, Ambrose, Augustine, and Leo—saying to the satisfaction of emperor and synod that there are two natural wills and operations in Christ <from his birth—one before all ages and timeless from the Father incorporeally, the other coming down from heaven and incarnate in the Virgin, the divine and human wills being inseparably united from the fact that in each of his natures that which wills exists according to his nature, and the divine and human operations being inseparably united from the fact that in each of his natures that which operates exists according to his nature>.

10. Next day the synod was in session in the same council chamber with the emperor; the synodal letter of the holy pope Agatho was read out, and to prove each point the statements of the Fathers were inserted; 125 of the western bishops had subscribed to this letter. After this the unspeakable Macarius was urged by the holy synod, the pious emperor, and the whole senate, to state whether he acknowledged one or two wills and operations. He would not listen and instead tried to say there was neither one nor two in the Saviour. Then the pious and serene emperor produced a volume to be read. In it was written the particular heretical dogma of Macarius, and he had put his signature to it, very clearly asserting that in the Lord there was one will; after his signature was that of the ex-patriarch Theodore, clearly in agreement with the contents. The patriarch George was questioned whether he embraced the faith taught by the apostolic see as stated in the documents of pope Agatho and the venerable holy Fathers. He answered that with permission he would give a suitable reply in writing. Meanwhile they went into recess.

11. On the 17th day of February, a Sunday, in the chapel of St Peter inside the palace, with the senate and patriarch in attendance, he received the legates of the apostolic see, who read out another petition sent by the holy pope to recommend them. On that day the holy patriarch George stated in writing that he believed the two natures, two wills and operations, and that he preached the same doctrine as the apostolic see and anathematized those who spoke of one nature, will, and operation.

12. On the 25th day of February the synod was in session with the pious emperor, and with them were the legates of the apostolic see; they summoned Macarius. When the emperor gave permission for them to divide, each taking the side he wanted, George, the patriarch of the imperial city, stood with his men on the orthodox side, while Macarius with his men stood on the other side, that of the heretics. The profession which the patriarch George had made and handed to the emperor was brought into the open and read. Macarius was urged to say what he felt and believed. He replied he would stick to the same perfidy he had previously expressed and would not acquiesce in the orthodox faith. **13.** At that point the holy synod and the emperor ordered his stole to be removed. Basil, the bishop from Crete, leapt up and removed it. With an anathema they threw him and his throne out of the synod. The Roman clerics threw his disciple Stephen out by the neck and expelled him from the synod. At that point so many jet-black spiderwebs fell among the people that everyone was astonished at the filth of heresies being expelled. And God's holy churches were with God's help united. **14.** In Macarius' place Theophanes, abbot of the monastery of Baias in Sicily, was ordained patriarch of the church of Antioch; while Macarius and his supporters—that is, the priests Stephen and Anastasius, the deacon Leontius, and the priests and cloistered monks Polychronius, Epiphanius, and Anastasius—were sent into exile at Rome. Then the names of the patriarchs were removed from the diptychs of the churches, the church pictures, and anywhere outside where they could be found—that is to say, the names of Cyrus, Sergius, Pyrrhus, Paul, and Peter, who until now had caused the spread of this error against the orthodox faith.

15. So great was the grace of almighty God granted to the envoys of the apostolic see, that to the joy of the people and of the holy council in the imperial city, on Sunday the Octave of Easter in the church of St Sophia, John bishop of Portus celebrated a public mass in Latin before the emperor and patriarchs. With one heart and voice they made their acclamations of praise for the victories of the pious emperors, this too in Latin.

2. In response to a petition he made, he received an imperial mandate by which, as he craved, the fee customarily paid for performing the ordination of the pontiff was abolished, but provided that when an election was held after his death, the man elected should not be ordained until the 'general decree' had been brought to the imperial city in accordance with the old custom; then, with their knowledge and on their mandate, the ordination could go ahead. **18.** He left one stipend to all the clergy, and to provide for the lights of the Apostles' and of St Mary's *ad praesepe*, 2160 solidi. He performed one ordination, 10 priests, 3 deacons; for various places 18 bishops. He was buried in St Peter's on 10 January. The bishopric was vacant 1 year 7 months 5 days.

82. 1. LEO the younger [II; 17. 8. 682 - 3. 7. 683], born in Sicily, son of Paul, held the see 10 months 17 days. He was a man of great eloquence, competently versed in holy scripture, proficient in Greek and Latin, and distinguished for his chanting and psalmody, which he interpreted elegantly and with the most sensitive and subtle touches. In speech too he was a man of education and refined in his choice of the lofty style. He gave encouragement to all good works and inspired a great flowering of knowledge among the people. He loved the poor, and was concerned to look after the destitute not merely with dutiful attention but through his own hard work and toil.

2. He received the acts of the sixth holy synod written in Greek; this was recently celebrated by God's providence in the imperial city, within the royal palace called Trullus, with the pious and clement emperor Constantine attending in his official capacity, and with him the legates of the apostolic see, two patriarchs, of Constantinople and Antioch, and 150 bishops. In it were condemned Cyrus, Sergius, Honorius, Pyrrhus, Paul, and Peter, also Macarius and his disciple Stephen, and Polychronius the new Simon—those who said or preached that there was one will and operation in the Lord Jesus Christ, or would again in future preach or defend this. From now on, two wills and operations must be spoken of in Christ our God, Governor and Saviour. With great application he translated the acts into Latin. Those defenders of heresy's evils, Macarius, Stephen, Polychronius, and Anastasius, as long as they refused to abandon their proposition, were confined in various monasteries. **3.** On the holy day of Epiphany this holy man absolved two men, Anastasius a priest and Leontius a deacon of the church of Constantinople, so they could share communion; they had been sent from the imperial city to Rome with Macarius and the rest without being anathematized by the holy synod; they now set forth in their own handwriting their faith in accordance with the holy synod's definition and anathematized all the heretics and their abovenamed followers, the men whom the holy synod and the apostolic see anathematized.

4. In his time an imperial mandate of the clement emperor was delivered whereby the church of Ravenna was restored under the control of the apostolic see: on the archbishop's death, the one elected should follow the old custom and come to Rome to be ordained. He issued a decree which is kept in the church archive, that the one ordained archbishop should not follow any custom of paying for the use of a *pallium* or the various church offices; and that the anniversary and requiem of the former bishop Maurus should not be observed. In order 'to cut off the offence', they restored to the holy see the *Typus* of independence which they had elicited for themselves.

5. He built a church in Rome close to St Bibiana's, where he deposited the bodies of Saints Simplicius, Faustinus, Beatrice, and other martyrs, and dedicated it in the name of the apostle St Paul on 22nd day of February; and there he presented gifts. <On the order of this beloved pontiff the church close to the Velabrum was built in honour of St Sebastian and the martyr George.>

6. In his time, on 16th day of April in the 11th indiction [683] the moon underwent an eclipse after [the Maundy Thursday mass of] the Lord's supper; nearly all night it laboured with a bloody countenance, and only after cockcrow did it slowly begin to clear and return to normal. **7.** He performed one ordination, on 27th day of June, 9 priests, 3 deacons; for various places 23 bishops. He was buried in St Peter's on 3 July. The bishopric was vacant 11 months 22 days. The holy man above described was ordained by three bishops, Andrew of Ostia, John of Portus, and Placentinus of Velitrae since the church of Albanum had no bishop.

83. 1. BENEDICT the younger [II; 26. 6. 684 - 8. 5. 685], born in Rome, son of John, held the see 10 months 12 days. From his early youth he had served in the church. In divine scripture and in chant while he was still a boy, and then in the office of the priesthood, he showed himself as befitted a man worthy of his name: in him grace and benediction from above truly overflowed. In both name and actions he was a worthy man to reach the dignity of the pontificate—a lover of the poor, humble, mild, with compassion for all and a most bountiful hand.

2. He restored St Peter's, and the church of the martyr St Laurence called that of Lucina. Also at St Valentine's on the Via Flaminia he provided over the altar an altarcloth with studs and thin bands, with a very precious border around it, adorned with gold buttons; similarly at St Mary's *ad martyres* another altarcloth of purple with a cross and chevrons and four gold-buttoned studs, with a very beautiful border all of silk; also at the above *titulus* of Lucina, another decorated altarcloth all of silk. He also provided 2 gold service chalices each weighing 1 lb.

3. He received <two> mandates of the great and clement emperor Constantine to the venerable clergy, people and most fortunate army of Rome, in which the emperor conceded that the one elected to the apostolic see should be ordained pontiff immediately and without delay. Like the clergy and army he received locks of the hair of the lord Justinian and of Heraclius, the clement emperor's sons, and also a mandate in which he intimated he had sent the hair.

4. In his time there appeared a star in the clear night sky, at about vigils, for some days between Christmas and Epiphany; it was totally overshadowed, like the moon beneath a cloud. Again in February after St Valentine's day, the star rose in daytime at midday in the west and sank in the eastern parts. Afterwards in March Mount Vesuvius in Campania erupted for some days, and all the places around were wiped out by its dust and ash.

5. On Easter Day this holy man honoured the clergy of various ranks with preferments. Immediately he fell ill and after some days he died. To all the clergy, the monasteries serving the poor, and the *mansionarii*, he left 30 lb of gold. He made 12 bishops for various places. He <died and> was buried in St Peter's on 8 May. The bishopric was vacant 2 months 15 days.

84. 1. JOHN [V; 23. 7. 685 - 2. 8. 686], born in Syria, from the province of Antioch, son of Cyriac, held the see 1 year 9 days, an energetic man, knowledgeable, and in every way temperate. It was in accordance with ancient custom, after the passing of many years and pontiffs, that he was elected by the commons in the church of the Saviour, called the Constantinian, and thereafter inducted into the Episcopium. **2.** While he was a deacon he was sent by pope Agatho of sacred memory to the imperial city <in the cause of the faith> with other priests to represent the apostolic see in the holy sixth synod, which by God's providence was gathered and celebrated there. When it ended the clement emperor let him depart thence; he came home bringing great joy to the church—the acts of the holy sixth synod itself, the clement prince's edict confirming the synod, and other imperial mandates which abolished many *annonocapita* for the patrimonies of Sicily and Calabria, the compulsory purchase-price of corn, and various other charges which the Roman church had been unable to pay every year.

3. Like his predecessor pope Leo, he was consecrated by three bishops, those of Ostia, Portus, and Velitrae. In his time the lord emperor Justinian

[II] began to reign on his father's death at the beginning of September in the 14th indiction [685]. With the Lord's help this clement prince established a ten years' peace by land and sea with the unspeakable Saracen people; and the province of Africa was subdued and brought back into the Roman empire.

4. Citonatus, archbishop of Caralis, had trespassed on an ordination for the church of Turris, performing it without the warrant of the pontiff— since anciently the right to perform this ordination belonged to the apostolic see, and although it had been temporarily granted to the church of Caralis, the effrontery of the archbishops had later brought about their suspension from it on the instructions of the pontiff in a decision of pope Martin of sacred memory. Because of this, after many years had passed, he held a council of *sacerdotes*, restored under the control of the apostolic see the new bishop whom that archbishop had ordained, and confirmed him in office; and their signed document is kept in the church archive.

5. This holy man was weakened by long-term illness, so that he could hardly even complete the ordinations of *sacerdotes*. To all the clergy, the monasteries serving the poor, and the *mansionarii*, he left 1900 solidi. He made 13 bishops for various places. He was buried in St Peter's on the 2nd day of August. The bishopric was vacant 2 months 18 days.

85. 1. CONON [21. 10. 686 - 21. 9. 687], born <in Greece> to a father who was a Thracesian, was brought up in Sicily and afterwards came to Rome, served in this church, and reached the dignity of the priesthood. He held the see 11 months. At his election, while the bishopric was under discussion, there was much argument, since the clergy favoured the archpriest Peter while the army were for Theodore, the next in seniority. The clergy assembled outside the doors of the Constantinian basilica and waited there, since men sent from the army to guard the locked main doors of the basilica were on the watch and would certainly not let anyone inside. The whole army had likewise assembled at the basilica of St Stephen the first martyr. They would not agree with the clergy, nor the clergy with them, on either of the above priests. **2.** Each side's negotiators came and went for a long time; nothing was going to produce agreement. Then the *sacerdotes* and clergy adopted a plan; singlemindedly they entered the Lateran Episcopium and elected and nominated the third in rank under the previous pontiff. He had a truly angelic appearance, venerable white hair, true speech, advanced age, an uncomplicated mind, and the quiet habits of the religious life, and at no time had he engaged in business or worldly affairs. Instantly all the judges and also the army officers came to hail him, and they all proclaimed his praises. When the army saw the unanimity of clergy and people in subscribing to the decree in his favour, they too gave way after a few days, agreed on this holy man and devoutly subscribed to the decree. With the clerics and people they sent the usual messengers to his Excellency Theodore the exarch.

3. He received an imperial mandate from the lord Justinian [II] in which the emperor intimated that he had come across the acts of the sixth holy synod, which his father lord Constantine of pious memory had held with God's help, and had them at hand; his Piety undertook to preserve and maintain the synod undefiled and unshaken for ever. In his time the emperor's Piety in an imperial mandate abolished 200 of the *annonocapita* paid each year from the patrimony of Bruttium and Lucania. Again he sent another mandate for the release of all the dependants of that patrimony and of Sicily; the army had been holding them as security for taxes.

4. It was against custom and without the clergy's consent, but at the instigation of evil men and to the repugnance of churchmen, that he appointed Constantine, a deacon of the church of Syracuse, as rector in the patrimony of Sicily. The man was fraudulent and evasive, but he even granted him permission to use the official saddle-cloth for travelling on horseback. Not long after the pontiff's death, the citizens and the occupiers of the patrimony stirred up a revolt because of him. Since it turned out that the judges disagreed about his case, the governor of the province confined him in close custody and sent him for trial to the judgment of the emperor.

5. This holy man was weakened by long-term illness, so that he could hardly even complete the ordinations of *sacerdotes*, and he died. Like his predecessor Benedict, he left a blessing in gold to all the clergy, the monasteries serving the poor, and the *mansionarii*. When his archdeacon had seen the pontiff weakened by illness, he was led on by covetousness for the legacy already announced but not yet paid, and he wrote to his Honour the new exarch John at Ravenna promising bribes to have himself elected to the pontificate. John gave orders to the judges he appointed for Rome and whom he sent to manage the city that on the pontiff's death his archdeacon was to be elected. He made 16 bishops for various places. He was buried in St Peter's on the 21st day of September. The bishopric was vacant 2 months 23 days.

86. 1. SERGIUS [I; 15. 12. 687 - 8. 9. 701], of Syrian origin from the region of Antioch, born to his father Tiberius at Panormus in Sicily, held the see 13 years 8 months 23 days. He came to Rome under the pontiff Adeodatus of holy memory and was numbered among the clergy of the Roman church; because he was studious and competent in the task of chanting, he was handed over to the precentor for education. He became an acolyte, rose through the ranks, and was ordained by the pontiff Leo of holy memory as priest for the *titulus* of St Susanna, called *duae domus*. In the period of his priesthood he celebrated the ceremonies of mass without stinting in the different cemeteries.

2. But after seven years, when Conon of blessed memory, prelate of the apostolic see, died, the Roman people as usually happens divided into two factions, and while one elected the archpriest Theodore, the other elected the archdeacon Paschal. Now Theodore and his supporters got to the patriarchate first and occupied its inner areas, while Paschal held the outer parts, from the oratory of St Silvester and the basilica of the house of Julius, which overlooks the grounds. Since neither would give way to the other, but each ferociously continued trying to dislodge the other, the dignitaries of the judges, the army of the Roman soldiery, the majority (if it may be said) of the clergy and particularly of the *sacerdotes*, and a crowd of the citizens, adopted a plan and made their way to the imperial palace. For a long time they discussed what should be done and how the struggle between the two elected rivals should be settled. It was God's will that with one mind they should settle on the person of the abovenamed Sergius, then a venerable priest. Taking him from the midst of the people, they brought him into the oratory of Christ's martyr St Caesarius, which is inside the imperial palace, and from there they led him to the Lateran Episcopium with praise and acclamation. **3.** Although the doors of the patriarchate were shut and barricaded on the inside, the faction which had elected the venerable Sergius was stronger and so had the advantage and forced an entry. When Sergius came in, one of the two men elected, the archpriest Theodore, immediately admitted defeat, and abased himself: he entered, greeted the elected holy Sergius, and kissed him.

But Paschal's hardness of heart would not let him do the same until, compelled and in confusion, willing or not, he entered and greeted his elected lord; yet Paschal did not desist from secretly sending to Ravenna messengers, and promises of money and various other gifts, to persuade the patrician and exarch John, surnamed Platyn, and his judges to come unannounced to Rome. And in such secrecy did he come to Rome that the flags and standards and soldiery of the Roman army did not go to meet him as was customary at the appropriate place, but only near the city itself. **4.** When the exarch arrived he realized that everyone had agreed on the person of the holy Sergius, and that the canvassing of himself had served no purpose, so, thanks to Paschal's wretched behaviour, he applied an imposition and penalty on the church of St Peter's; what Paschal had promised the exarch, that is, 100 lb of gold, he exacted on the part of the church, with the holy bishop-elect Sergius protesting that he had not promised to give anything and that there was no possibility of it. To move the minds of those who saw it to remorse, he had the chandeliers and crowns which from of old had hung before the holy altar and confessio of St Peter taken down and handed over as a pledge. **5.** Not even this deflected the exarch's hardness, until he had received precisely the stated 100 lb of gold. So although, as has been related, the wretched Paschal caused a loss and penalty to Christ's church, yet by Christ's favour, the priest Sergius, the one elected to the see of St Peter, was ordained pontiff. But not long afterwards, Paschal was deprived even of the office of archdeacon, by the judgment of God and of St Peter the prince of the apostles, because of certain magical practices, the groves he was attending to, and the fortune-telling that he was indulging in with other soothsayers. He was confined in a monastery, and after five years the hardness of his heart caused him to die unrepentant.

6. In his time the emperor Justinian ordered a council to be held in the imperial city, at which the legates of the apostolic see had forgathered, and to whose acts they were deceived into subscribing. He too was under pressure to subscribe, but he absolutely refused since certain chapters which went outside the usages of the church had been annexed to the acts. As if they were synodal definitions, six copies of the acts had been written out, signed by the three patriarchs of Constantinople, Alexandria, and Antioch and by the other prelates who had then forgathered there, confirmed by the hand of the emperor and placed in the despatch-box called *scevrocarnalis*. He sent them to Rome to be confirmed and signed at the top by the pontiff Sergius as head of all *sacerdotes*. **7.** As has been said, the blessed pontiff absolutely refused to agree with the emperor Justinian, nor did he tolerate those copies to be received or opened for reading. Instead he rejected them and set them aside as invalid, choosing to die sooner than consent to erroneous novelties. In scorn for the pontiff the emperor sent the *magistrianus* Sergius to Rome, and he took John, the beloved of God and bishop of Portus, and Boniface, counsellor of the apostolic see, away to the imperial city. Then he sent Zacharias, his ferocious chief *spatharius*, with a mandate to bring the pontiff as well to the imperial city. But God's mercy went before him, and St Peter, the apostle and prince of the apostles, supported him and preserved his church unmutilated: the hearts of the Ravennate soldiery were stirred up, along with those of the Pentapolitan duchy and of the parts all around, not to allow the pontiff of the apostolic see to go up to the imperial city. **8.** When a crowd of the soldiery forgathered from every side, Zacharias the *spatharius* was terrified, and fearing he might be killed by that mob of soldiers he craved that the gates of the city be shut and the pontiff be held. But in fear he took refuge in the pontiff's bedroom, and in tears he begged the pontiff to have mercy on him and not let anyone take his life. The army of Ravenna entered the city by St Peter's Gate with weapons, and the crowd came to the Lateran Episcopium, burning to see the pontiff whom they understood from a rumour that was going around had been smuggled out by night and put on a ship. Since both the upper and lower doors of the patriarchate had been shut, they threatened to pull them to the ground if they were not quickly opened; then in extreme terror and despair for his survival Zacharias the *spatharius* got under the pontiff's bed so that he went out of his mind and lost his senses. The blessed pope comforted him and told him to have no fear. **9.** The pontiff went outside to the basilica named after the lord pope Theodore; opening the doors and sitting on a seat beneath the Apostles, he honourably received the common soldiers and the people who had come to see him. Giving a suitable and gentle reply he calmed their feelings; though they, driven by enthusiasm, for love and reverence both for God's church and for the holy pope, did not give up picketing the patriarchate until they had expelled the *spatharius* Zacharias out of Rome with injuries and insults. And at that very same time the one who had sent him was by the Lord's retribution deprived of his realm. Thus by Christ's favour was God's church, with its prelate, preserved undisturbed.

10. In the shrine of St Peter the apostle this blessed man discovered, by God's revelation, a silver casket lying in a very dark corner; because of tarnishing during the years that had gone by, it was not even clear whether it was silver. So after praying he removed the seal impressed on it. He opened the reliquary and inside he found placed on top a feather cushion made all of silk, which is called *stauracis*. He took this away and lower down he saw a cross, very ornate with various precious stones. From it he removed the four plates in which the jewels were embedded, and he found placed inside a wonderfully large and indescribable portion of the saving wood of the Lord's Cross. From that day, for the salvation of the human race, this is kissed and worshipped by all Christian people on the day of the Exaltation of the Holy Cross in the basilica of the Saviour called Constantinian.

11. He provided the gold image of St Peter which is on the women's side, and also the great gold censer with columns and a lid, which he hung in front of the three gold images of St Peter; on feast days when the ceremonies of mass are celebrated, incense is unstintingly placed in it and a fragrant odour rises to almighty God. In the apse of this basilica, above the throne, he placed a silver canopy weighing 120 lb. He provided 6 silver lights in the basilica, weighing 170 lb, which are above the beams at the entrance to the confessio. Around the altar of the basilica to cover all four sides he provided 8 veils, 4 of white and 4 of scarlet cloth. He carefully renewed and repaired the awning and chambers which are all around the basilica, which had for a long time been damaged by dripping rainwater and building rubble. He renewed the mosaic which had been partly destroyed on the front of the atrium of the basilica. He also renewed the windowpanes of the basilica, both those above the throne and those above the silver main doors. **12.** He reburied the body of the highly esteemed Father and pontiff St Leo, which had been placed inconspicuously in the lower areas of the *secretarium* of the basilica, after carefully constructing a tomb in a public part of the basilica as revealed to him, and he decorated the tomb itself. He provided a great gold paten, with pearls around it and a cross of jacinth and emerald in the middle, weighing 20 lb.

He carefully renewed and repaired the awning and chambers around St Paul's basilica; for a long time these had been worn out by age. He also had beams brought from Calabria and renewed those in this basilica that he found to be the oldest. He replaced the very old image of the apostles which was above the basilica's doors.

13. He built an ambo and a canopy in the basilica of Saints Cosmas and Damian, and there he presented many gifts; he roofed and strengthened the cupola of this basilica by casting sheets of lead.

The canopy of St Susanna's basilica had been of wood; he built it of marble; and he also presented there various sacred equipment of gold and silver, and real estate.

The basilica of St Euphemia had for a long time been roofless; he roofed it and renovated it.

The basilica of St Aurea at Ostia had also been roofless and damaged; he roofed it and attentively renovated it.

The oratory of St Andrew the apostle, situated on the Via Labicana, he rebuilt from the ground.

14. He laid it down that at the time of the breaking of the Lord's body the clergy and people should sing 'Lamb of God, who takest away the sins of the world, have mercy on us'. He decreed that on the days of the Lord's Annunciation, of the Falling-asleep and Nativity of St Mary the ever-virgin mother of God, and of St Simeon (which the Greeks call *Hypapante*), a litany should go out from St Hadrian's and the people should meet up at St Mary's. He provided 4 silver arches in the basilica of St Laurence the martyr called the *titulus* of Lucina.

15. In his time the archbishop of the church of Aquileia, and the synod which comes under him, who, in error as they were, had not the faith to accept the holy fifth universal council, were instructed by the spiritual teachings and admonishments of this blessed pope; they were converted and agreed to accept that same venerable council. Those who were previously held by wickedness and error were enlightened by the doctrine of the apostolic see; now that they were peaceably in harmony with the truth, they were allowed to go home.

For the use and decoration of Christ's churches, he provided many altarcloths and gold and silver vessels for various churches. **16.** He ordained Damian as archbishop of the holy church of Ravenna. He ordained Beorhtweald as archbishop of Britain, and Clement [Willibrord] for the race of the Frisians. For various provinces he ordained 97 bishops. He performed two March ordinations, 18 priests, 4 deacons. <He held the see 13 years 8 months 23 days.> He was buried in St Peter's on 8 September in the 14th indiction [700] while Tiberius was emperor. The bishopric was vacant 1 month 20 days.

87. 1. JOHN [VI; 30. 10. 701 - 11. 1. 705], born in Greece, held the see 3 years 2 months 12 days. <He was bishop in the time of the emperor Tiberius.> In his time the chamberlain and patrician Theophylact, exarch of Italy, came from the districts of Sicily to Rome. Knowing that he was coming, the soldiery of the whole of Italy riotously forgathered in this city of Rome, meaning to cause the exarch trouble. To prevent his being injured, the pontiff interposed himself in person, closed the city gates, sent *sacerdotes* out to the encampment where they had forgathered, and with salutary admonitions pacified their riotous mutiny. **2.** But a just punishment for their action was meted out to some suspect individuals who had laid information against certain inhabitants of Rome and had offered the exarch a chance to strip them of what they owned.

Then Gisulf, duke of the Lombard people at Beneventum, came with all his might into Campania; he was causing much burning and devastation, had taken quite a number of captives, and was building an encampment as near Rome as the place called Horrea. Since there was no one who could resist him, the pontiff sent *sacerdotes* with apostolic gifts, ransomed all the captives from their hands, and made him go back home with his army.

3. He built a new ambo in the basilica of St Andrew the apostle, situated below the church of St Peter prince of the apostles.

Over the altar of St Mark's church he provided an altarcloth;

and white veils in St Paul's basilica, between the columns of the altar on right and left.

He performed one ordination of priests and deacons, that is, 9 priests, 2 deacons; and for various places he made 15 bishops. He was buried at St Peter's <on <the 2nd day of August> in the 3rd indiction [704-705] in the reign of the emperor Tiberius>. The bishopric was vacant 1 month 18 days.

88. 1. JOHN [VII; 1. 3. 705 - 18. 10. 707], born in Greece, son of Plato, held the see 2 years 7 months 17 days. <He was bishop in the time of the emperor Tiberius and the second reign of Justinian [II].> He was a man of great learning and eloquence.

Inside St Peter's church he built an oratory of the holy mother of God, coloured its walls with mosaic, expended there a large amount of gold and silver, and set up images of the venerable Fathers on right and left.

He restored the basilica of St Eugenia which had for a long time been roofless and damaged.

2. He also worked on the cemetery of the martyrs Saints Marcellian and Mark, and that of the pontiff St Damasus.

He also provided images in various churches; whoever wants to know what he looked like will find his face depicted on them.

He adorned with painting the basilica of the holy mother of God which is called *Antiqua*, and there he built a new ambo, and above the same church an Episcopium which he wanted to build for his own use, and there his life and the time of his pontificate came to an end. He provided an excellent gold chalice weighing 20 lb and decorated it with jewels.

3. In his time Aripert, king of the Lombards, by a donation made out in letters of gold, restored to the legal ownership of St Peter prince of the apostles the patrimony of the Cottian Alps; for a long time this had been alienated from the church's ownership and held by that same people.

4. In his time the emperor Justinian came from the districts of Chazaria through the places of Bulgaria along with Tervel as far as the imperial city, and got back the realm that was his own—he had been expelled from it. He also captured Leo and Tiberius who had usurped his place, and had their throats cut in the middle of the Circus when all the people were present. Thus he acquired the principate from which he had previously been ejected in tumult. **5.** Immediately after he entered the palace and obtained the *imperium*, he dealt with the matter of the copies of the acts he had previously sent to Rome in the time of the lord pontiff Sergius of apostolic memory, in which there were written various chapters in opposition to the Roman church. He despatched two metropolitan bishops, also sending with them a mandate in which he requested and urged the pontiff to gather a council of the apostolic church, and to confirm such of them as he approved, and quash and reject those which were adverse. But he, terrified in his human weakness, sent them back to the prince by the same metropolitans without any emendations at all. After that he did not endure long in this life. **6.** He made 19 bishops for various places. <He was buried at St Peter's in front of the altar of the holy mother of God which he had constructed, on 18 October in the 6th indiction [707] under Justinian <governing the Roman state>.> The bishopric was vacant 3 months.

89. 1. SISINNIUS [15. 1. 708 - 4. 2. 708], born in Syria, son of John, held the see 20 days. <He was bishop in the time of the emperor Justinian [II].> This man was so crippled by a gouty humour that he could not take his food with his own hands. Yet he had a resolute mind and was concerned for the inhabitants of this city. He ordered the burning of lime for the restoration of the walls <of this city>. **2.** But he died a sudden death. He made one bishop, for the island of Corsica. <He was buried in St Peter's> <on 6 November> <on ... in the 6th indiction [707-8] in the reign of Justinian.> The bishopric was vacant 1 month 18 days.

90. 1. CONSTANTINE [25. 3. 708 - 9. 4. 715], born in Syria, son of John, held the see 7 years 15 days. <He was bishop in the time of the emperors Justinian [II], Philippicus and Anastasius [II].> He was exceptionally gentle. In his time there was a three years' famine in Rome, but afterwards there was such productiveness that the luxuriance consigned the earlier shortage and barrenness to oblivion.

2. He ordained Felix as archbishop of Ravenna, but Felix refused to provide at the church office the written bonds in the form customary for his predecessors, and thanks to the influence of the judges he expressed his own preferences. His bond was placed by the pontiff in the holy confessio of St Peter the apostle, but after a few days it was found to be grimy as if charred by fire. The citizens of Ravenna were punished for their haughtiness with the vengeance they deserved: the emperor Justinian despatched the patrician Theodore, general of the army of Sicily, with a fleet; he captured Ravenna, arrested and confined that presumptuous archbishop on a ship, put all the rebels he could find there in shackles, seized their wealth, and sent them to Constantinople. By God's judgment and the sentence of Peter prince of the apostles, those who had disobeyed the apostolic see died a bitter death; the archbishop received a punishment worthy of his deeds—he was blinded and sent into exile over to the region of Pontus.

3. At that time the emperor sent the pontiff Constantine a mandate in which he bade him go up to the imperial city. In obedience to the emperor's commands the holy man immediately had a fleet prepared to tackle the journey by sea. He left Portus Romanus on the 5th day of October in the 9th indiction [710]; in his retinue were Nicetas bishop of Silva Candida, George bishop of Portus, the priests Michael, Paul, and George, the deacon Gregory, the *secundicerius* George, John the chief of the *defensores*, Cosmas the *sacellarius*, Sisinnius the *nomenclator*, Sergius the *scriniarius*, the subdeacons Dorotheus and Julian, and a few clerics from the remaining ranks of the church. **4.** So they reached Naples where the patrician and exarch John, surnamed Rizocopus, encountered him. John went to Rome, cut the throats of the deacon <and *vicedominus*> Saiulus, the *arcarius* Peter, Sergius the abbot and priest, and Sergius the *ordinator*; he went on to Ravenna where by God's judgment on his atrocious deeds he died an ignominious death.

The priest George was left at Naples, while the pontiff and his men went on to Sicily, where the patrician and *strategos* Theodore, though weakened by illness, met the pontiff and with great reverence greeted and welcomed him; he obtained a speedy cure. Leaving there by Rhegium and Croton, he crossed the gulf to Callipolis, where bishop Nicetas died. **5.** While he spent the winter at Hydruntum, he received a sealed mandate from the emperor by Theophanius the regionary; its contents were that wherever the pontiff went all the judges were to give him as honourable a welcome as they would if they saw the emperor present in person. Leaving there, and reaching the areas of Greece, at the island called Ceos the patrician Theophilus, *strategos* of the Caravisiani, met and greeted him most honourably; after a welcome such as the mandate required, he completed the journey he had begun. They sailed from there to the 7th mile from Constantinople. The emperor Tiberius, son of Justinian Augustus, came out to that spot with the patricians and the entire senate, Cyrus the patriarch, the clergy, and a multitude of people, all rejoicing and keeping festival day; the pontiff and his dignitaries entered the city on imperial saddle-horses, with gilded saddles and bridles, and with official saddle-cloths; the apostolic pontiff was wearing the camel-hair cap he usually travels with at Rome, and from the palace he moved to the house of Placidia as was agreed. **6.** When the lord emperor Justinian heard of his arrival, he was filled with great joy. From Nicaea in Bithynia he sent a mandate full of thanksgiving, saying that the pontiff should go to Nicomedia; he himself would come there from Nicaea. Which is what happened.

On the day they saw each other, the Christian Augustus, crown on head, prostrated himself and kissed the feet of the pontiff. Then they rushed together in mutual embrace, and there was great joy among the people as everyone gazed at their good prince in his great humility. On Sunday he performed mass for the emperor; the prince communicated at his hands and craved the pontiff to pray for his sins. He renewed all the church's privileges and gave the pope leave to return home. **7.** After leaving the city of Nicomedia, the pontiff was worn down by frequent bouts of illness, but the Lord granted him recovery and finally he reached the port of Caieta in safety; there he found the *sacerdotes* and the greater part of the Roman people. On the 24th day of October in the 10th indiction [711] he entered Rome, and all the people rejoiced and were glad. On his outward and return journey he performed the ordinations of 12 bishops for various places.

8. But after three months the doleful news resounded that the Christian and orthodox emperor Justinian had been assassinated, and that the heretic Philippicus had been raised up to the imperial dignity. When his mandate came containing false doctrine, he received it but with the council of the apostolic see he rejected it. It was for this reason that the whole population of Rome, in their burning enthusiasm for the faith, erected in St Peter's the image which the Greeks call *Botarea*: it includes the six holy universal synods. **12ª.** He replaced a gold paten weighing 12 lb.

9. Then Felix, archbishop of Ravenna, who had repented, was brought back from exile; though deprived of his eyesight, he was restored to his throne; he too provided the normal tokens and expressions of his faith which all bishops put in the church office, and thus he deserved to be reconciled and absolved.

In his time two kings of the Saxons came with many others to pray to the apostles; just as they were hoping, their lives quickly came to an end. Benedict, archbishop of Milan, also came to pray and present himself to his pontiff; he was in dispute over the church of Ticinum, but he was shown to be in error, because the consecration of the bishop of the church of Ticinum from ancient times has belonged and belongs to the apostolic see.

10. The Roman people had determined never to receive the name of the heretic emperor, his letters or the gold coins with his image—so his picture was not brought into church, nor was his name mentioned at the ceremonies of mass. It then occurred that a certain Peter sent to Ravenna to get the dukedom of Rome, and received an instruction to that effect. Once it became known that Peter had obtained his promotion in the name of the heretic emperor, the majority of the Roman people, burning with enthusiasm for the faith, determined not to accept him as duke. It happened that when the former duke Christopher and Agatho and his men were struggling to achieve this end, a civil war started: they fell upon each other on the Via Sacra in front of the palace, and more than 30 of each faction were beaten and killed, until the pontiff sent *sacerdotes* with gospels and the Lord's Cross and in this way pacified the factions. Peter's faction were in difficulty and had no hope of survival. But on the pontiff's order the other faction, called the Christian one, fell back; so Peter's faction, defenders of the heretic, were able, though battered, to withdraw.

11. Not many days later, written news came from Sicily saying that the heretic Philippicus had been deposed from the heights of the principate, and that the orthodox emperor Anastasius had assumed the reins of royal power. Among the orthodox there was great exultation, while the day of darkness came down on all the heretics. After some time the chamberlain and patrician Scholasticius, exarch of Italy, came to Rome with the mandate of Anastasius, in which the prince declared himself one who proclaimed the orthodox faith and acknowledged the holy sixth council; he presented the mandate to the pontiff and made his way to Ravenna. While this was happening, Peter acquired the dukedom, promising he would not attempt to create any opposition.

12^b. He performed one ordination, 10 priests, 2 deacons; for various places 64 bishops. \<He was buried at St Peter's\> \<on 8 January\> \<on 9 April in the 13th indiction [715] when Anastasius was emperor.\> The bishopric was vacant 40 days. \<To this point it is 129 years 7 months since the Lombards arrived.\>

APPENDIX 1

THE LIBERIAN CATALOGUE

(*From the 'Chronographer of 354'; see introduction p. xii. The manuscript text has some lacunae, which can be partly restored from the LP; such passages are given in angle brackets. In square brackets is added some material from the burial lists of bishops and martyrs preserved in the work of the same chronographer. To save space, consular dates are here translated into A.D. The serial numbers are those of the corresponding lives in the LP.*)

Our Lord Jesus Christ suffered while Tiberius Caesar was emperor in 29 on 25 March, and after his ascension St Peter undertook the episcopate. From that time on it is set down successively which bishop was in charge for how many years and in whose emperorship.

1. PETER 25 years 1 month 9 days. He was bishop in the time of Tiberius Caesar, Gaius, Tiberius Claudius, and Nero from 30 to 55. He suffered with Paul on 29 June in the same year while Nero was emperor. [Birthday of Peter's *cathedra* 22 February; Peter at the Catacombs and Paul on the Via Ostiensis 29 June 258.]

2. LINUS 12 years 4 months 12 days. He was bishop in the time of Nero from 56 to 67.

4. CLEMENT 9 years 11 months 12 days. He was bishop in the time of Galba and Vespasian from 68 to 75.

3. CLETUS 6 years 2 months 10 days. He was bishop in the time of Vespasian and Titus and the beginning of Domitian from 77 to 83.

5. ANACLITUS 12 years 10 months 3 days. He was bishop in the time of Domitian from 84 to 95.

6. EVARISTUS 13 years 7 months 2 days. He was bishop at the end of Domitian and in the time of Nerva and Trajan from 96 to 108.

7. ALEXANDER 7 years 2 months 1 day. He was bishop in the time of Trajan from 109 to 116.

8. XYSTUS 10 years 3 months 21 days. He was bishop in the time of Hadrian from 117 to 126.

9. TELESPHORUS 11 years 3 months 3 days. He was bishop in the time of Antoninus <and> Marc<us> from 127 to 137.

10. HYGINUS 12 years 3 months 6 days. He was bishop in the time of Verus <and Marcus from 138 to 149.>

<**12.** ANICETUS ...He was bishop in the time of Verus and Marcus> from 150 to 153.

11. PIUS 20 years 4 months 21 days. He was bishop in the time of Antoninus Pius from 146 to 161. In his episcopacy his brother Hermas wrote a book in which is included the order that an angel of the Lord imposed on him when he came to him in shepherd's apparel.

13. SOTER 9 years 3 months... <He was bishop in the time of Verus from 162 to 170.>

<**14.** ELEUTHER 15 years...> 2 days. He was bishop in the time of Antoninus and Commodus from 171 to 185.

15. VICTOR 9 years 2 months 10 days. He was bishop in the time of...<from 186 to 197.>

<**16.** ZEPHYRINUS...years 2 months 10 days. He was bishop in the time of Severus and> Antoninus from 198 to 217.

17. CALLISTUS 5 years 2 months 10 days. He was bishop in the time of Macrinus and Heliogabalus from 218 to 222. [Martyr, buried at the 3rd mile on the Via Aurelia 14 October.]

18. URBAN 8 years 11 months 12 days. He was bishop in the time of Alexander from 223 to 230.

19. PONTIAN 5 years 2 months 7 days. He was bishop in the time of Alexander from 231. Then Pontian the bishop and Hippolytus the priest were carried off into exile to Sardinia, the island Vocina (*or* Nocina; *perhaps* nociva, harmful), in 235. In that island he was unrobed on 28 September; in his place Anteros was ordained on 21 November in the same year. [Martyrs, Hippolytus buried on the Via Tiburtina and Pontian at Callistus' 13 August.]

20. ANTEROS 1 month 10 days. He fell asleep on 3 January 236.

21. FABIAN 14 years 1 month 10 days. He was bishop in the time of Maximinus, Gordian, and Philip from 236 to 250; he suffered on 21 January. He divided the regions among the deacons and ordered many works to be carried out in the cemeteries. After his passion the priests Moyses and Maximus and the deacon Nicostratus were arrested and put in prison. Then Novatus came over from Africa and separated Novatian and some of the confessors from the church after Moyses had died in prison— he was there 11 months 11 days. [Martyr, buried at Callistus' 20 January.]

22. CORNELIUS 2 years 3 months 10 days from 251 to 252. In his episcopacy Novatus ordained Novatian in the city of Rome, outside the church, and also Nicostratus in Africa. When this happened the confessors who had separated from Cornelius with the priest Maximus—the one who was with Moyses—returned to the church. After this they were expelled to Centumcellae; there he fell asleep in glory.

23. LUCIUS 3 years 8 months 10 days. He was bishop in the time of Gallus and Volusian to 255. He was exiled and later by God's will he came back safe to the church...5 March in the same year. [Buried at Callistus' 5 March.]

24. STEPHEN 4 years 2 months 21 days. He was bishop in the time of Valerian and Gallienus from 253 to 255. [Buried at Callistus' 2 August.]

25. XYSTUS 2 years 11 months 6 days. He began in 256, to 258 and suffered on 6 August. <The priests were in charge> from 258 to 21 July 259. [Martyrs, Xystus buried at Callistus' 6 August, Agapitus and Felicissimus at Praetextatus' on 6 August, Laurence on the Via Tiburtina

10 August.]

26. DIONYSIUS 8 years 2 months 4 days. He was bishop in the time of Gallienus from 22 July 259 to 26 December 269. [Buried at Callistus' 27 December.]

27. FELIX 5 years 11 months 25 days. He was bishop in the time of Claudius and Aurelian from 269 to 274. [Buried at Callistus' 30 December.]

28. EUTYCHIAN 8 years 11 months 3 days. He was bishop in the time of Aurelian from 275 to 7 December 283. [Buried at Callistus' 8 December.]

29. GAIUS 12 years 4 months 7 days. He was bishop in the time of Carus and Carinus from 17 December 283 to 22 April 296. [Buried at Callistus' 22 April.]

30. MARCELLINUS 8 years 3 months 25 days. He was bishop in the time of Diocletian and Maximian from 30 June 296 to 304 when there was the persecution, and the bishopric was vacant 7 years 6 months 25 days. [Buried at Priscilla's 15 January—*but this almost certainly refers to Marcellus.*]

31. MARCELLUS 1 year 6 months 20 days. He was bishop in the time of Maxentius from 308 to 309.

32. EUSEBIUS 4 months 16 days from 18 April to 17 August. [Buried at Callistus' 26 September.]

33. MILTIADES 3 years 6 months 8 days from 2 July 311 <'the 8th consulship of Maximian alone, which from September was the consulship of Volusianus and Rufinus'> to 11 January 314. [Buried at Callistus' 10 January.]

34. SILVESTER 21 years 11 months. He was bishop in the time of Constantine from 31 January 314 to 1 January 335. [Buried at Priscilla's 31 December.]

35. MARCUS 8 months 20 days. And he was bishop in the time of Constantine from 18 January 336 to 7 October the same year. [Buried at Balbina's 7 October.]

36. JULIUS 15 years 1 month 11 days. He was bishop in the time of Constantine from 6 February 337 to 12 April 352. He carried out many works: the basilica at the 3rd mile on the Via Portuensis, the basilica called Valentine's at the 2nd mile on the Via Flaminia, the basilica Julia in region 7 close to the Forum of the divine Trajan, the basilica across the Tiber in region 14 close to Callistus', the basilica at Callistus' at the 3rd mile on the Via Aurelia. [Buried at the 3rd mile on the Via Aurelia at Callistus' 12 April.]

37. LIBERIUS...He was bishop in the time of Constantius from 22 May 352 to...

APPENDIX 2

THE LAURENTIAN FRAGMENT

(Part of a series of papal biographies composed between 514 and 519, on which see pp. xiv-xv. The only manuscript, at Verona, was written shortly after 555, but lacks the first 18 of its 23 pages; the scale of the earlier lives must have been much less than that of those in the LP, though Mommsen's suggestion that the lost pages contained little more than an up-dated Liberian Catalogue lacks proof. It will be noted that the serial numbers of the lives differ from those in the LP; the section numbers given here are new. This account of the Laurentian schism should be compared with that in the LP, 53:1-5, that in the Epitome of the first edition of the LP (Appendix 3, 53:1-5), and with the brief, pro-Symmachus, version in the Anonymi Valesiani pars posterior, *65, given in the Loeb edition of Ammianus Marcellinus, vol. III, p. 548.)*

<51. ANASTASIUS II ...he wrote a letter to> the emperor Anastasius and sent it by bishops Cresconius and Germanus; it was backed up with so much corroboration from the heavenly scriptures that anyone who reads through it attentively and in the fear of God can see that the persistence up till now of so atrocious a schism between the churches of the East and of Italy is quite pointless.

52. **1.** SYMMACHUS held the see 15 years 7 months 27 days. Laurence, a priest of the Roman church, was also ordained bishop with him and such an enormous and savage disagreement took hold of the clergy and Roman people that neither the thought of God nor the fear of the king [Theoderic] could prevent the factions colliding. **2.** Then both of them, Symmachus and Laurence, were compelled to go to court to submit to the king's decision; there Symmachus won his case by spending a lot of money, while Laurence was severely threatened and cajoled, and forcibly despatched to govern the church of Nuceria, a city in Campania.

3. Some years later, however, Symmachus was accused before the king of committing many crimes. On the pretext that Symmachus had failed to celebrate Easter with the whole church, the king summoned him to court to give an explanation for the disagreement about so great a festival, and he made him take up residence at Ariminium. **4.** While Symmachus and his clergy were staying there for a time, he was walking in the morning hours along the seashore when he saw the women with whom he was accused of committing sin passing by; at the king's bidding they were going to court. So he pretended he did not know what he had seen, and in the middle of the night when everyone was asleep he took to flight with only one accomplice; he went back to Rome and shut himself inside the precinct of St Peter the apostle. **5.** Then the priests and deacons and also the rest of the clergy whom he had brought down with him went to the king and swore that Symmachus had fled without their knowledge; the king used them to take instructions to both senate and clergy about Symmachus' partial condemnation.

6. He was also accused by the whole Roman clergy of squandering the estates of the church contrary to the decree observed by his predecessors, and of thereby entangling himself in the bonds of an anathema. During Eastertide virtually everyone requested the king to provide the venerable Peter, bishop of Altinum, as visitor to the Roman church; and after the holy festival, at the desire of senate and clergy and at the king's bidding, a synod forgathered in the city of Rome to pass judgment on his excesses. **7.** Many bishops and senators took action simply to stop Symmachus having to submit to a hearing; they openly claimed in his defence that a Roman pontiff could not be heard by anyone even if he was as bad as he was accused of being. But the more select bishops decided, both from the religious point of view and at the king's bidding, that so important a matter, which was being talked about almost everywhere, should clearly be dealt with and not be left unexamined. **8.** Since its disagreement on this was serving to fuel the discord between the factions, the synod finally decided that the written charge which Symmachus' accusers were presenting should be accepted and formally published in the acts. Once this had been done Symmachus himself was then summoned by the bishops to come to trial. But the clerics who were on the lookout for him stopped him attending, and so the bishops warned him a second and third time, as the canons required, to come to the synodal hearing; he saw fit not to reply. **9.** Then a number of bishops realized they were getting nowhere in the matter, and once and again they advised the clergy who had left Symmachus' fellowship to go back to him and forget about a trial. But they replied that they could never do this until a person who had been arraigned on such great charges was canonically examined, and either absolved if found innocent or deprived of the *sacerdotium* if found guilty.

But the bishops saw that divisive activities were ever on the increase, would not brook delays, decreed what they thought would suit Symmachus, and thus left the city in total chaos.

10. So the more select clergy and senators, who had avoided Symmachus' fellowship, sent a memorial to the king in favour of Laurence, who at the time was staying at Ravenna to be away from Symmachus' violence and persecution; they asked for him to preside over the Roman church in which he had long ago been elected supreme pontiff, since the canons also laid down that every bishop should remain in the place where he had originally been consecrated or if by any machinations he had been removed from it every effort should be made to reinstate him. **11.** So Laurence came to the city and for about four years he held the Roman church. It is not the purpose of the present account to relate the civil wars that were fought and the terrible murders that were perpetrated during that time.

12. While the factions in their mutual disagreement were coming into collision and kept on requesting the king's protection for their activities, Symmachus eventually addressed a memorial to the king by Dioscorus, a deacon of Alexandria, claiming that his case was being totally prejudiced, particularly in the matter of the titular churches which Laurence was occupying in the city This wheedling captivated the king's mind and he sent instructions to the patrician Festus stating that all the titular churches were to be given back to Symmachus and that he would allow there to be only one pontiff at Rome. **13.** When Laurence learnt of this, he did not want the city to be troubled by daily strife and without delay he went of his own accord to the estates of the same patrician Festus; there he lived, fasting a great deal, until he met his appointed end. **14.** But afterwards, although Symmachus was the victor, disgusting stories blackened him on many counts, particularly about the woman they commonly called Conditaria [pickled-food dealer, Spice Girl] and about the orders in the church which he was prostituting by openly accepting cash for them. For these reasons the Roman church remained divided to the very end of his life.

15. He built and decorated the church of St Martin close to St Silvester's with the money of the illustrious Palatinus, and at that person's plea he dedicated it. He renovated many of the cemeteries, especially that of St Pancras, and he also built many new structures there.

53. HORMISDAS held the see 9 years 17 days.

54. JOHN held the see 2 years 9 months 16 days.

55. FELIX held the see 4 years 2 months 12 days.

56. BONIFACE held the see 2 years 26 days.

57. JOHN held the see 2 years 4 months 6 days.

58. AGAPITUS held the see 11 months 8 days.

59. SILVERIUS held the see 9 months.

60. VIGILIUS held the see 18 years 2 months 9 days. He died at Syracuse on the night of Monday 7 June in the third indiction [555].

APPENDIX 3

EXTRACTS FROM THE EPITOMES OF THE FIRST EDITION OF THE LIBER PONTIFICALIS

(See pp. xiii, xlvi. The most significant variations between these epitomes and the second edition occur in the early sixth-century lives, where the second editor was in virtually as good a position as the first to call on living memory. It is clear from the epitomes that in the lives of Hormisdas and John I the first edition contained important passages which the second editor did not preserve. It seems worthwhile to translate in full Epitome F's version of three of the last four lives from the first edition, and to precede this with extracts from the earlier lives where Epitome F suggests that the text of the first edition differed significantly from that of the second; brackets enclose some additions from Epitome K.)

1. ST PETER. **6.** ...He performed three December ordinations...

5. ANECLITUS. **1.** ...held the see 12 years 10 months 3 days...

6. EVARISTUS. **1.** ...born in Greece, an Antiochene, son of...

9. TELESPHORUS. **2.** ...hymn (that is, Glory be to God on high etc.) should be sung when entering on the sacrifice, but only at night on the Lord's birthday...

10. HYGINUS. **1.** ...from the consulship of Magnus and Camerinus to that of Orfitus and Camerinus...

[12 ANICETUS is placed before 11 PIUS]
11. PIUS. **2.** In his episcopacy, his brother Hermas wrote...

12. ANICETUS. **2.** ...9 bishops. He was buried close to St Peter's body on the Vatican on 20 April... *[no reference to martyrdom]*

13. SOTER. **3.** ...11 bishops. He was buried close to St Peter's body on 22 April...

15. VICTOR. 2. He decreed like Pius that the holy Easter... ...or in springs or in a lake, to become a full Christian, provided only that... **3.** He held a council and questioning took place on Easter or on the first day with Theophilus bishop of Alexandria about the moon.

18. URBAN. 3. ...and through his teaching many were crowned with martyrdom.

[20 ANTEROS is placed before 19 PONTIAN in F (not K)]
19. PONTIAN. 3. ...The bishopric was vacant 10 days from the day of his burial from [to?] 21 November.

20. ANTEROS. 2. ...because of a certain priest Maximus he was crowned with martyrdom.

21. FABIAN. 1. ...held the see 14 years 1 month 11 days...

22. CORNELIUS. 4. ...on 29 June. After this occurrence he performed one ordination, 8 priests.

27. FELIX I. 2ᵃ. He decreed that mass be celebrated over the tombs of martyrs. ... **2ᵇ.** He was buried in his own cemetery on the Via Aurelia at the 2nd mile on 30 May.

28. EUTYCHIAN. 3. *[no reference to martyrdom]*

29. GAIUS. 3. ...Fleeing from the persecution of Diocletian he lived in the crypts and as a confessor went to his rest.

31. MARCELLUS. 1. ...son of Marcellus...

32. EUSEBIUS. 1. ...He was bishop in the time of Constantine... **3.** He performed three ordinations...

33. MILTIADES. 1. ...from 7 July in the 9th consulship of Maximinus to the 2nd of Maxentius which...

34. SILVESTER. 4. ...In his time a council was held with his consent at Nicaea...

40. SIRICIUS. **1.** ...He issued a decree about the church and sent it throughout the provinces. **2.** He decreed that no priest was allowed to consecrate without the consecrated element of the bishop of each place. **3.** He decreed that a heretic should be reconciled...

42. INNOCENTIUS. **8.** ...He was buried Ad Ursum Pileatum on 27 June...

43. ZOSIMUS. **1.** ...He decreed that deacons should have their left arms covered with *pallia* half wool, half linen, throughout the parishes and that the [Easter] candle should be blessed...

44. BONIFACE I. **4.** A synod was held and Eulalius was deposed by 52 bishops because he had not been justly ordained, and with the consent of all Boniface held the see as prelate and Eulalius was established as bishop of Nepet...

46. XYSTUS III. **1.** ...held the see 8 years 19 days. He was arraigned on a charge by one Bassus and on the instruction of the emperor Valentinian with much investigation a synod was held and he was cleared by the 56 bishops and they ejected Bassus from communion.

47. **1.** LEO [I], born in Tuscia, son of Quintianus, held the see 21 years 1 month 13 days. He issued a decree about the church. **2.** He discovered two heresies, Eutyches and Nestorius, and by the request of the emperor Marcian, an orthodox prince, on his instruction a council of holy bishops was held in Chalcedon of the East in the basilica of the martyr St Euphemia, and he gathered 266 *sacerdotes* and the signatures of 406 other bishops were circulated; and they condemned Eutyches and Nestorius. **3.** After 42 days again being gathered together with the signatures, those who were present expounding the faith, 1200 bishops with the pious emperor Marcian who declared his faith with the empress Placidia publicly in the sight of the holy *sacerdotes* bishops, where again Eutyches was condemned. **4.** Afterwards the emperor Marcian along with 150 bishops requested and sent mandates requesting pope Leo to send him the expounded faith of the catholic and apostolic faith. And blessed Leo expounded and sent the Tome and confirmed the holy synod. **5.** He produced many letters expounding the correct catholic faith which are kept today in the archive of the Roman church, and a decretal which he

broadcast through the whole world.

48. HILARUS. 1. ...son of Crispinianus...

50. FELIX III. 2. In his episcopacy there came another report from the districts of Greece, that Peter of Alexandria had been reinstated to communion by Acacius. Then the revered pope Felix sent a *defensor* following a decree of the synod of his see and condemned Acacius as well as Peter. 3. Three years later there came another report from the emperor Zeno, that Acacius had repented and should be readmitted. Then pope Felix held a council and with its agreement sent two bishops, Misenus and Vitalis...

53. 1. SYMMACHUS, born in Sardinia, son of Fortunatus, held the see 15 years 7 months (27) days. He was bishop in the time of the heretic Theoderic and the Eutychianist emperor Anastasius. He loved the clergy and the poor; he was good, prudent, humane and gracious; 2. and Laurence was ordained bishop in rivalry with him. That was why some part of the clergy and senators were split, some with Symmachus, others with Laurence. Once the dispute had begun they agreed together that both should go to Ravenna for king Theoderic to arbitrate. When they arrived, he made the fair decision that the one who was ordained first and whose faction was agreed to be the largest should hold the apostolic see. In applying this principle, an investigation into the facts found in favour of blessed Symmachus, and he was the prelate. Then (blessed) pope Symmachus assembled a synod and, guided by sympathy for Laurence, set him up as bishop in the city of Nuceria.

3. But four years later some of the clergy and some of the senate were driven by jealousy and treachery to bring a charge against Symmachus; they suborned false witnesses whom they sent to the heretic king Theoderic at Ravenna with their accusation against blessed Symmachus; and they privately recalled Laurence to Rome. They created a schism and some part separated themselves from communion with Symmachus, sending (the heretic) king Theoderic a report and asking him for Peter of Altinum as visitor to the apostolic see. 4. Then blessed Symmachus gathered 115 bishops, and a synod was held in which he was acquitted of the false charge, while Peter of Altinum was condemned as an intruder into the apostolic see as was Laurence of Nuceria. Then blessed Symmachus was gloriously reinstated to sit in St Peter's as prelate of the

apostolic see by all the bishops, priests, deacons and clergy. (**5.** Then Festus the patrician began to cause slaughter in Rome of the clergy who were in communion with blessed Symmachus, and he displaced dedicated women from their houses, stripped women and beat them with clubs, and he killed many *sacerdotes* there.)

(Blessed Symmachus was bishop from 22 November in the consulship of Paulinus to 20 July in that of Senator. **6.** He built the basilica of St Andrew the apostle at St Peter's and dedicated both it and very many others with much gold and silver. He was a builder of churches **11.** and he augmented the clergy, tripled the gift to the priesthood, and tripled the clothing and alms given to the poor, and did many other good things which it would take too long to recount.) **12.** He performed four December ordinations in Rome, (98) priests, (16) deacons; for other places 117 bishops. He was buried in peace in St Peter's on 19 July. The bishopric was vacant 7 days.

54. 1. HORMISDAS, born in Campania, son of Justus, from the city of Frusino, held the see 9 years (17) days. **2.** (In his letters he carried on polemics with the heretic emperor Anastasius.) In his episcopacy, pursuant to the decree of a synod he sent to Greece a warrant in accordance with the apostolic see's humanity, and reconciled the Greeks, who were held under an anathema because of Peter of Alexandria and Acacius of Constantinople. This pope betook himself to king Theoderic at Ravenna and on the advice of the king he despatched Ennodius bishop of Ticinum, Fortunatus bishop of Catina, Evantius priest of the city, and Vitalis deacon of the city. They reached the emperor Anastasius to arrange for a reinstatement by a document [of repentance], but achieved nothing. **3.** Again a second time Hormisdas sent bishops Ennodius and Peregrinus, and Pollio subdeacon of the city, and they carried 19 letters on the faith and secret admonishments, with a document [of repentance] by which they might come back; but if they should refuse to accept the admonishments in the letter, they should publish them throughout the cities. The emperor Anastasius refused to agree to it, since he too was in agreement with the heresy of Eutyches. So he wanted to corrupt them with a bribe. But they spurned the prince and absolutely refused to take the cash. Burning with rage the emperor threw them out by a dangerous district and put them on a ship in danger of their lives, along with the *magistrianus* and *praefectianus* Heliodorus and Demetrius. **4.** The emperor's orders included a prohibition on going to any city; yet they stealthily used the services of catholic monks to publish the 19 letters on the faith throughout all the cities. But the bishops of the cities who agreed with the heretic emperor were afraid and they took and sent them to Constantinople into Anastasius' hands. Anastasius was driven by fury with pope Hormisdas and included in the imperial mandates he wrote: 'It is our wish to give orders, not to take them'. Anastasius was struck by a divine blow (thunderbolt) and died.

5. And so the orthodox Justin assumed the *imperium*; and he sent Gratus of illustrious name to the apostolic see to pope Hormisdas, and his hope was that envoys might be sent by the apostolic see, but on the advice of king Theoderic. He despatched Germanus bishop of Capua, John the bishop, Blandus the priest, Felix deacon of the apostolic see and Dioscorus deacon of the same see—these he instructed on every aspect of the faith—along with the document by which the Greeks might come back into communion with the apostolic see. As they approached Constantinople a crowd of monks and a crowd of illustrious men, including the emperor Justin and the master of the soldiers Vitalianus, met them at the place called Castellum Rotundum and accompanied them into Constantinople. In glory and praise they entered the city, along with the illustrious Gratus; and gloriously were they thus received on entry to the city by the orthodox emperor Justin. 6. So all the clergy of Constantinople, along with bishop John, aware that they had had such a welcome, locked themselves in the great church called St Sophia, and after discussion sent this message to the emperor: 'Unless we get an account of why our city's bishop Acacius has been condemned, there is no way we will come to agree with the apostolic see'. Then after discussion with the emperor Justin in the presence of all the illustrious men, the envoys of the apostolic see chose from their own number the deacon Dioscorus to give the account; and he explained to them Acacius' mistakes so well that they all cried out along with the emperor Justin: 'Damned be Acacius now and for ever!' 7. Now that he had accepted the truth, Justin gave orders that all the bishops in his realm should act according to the document without delay and return into communion with the apostolic see. And so it happened: there was agreement from east to west and peace was achieved in the church. The text of the document is kept safe today in the church archive.

9. He discovered Manichaeans whom he tried with an investigation under blows, and he burnt their books before the doors of the Constantinian basilica. In his time the episcopate of Africa was reinstated

after 74 years—they had been wiped out by the heretics at the time of the persecution. **10.** At that time a gold crown with precious jewels came as a gift from the king of the Franks. (Pope Hormisdas provided various ornaments of gold and silver in many basilicas in the Roman church.) **12.** He performed ordinations, priests, bishops for (various) places. He was buried in St Peter's on (6) August (in the consulship of the younger Maximus). The bishopric was vacant 6 days.

55. 1. JOHN [I], born in Tuscia, son of Constantius, held the see 2 years 8 months 15 days from the consulship of Maximus to that of (the younger) Olybrius. He was summoned to Ravenna by king Theoderic; at the king's request he agreed to be sent to Constantinople on an embassy to the emperor Justin, a devout man, who in the depths of his love for the Christian faith, wanted to drive heretics out: in deep fervour he dedicated the churches of the Arians as catholic. **2.** After that the Arian Theoderic in anger (with the Christians) wanted to put the whole of Italy to the sword. Then the venerable pope John set out and travelled in tears and groaning, and also the devout men, (ex)consuls and patricians, Theodore, Importunus, Agapitus and another Agapitus. The message they were given to take on their embassy was that (their) churches in the areas of Greece were to be restored to the heretics and if this was not carried out the emperor Justin (king Theoderic) would destroy the whole of Italy with the sword. (**3.** When all the above men with pope John entered Constantinople, they came out to meet them at the 12th mile in honour of the apostles; it was their wish since blessed pope Silvester in the time of Constantine that they should deserve to receive the vicar of St Peter in the area of Greece; and the emperor Justin prostrated himself before the blessed John; **4.** and at his hands he was crowned.) **5.** To him, and also to so many distinguished exconsuls and patricians of the city of Rome (who had come with blessed pope John), to Flavius Theodore who outranked the illustrious men in the splendour of all his dignities, to the illustrious exconsul Importunus, to the illustrious exconsul Agapitus and to the other Agapitus the patrician, he granted all that they asked. To save the blood of the Romans, he restored (their) churches to the heretics. And when what the heretic king Theoderic wanted was carried out in the areas of Greece, particularly that *sacerdotes* and Christians be put to the sword, while the blessed bishop John and the illustrious men were still at Constantinople, king Theoderic arrested two senators, exconsuls and patricians, Boethius and Symmachus, and slew them with the sword; he even ordered that their bodies be hidden. **6.** The above illustrious men and bishop John, after achieving everything in an orderly way—though Agapitus the patrician died in Greece—arrived and were received by king Theoderic with treachery and great hatred; he received bishop John and the devout illustrious senators whom he received with such great wrath and thus wanted to put them to the sword but fearing the orthodox emperor Justin's wrath, he did not do so, but he destroyed them all in prison, so that blessed pope John, tortured by maltreatment in prison, grew weak and died. He died at Ravenna in glory on 18 May in the prison of king Theoderic. After this, it was almighty God's will that king Theoderic was suddenly struck down by the Deity (by a thunderbolt) and died on the (98th) day after bishop John's death in prison. (**7.** Blessed John brought from Greece gold, jewels and silver and decorated many basilicas.) **8.** He performed ordinations (of bishops) for (various) places. The bishopric was vacant (58) days.

56. FELIX [IV] ...*In this last life from the first edition Epitome K contains the remark*: **2.** ...He was ordained on the order of king Theoderic and died in the time of king Athalaric on 12 October in the said consulship.

GLOSSARY OF TECHNICAL TERMS
IN THE TRANSLATION

acolyte (*acolitus*) - **15**:2, **29**:2, **34**:8, **71**:1, **86**:1; clerics inferior to subdeacons in the Latin church; their duties included lighting candles and supplying wine at the eucharist. Despite the Greek name (ἀκόλουθος, 'follower') the Greek churches originally had no such officer. At **15**:2 and **29**:2 the LP renders the word by the Latin *sequens*, but on **71**:1 it distinguishes an acolyte from subdeacons described as *sequentes* (here translated 'attached'), who were so called to differentiate them from the 'regionary' subdeacons.

agens in rebus - **37**:3; a carrier of imperial despatches; from Constantius II's time on, these *agentes* were liable to be used as secret service agents; cf. *magistrianus*.

altar (*altare*); the table for celebration of the eucharist. Augustine uses the terms *altare* and 'Lord's table' indifferently, but very rarely uses *ara* for the Christian altar, though other Christian Latin writers use this word also without inhibition. In the fourth century altars were much more commonly of wood than of any other material (cf. Optatus 6.1, and Augustine's story of Maximin of Bagai whose wooden altar was smashed over his head by the Donatists), but from that time on at least in major churches stone or even silver altars became more frequent. The altar was generally sited on the chord of the apse or slightly forward in the transept (if any) or in the nave itself, so that the celebrant (when not seated at his throne in the apse) faced the congregation across it; there was only one altar in a church, though eventually side-chapels would have their own altars. The LP (**34**:10) has 7 silver altars at the Lateran; though some have thought these were real altars and even that one was used for each day of the week(!), 6 of them were probably tables for placing the offerings of the people (Krautheimer, *Corpus*, V 88); the main altar was probably on the site of the present high altar, slightly forward in the west end of nave (the Lateran then had no transept).

ama - first at **34**:3, then frequent till **54**:11; a vessel to receive the wine presented by the congregation at mass; the word had earlier been used for a wine-cup or wine-measure. Those in the LP are of silver, rarely of gold, and weigh on average about 13 lb; their capacity is specified twice (**34**:10), as 1 and 3 *medimni*; from the weights regularly given, these capacities (approximately 50 to 150 litres) would seem to cover the likely range—for large congregations they would need to be of considerable size. The people would bring their offerings in *amulae* (small flasks); a deacon would pour the wine from these into the larger *amae* and return the *amulae* to their owners. The rather smaller quantities of wine actually needed for the mass would then be poured (through a strainer) into a cup or chalice (*calix*) which would stand on the altar (the surplus wine might be distributed to the poor). This chalice would be of precious metal and of some weight especially when filled—the celebrant would be assisted by deacons when it had to be lifted. For this reason and also to save time, the wine consecrated in the large chalice would be poured into a number of service chalices (*calices ministeriales*) of gold or silver (average weight 2 lb) for distribution to communicants. The *scyphus* of gold or silver (those in the LP weighing on average 10 lb) was for additional wine to be placed on the altar when it was foreseen that the main chalice would not hold all that was required to be consecrated. But the LP seems not quite consistent in its terminology: the chalices mentioned (average weight 4½ lb) actually divide up into lighter and heavier ones (none weighs between 5 and 10 lb); I suspect that the lighter ones are in fact service chalices (at **34**:10 some are described as *minores*) and the heavier ones are *scyphi*; and it also seems clear that the LP refers to the principal chalice on the altar sometimes as 'chalice', sometimes as *scyphus*.

ambo - **62**:2, **86**:13, **87**:3, **88**:2; an elevated reading-desk, not unlike a pulpit, and generally approached by two separate sets of steps.

annonocapita - **84**:2, **85**:3; apparently poll-taxes (on persons and livestock) payable in goods rather than in money, and hence the fiscal units (established through census registration) by which the taxes were calculated, like the pounds in which the rateable value of property was expressed. Compare 'registrations of land and persons' (*diagrafa* and *capita*) at **78**:4.

apocrisiarii - **60**:6,7, **75**:6, **76**:2,4, **78**:1; the representatives of the pope at Constantinople, perhaps more at the court of the Byzantine emperor than at the patriarchate, who had the task of reporting to Rome what was afoot there; at **78**:1 the LP renders the word (ἀποκρισιάριοι, 'answerers') by *responsales*. The main *apocrisiarius* alluded to at **76**:2 as being persecuted by the emperor Constans II was Anastasius, who was exiled to Trapezus (Trebizond); the reference by the emperor at **76**:4 to pope Martin as a former *apocrisiarius* was to avoid recognizing him as pope.

apse (*apsis*) - **34**:10,24, **53**:8-10, **72**:3, **73**:5, **86**:11; the semicircular extension of a church at the opposite end of the nave from the main entrance, and containing the bishop's throne and seats for the other ministers. It would be roofed by an apse-vault (*camera* - **34**:10,17; **47**:6; **53**:8), in shape half a dome; the LP sometimes refers to the apse-vault simply as an apse (at its first occurrence in **34**:10 the word 'vault' refers to the structure of the *fastigium*, not to the apse of the basilica). At **46**:5 the LP uses *apsis* to refer to something much smaller, translated 'niche'.

arcarius - **81**:17, and (Peter) **90**:4; treasurer of an institution (here, the church); from *arca*, state treasury, public revenue; cf. *sacellarius*.

arch (*arcus*) - first at **48**:3, then frequent; apparently small decorative structures of precious metal on top of shrines.

arenarium - **23**:5, **34**:24, **75**:4; literally 'sandpit', but *arena* means not only sand but also the volcanic 'tufa' into which the galleries of cemeteries (catacombs) could be excavated; *arenarium* seems to mean the surface layers of the ground above a subterranean gallery ('crypt') of a cemetery.

Arian heresy - **34**:5, **37**:2,5; the term was used by the orthodox to cover varieties of views which sprang from those of the early fourth-century Arius, a priest at Alexandria; basically Arians denied the eternal existence of Christ and thus regarded him, if as God, not as God in the same sense as the Father. Once the empire returned officially to orthodoxy, these views remained those of barbarians who invaded the empire later: hence Theoderic the Ostrogothic king (**55**:1,2) is a 'heretic'.

atrium - **53**:7,8, **80**:1, **86**:11; the first main room in a Roman-style house, with the centre open to the sky and containing a pool for rainwater; hence, an open courtyard (possibly walled rather than colonnaded) in front of a church.

awning (*tegnum*) - **53**:7, **86**:11; apparently lateral porticoes at St Peter's and St Paul's.

basilica; originally an assembly hall such as might be appropriate for the emperor (βασιλεύς) to use when giving an audience; there were at least three such for the pope at the Lateran Episcopium: **78**:3 'of Vigilius', **86**:2 'of the house of Julius', **86**:9 'of pope Theodore'. More or less standardized architectural features (a longitudinal design with aisles and a clerestory-lit nave) which would make such an arrangement suitable for church worship, rather than thoughts of Christ as βασιλεύς, seem to have caused the Christian use of the word; it then came to be used for a church building of any design. 'Royal hall' (*aula regalis*, **34**:17) on the gold cross at St Peter's is evidently a translation. It was sometimes used to describe only those churches at Rome which were not *tituli* (q.v.), but the LP is not consistent and uses it for *tituli* also.

basin - **34**:13 (*fiala*, supporting a candle), **34**:28 (*pelvis* for baptism, cf. 'handbasin'), **48**:4 (*lacus*, structural element at the Lateran Font).

bonds (*cautiones*) - **36**:3, **61**:5; sureties, bonds of security, acknowledgments of debts, obligations or promises; a specific use of the word (**90**:2) is for the written sureties left by bishops in the hands of the pope.

Botarea - **90**:8 a name of unknown meaning for the 'image' erected in 712 at Rome which placed the 6th General Council (**81**) in the context of the earlier five, in reaction against the removal of the image of that council at Constantinople by the monthelete emperor Philippicus. The word may be corrupt: a derivative of Greek κιβωτός (a chest) has been suggested. If so perhaps it was a box containing the conciliar decrees and painted on the outside.

camel-hair cap (*camelaucum*) - **90**:5; otherwise known as the *frigium* (*phrygium*), a large white bonnet worn by the pope when not at a liturgical function, and the ancestor of the medieval tiara (though without the crown).

candelabra, **candle** (*candela*), **candlestick chandeliers** (*canthara cereostata* or *fara c.c.*), **candlesticks** (*cereostata*); see 'lights'.

canopy (*ciborium*) - **53**:6,9, **66**:4, **72**:3,5, **86**:13; a dome above an altar (which itself may be over a tomb), supported on columns. At **86**:11 'canopy' also translates the rare word *appallarea*, for a structure set above a throne.

Caravisiani - **90**:5; name of a naval theme (Byzantine military district), first recorded in 687.

cartularius - **73**:1, **75**:1,2 (Maurice), **75**:2 (Thomatius); title of an imperial officer, strictly one in charge of military registers, in practice in command of the Byzantine army in seventh-century Rome; by the early eighth century this army came under a duke (q.v.), and the *cartularius* was merely a minor military official.

cataadioces - **68**:1 (father of Boniface III); apparently (for *catadioecetes*?) a financial officer (if the text is sound; read *Cappadoce?*—but he can hardly be identified with either of the patriarchs of Constantinople known as John the Cappadocian or with the similarly named praetorian prefect of Justinian).

catabulum - **31**:3,5; imperially-owned stable, required for providing animals for transport (e.g. of corn from the granaries to the public bakeries in Rome).

cathedra - **1**:1,5, **4**:3, **75**:3, **Appendix 1**:1; the chair or throne on which a bishop sat when presiding over, or teaching, a congregation; the early occurrences refer to the chair of St Peter, but the *cathedra* now preserved in St Peter's is of later date than the composition of the LP.

cellars (*cellae*) - **43**:1, certainly meaning wine-cellars; but at **34**:19 *cellae* ('rooms') may refer either to apartments or to storehouses.

censer (*thymiamaterium*) - **34**:12,13,18, **46**:3, **86**:11; a container for burning incense; a standing object rather than one held in the hand and swung on chains, though **34**:18 could be an early reference to the 'apostolated thurible' suspended into St Peter's grave (see *The Lives of the Ninth-century Popes*, **105**:43,45 and **100**:6 with n. 16). The censer at **86**:11 is suspended in front of statues in St Peter's; a *subfiturium* ('incense-burner') at **54**:10 is apparently hung above the confessio in the same church.

chalice (*calix*); see on *ama*; there are also mentioned 3 silver 'chalices for baptism' weighing 2 lb each, and other chalices and *scyphi* occur in that same baptismal context (**42**:5); rather than suppose that these were for mass said in a baptistery, I would guess that they were for the drink of milk and honey which was sometimes offered to the newly baptized.

chamberlain (*cubicularius*) - **61**:8 (Narses, eunuch), **70**:2 (Eleutherius, patrician), **76**:4 (Olympius, exarch), **76**:8 (Theodore), **87**:1 (Theophylact, patrician and exarch), **90**:11 (Scholasticius, patrician and exarch)—originally a eunuch of the imperial bedchamber (brought from outside the empire, since castration was not permitted on Roman territory); close contact with the emperor gave the eunuchs great influence and wealth; by the seventh century 'chamberlain' had evidently become a title of honour, and later in the eighth century it would be used as such at Rome.

chandeliers (*canthara* or *fara canthara*); see 'lights'.

chevron (*gammula)* - **83**:2; a diminutive of the Greek letter *gamma*, and clearly from the context a decoration shaped like the upper-case form of the letter, making up a cross gammadion, or fylfot (swastika) pattern.

chief of the imperial bedchamber (*praepositus sacri cubiculi*) - **34**:14; chief eunuch at court, at the head of the chamberlains (q.v.). Festus is the earliest known.

chrism, oil of (*chrisma, oleum chrismae*) - **34**:6, **42**:5; oil used for anointing during the ceremonies of baptism, signifying that those baptized were 'in Christ'; at least by the seventh century the bishop consecrated this oil at a special ceremony held on Maundy Thursday, so that it would be available for the great baptismal ceremonies on Easter Eve.

chrism-paten (*patena chrismalis*) - **34**:3,28 (*patena ad chrismam*) **42**:5;

the dish, usually of silver, containing the oil of chrism; the 4 mentioned in the LP average 5¼ lb, very much lighter than the ordinary eucharistic paten (q.v.).

confessio - **46**:4,5, **48**:2,3,5, **52**:1, **53**:6-9, **54**:10, **55**:7, **57**:3,4, **72**:1,2, **75**:4, **86**:4,11, **90**:2; originally the burial-place of one who had 'confessed' Christ by martyrdom; hence the name for an area in front of an altar above a martyr's tomb, excavated to give closer access to, or sight of, the grave; some or all of the area might then be decorated with silver. In the LP the earliest are at the tombs of Peter, Paul and Laurence (**46**:4,5), all in the time of Valentinian III or Xystus III; thereafter they are frequent, even when there was no actual grave, e.g. for a fragment of the Cross (**48**:3).

consul; the title of the two chief magistrates in the Roman republic; as they were elected annually, their names were used in the absence of a fixed era to denote the year in which they held office; hence the dating by consulships in parts of the LP. Under the Roman emperors they possessed little power, but the system was maintained to give prestige to distinguished senators. The office was often held by emperors, particularly in the first year of their reigns, and by the mid sixth century it was held by no one else (though later the title was bestowed as an honour, perhaps specifically on some of those who served in the imperial lawcourts). Since from the mid sixth century there were in many years no consuls at all, events were often dated as so many years after the last consuls had held office, but this dating system was then abandoned and indictions (q.v.) were used instead.

count (*comes*) - **61**:1 (the ex-king Vitiges); a title of honour or of actual office created by Constantine; the holder might have either civilian or military responsibilities, the rank it connoted being more specific than the duties; in the case of Vitiges it is clear that the title is purely honorific; cf. 'patrician'.

crown (*corona*); see 'lights'; but also used for the 'crown' of martyrdom (**1-30** *passim* and **38**), for the 'ring' of eucharistic bread (**16**:2), and perhaps for a royal diadem (**34**:9, cf. **55**:4), in which sense *regnum* is also used (**54**:10; **75**:1,2, **90**:6).

crown lamps (*fara coronata*), **crown light** (*corona fara* or *corona faralis*), **crown which is a chandelier** (*corona quae est farus cantharus*); see 'lights'.

crypt (*crypta*) - **22**:6, **25**:4, **29**:3, **30**:4, **32**:3, **33**:3, **34**:24, **46**:9[b], **48**:13; a gallery or chamber in a subterranean cemetery.

cubicularius; at **47**:8 the LP explains the word as meaning 'warden'; but everywhere else the sense is different, and it has been translated 'chamberlain' (q.v.).

curia; a city council, also the building in which one (especially the Senate of Rome) met; at **44**:5 'under obligation (*obnoxius*) to a *curia*' means liable to the sometimes crippling financial burdens (*munera*) imposed by the government on members of city councils; there were restrictions in civil law on such persons becoming clerics, but the church was also concerned that it should not find itself responsible for its clerics' liabilities.

dalmatic (*dalmatica*) - **28**:2, **34**:7; a vestment shaped like a tunic, with long sleeves, and ornamented with two strips of red material.

declarations (*allegationes*) - **36**:3; any declaration made for an official purpose.

deeds (*instrumenta*); documents, instruments; at **36**:3 this is a general word covering the six terms following (donations, exchanges, transfers, wills, declarations, manumissions, qq.v).

defensor - **50**:2, and (John) **90**:3; one of the legal officers of the church. At Rome they were laymen or if ordained then in orders below those of the subdeacons. There was one for each of the seven regions, the senior being the *primicerius* or *primus*. Much as the seven deacons were concerned with the spiritual and material welfare of the poor, of widows and of orphans, the seven *defensores* concerned themselves with their legal rights, and in practice also with the defence of the rights and property of the church itself. They acquired coercive powers—already Pelagius I sent two to arrest a bishop who had been ordered to Rome for trial. Under Gregory I (who formed them into a corps) they are found supervising monasteries and vacant bishoprics, and are involved in various legal matters such as dealing with testamentary affairs and contracts, advising the bishop when dealing with disputes in his court, judging legal cases themselves, and even protecting clerics against local bishops; they could also be employed on special missions. Like the notaries, they came to be heavily involved with the *rectores* in the administration of the papal patrimonies and, later, of the papal State.

diocese (*diocesis*); in its civil sense (**34:**19), one of the dozen or so groupings of provinces into which the empire was divided by Diocletian; each was governed by a *vicarius*, so called as 'deputy' to a praetorian prefect (q.v.); note that Egypt ceased to be in the diocese of the East before the end of the fourth century. In its ecclesiastical sense in the LP, 'diocese' means 'parishes'—**26:**2, **31:**2; on the latter, see Kuttner (1945) 147. The later meaning, 'territory of a bishop', does already occur in Augustine and fifth-century writers, but for this *paroecia* was commoner.

diptychs - **81:**14; folding wax tablets listing those, especially the dead, to be prayed for at mass.

dolphins (*delphini*); see 'lights'.

donations (*donationes*); at **36:**3, records of donations, charters.

duae domus - **86:**1; 'two houses'; the legend of the foundation of the *titulus* of St Susanna and of the saint's martyrdom claims that the building was on the site of two adjoining houses which had belonged to Susanna's father Gabinius and the latter's brother pope Gaius (cf. **29:**4); whatever be made of the legend, archaeology has shown that there were two houses consecutively occupying the site, one from the late first, one from the early third century; the second of these was replaced in the fourth century by a large hall, of which the nucleus survives in the present church on the site. Cf. A. Bonanni in the *Akten des XII internationalen Kongresses für christliche Archäologie.*

duke (*dux*) - **90:**10 (Christopher, Peter); in imperial territory, an army commander whose territory was a duchy (*ducatus*); the Pentapolitan duchy (**86**:7) was the area south-east of Ravenna; see also *cartularius*. Among the Franks and Lombards, *dux* may refer to an army commander subject to a king or to the military ruler of a particular territory who might achieve a measure of independence from a king: the Frank Amingus (**63**:2) and the Lombard Gisulf (**87**:2).

Ecthesis - **76**:2; exposition (of writings, of teaching), explanation or publication; hence the title of Heraclius' edict in 638 in favour of monotheletism, the heresy which argued that Christ has two natures but one Will or Operative Principle, a view which it had been hoped might reconcile the monophysites (who argued that Christ had one nature, that of God) with the (orthodox) dyophysites (who upheld two natures, those of God and Man). The monothelete idea had been proposed by Sergius patriarch of Constantinople to pope Honorius and had gained his approval. Honorius was dead when the *Ecthesis* reached Italy; the ensuing delay before the ordination of pope Severinus was caused as much because the exarch Isaac was expected to gain his assent to the document before allowing the ordination as because (**73**:1-5) Isaac and Maurice wanted the opportunity to sack the Lateran. Honorius' acquiescence in monotheletism is ignored by the LP in that pope's life, and even in the account of the sixth Ecumenical Council (**81**:14), but is acknowledged at **82**:2. The *Ecthesis* was abrogated by the *Typus* (q.v.).

Episcopium - **73**:1-4, **75**:5, **76**:3, **84**:1, **85**:2, **86**:2,8; the building or palace close to the Lateran basilica at which the pope resided; at **86**:2,3,8,9 it is also called the 'patriarchate' (*patriarchium*). *Episcopium* is used also of John VII's new residence at S Maria Antiqua (**88**:2). The 'episcopal rooms' (*episcopia*) at St Peter's (**53**:7) are presumably a suite for Symmachus at the time he was confined to the Vatican by the troubles of the Laurentian schism; cf. *praetorium*.

estate, in lists when accompanied by a name, represents *massa*, a grouping of several farms (*fundi*); the average revenue of the 30 *massae* listed is 456 solidi. Elsewhere 'estate' is for *praedium*.

Eutyches, Eutychian heresy - **47**:2,3, **48**:1, **49**:3, **51**:6, **54**:3; Eutyches, an archimandrite (head of a group of monasteries) near Constantinople, was with Dioscorus patriarch of Alexandria one of the chief proponents of monophysitism, which Leo I attacked in his Tome (q.v.).

exarch (*exarchus*); the military commander of Italy under Byzantine rule, usually resident at Ravenna; the following are named: Romanus **66**:2; John **70**:2; Isaac **73**:1; Theodore Calliopas (two tenures) **75**:2, **76**:8; Olympius **76**:4-7; Theodore **85**:2; John Platyn **85**:5, **86**:3-5, Theophylact **87**:1,2; John Rizocopus **90**:4; Scholasticius **90**:11.

exchanges (*commutationes*); at **36**:3, records of exchange contracts or substitutions, and/or of the properties so acquired.

exorcism, oil of (*oleum exorcidiatum*) - **42**:5; used at an early part of the ceremonies of baptism; those to be baptized were anointed with it to the accompaniment of formulae in which the devil was adjured to depart from them; also called the oil of the catechumens, it was eventually consecrated by the bishop in the same ceremonies as the oil of chrism (q.v.).

farm (*fundus*); 25 are listed with revenues. One has the huge revenue 1120 *solidi* (it need not be assumed that the land was a single block), the other 24 average 55 *solidi*.

fastigium - **34**:9-10, **46**:4 (Lateran); 'literally, the ridge of a roof or a gable; a structure...consisting of a colonnaded screen across the chord of the apse and centred either on a canopy or on a pedimented section' (Krautheimer (1986) 518; on p. 40 he prefers the latter possibility: 'an arched and pedimented lintel colonnade, like that under which the Emperor revealed himself to his subjects at court, as it survives in Diocletian's palace at Spalato (Split)'). The former explanation would make the Lateran *fastigium* not unlike the canopy which existed at St Peter's. But the latter does seem more probable: it will have been a gabled colonnaded screen sheltering the figures (perhaps beneath a vault (*camera*), see on 'apse-vault' above), the chandeliers and the crowns hanging over them, as mentioned in the LP's description. Krautheimer, *Corpus*, V 88, suggests that the crown lights hung over the angels in this structure, and presumably also over the apostles; the huge chandelier under the golden vault would have hung over the two figures of Christ seated back to back. The enormous antique bronze columns now framing the Altar of the Sacrament were almost certainly part of the structure.

Either way the *fastigium* was certainly inside the chancel, between apse and altar; Christ on a chair (as a teacher) faced the altar and congregation, Christ on a throne faced the bishop and clergy in the apse. That the *fastigium* was Constantinian need not be doubted; but some have questioned whether the figurative additions to it were earlier than the fifth century. Cf. M. Teasdale Smith (1970) and P. Liverani (1992-1993).

fermentum - **33**:2, **40**:2; as the LP explains at both places, a piece of eucharistic bread consecrated by the bishop and then sent to another church. It was there added to what was consecrated by a priest at his own mass; the purpose was to express the unity of a bishop and his priests and the congregations which they all led, when it was not possible for them to be present at the same mass.

font (*fons*); used in the LP to refer both to the sunken area or hollowed-out basin containing the water in which one being baptized was immersed, and to the building (which in other places the LP calls the baptistery, *baptisterium*) in which the font was the main feature; it is generally, but not always, clear which is meant. Fonts and/or baptisteries are mentioned at the following locations: St Pudentiana **11**:4; the Lateran **34**:13-14, **46**:7, **48**:2,5,12, **74**:2; St Agnes **34**:23; St Mary Major **46**:3,7; St Sabina **46**:8; St Peter's **53**:7; St Agatha via Aurelia **53**:8.

foot (*pes*); at 296 mm, slightly shorter than the English foot (304.8 mm).

formata - **8**:2; the LP explains this as a document certifying to the congregation of an existing bishop that he was in good standing with the Roman see; but it seems that it normally certified that a new bishop was validly and lawfully ordained. The word was also used to mean a letter of recommendation from a bishop carried by a cleric going abroad.

handbasin (*aquamanile*) - **42**:5, **45**:2, **46**:3,6; for washing the hands of the celebrant at a liturgical function—at baptisms, because he had to touch oil.

Hypapante (ὑπαπαντή, encounter) - **86**:14; though describing the feast as that of St Simeon (see Luke 2.22-40), the LP's record of Sergius' institution of the procession on that day (2 February, Candlemas, the

Purification) is in the context of the three other feasts of the Virgin, for the celebration of all of which at Rome the LP is the earliest evidence; the evidence of the Roman Antiphonal of the Mass suggests that this feast is itself earlier than the other three.

illustrious (*illustris*) - **42**:3,6 (Vestina), **53**:10 (Albinus), **54**:5, **Appendix 3 54**:5 (Gratus; and a group including the emperor Justin I and Vitalianus), **63**:1 (the father of John III), **Appendix 2 52**:15 (Palatinus), **Appendix 3 55**:5,6 (Flavius Theodore and others)—a title for senators who had gained very high rank from the offices they had held (such as consul, praetorian or city prefect, master of the soldiers), whether they held such offices in reality or by an honorary grant.

images, designs, representations etc. (see also dolphins, *Botarea*): True Cross **32**:2, **34**:22, **48**:3, **53**:7, **86**:10; crosses **34**:17,21, **48**:2, **48**:3, **53**:7, **55**:3, **61**:2, **62**:2, **83**:2, **86**:10,12, **90**:10; Saviour **34**:9,10,13, **46**:4, **53**:8; angels **34**:10; St John the Baptist **34**:13; medallions of prophets **34**:11; apostles **34**:9,10, **46**:4, **53**:8, **86**:12; medallions of acts **34**:18; St Peter **86**:11; St Laurence **46**:5; medallions of passio of St Laurence **34**:24; the Fathers **88**:1; John VII **88**:2; Philippicus **90**:10; lambs **34**:13, **48**:3, **53**:7; doves **34**:18, **42**:4, **48**:5; stags **34**:13, **42**:5, **46**:3, **48**:5; palms **53**:7; portals **46**:4; chevrons **83**:2; medallions (unspecified) **34**:23,26; picture (unspecified) **53**:8; relief decoration **34**:29, **39**:4, **42**:5; used by Manichaeans **53**:5.

imperium - **54**:5, **88**:5, **Appendix 3 54**:5; means both 'emperorship' and 'empire'.

indiction (*indictio*); a cycle of 15 years, originating with Diocletian's reform of the tax-system; from the sixth century onwards the cycle is commonly used for dating documents. The number attached to the word refers to the year within the cycle; unfortunately the number of the cycle itself was not expressed, so it is the context which makes it clear that, e.g., at **60**:6 the 15th indiction means 537 rather than 522 or 552 or any other year at 15-year intervals. Furthermore the indiction year began in September (though **86**:16, if not an error, implies later), so where the month is not given, the modern date has to be expressed as two calendar years, e.g. at **61**:7 the 13th indiction is 549-550, i.e. September 549 to

August 550. The first occurrence in the LP is at **57**:5, where the 11th indiction, 532-533, is an error for the year 530.

judges (*iudices*); at **34**:7 in its legal sense, but thereafter the word is used to mean any high state officials, and tends to be used to mean the leading laymen of a city even if they were holding no actual office, **70**:2, **73**:3, **75**:2, **79**:2, **85**:2,4,5, **86**:2,3, **90**:2,5 (none is actually named); at **85**:4 the Latin word is used in two senses, for the high officials (who as it happens are involved in a legal case) and in the singular for the civil governor of Sicily (the latter instance is therefore translated 'governor'); this is the last mention of such a civil governor before Sicily was raised to be a theme about 700, T. S. Brown (1984) 13.

lamps (*lampades*), **lantern** (*lucerna*); see 'lights'.

lb (*libra*); the Roman pound of 327.45 g (whereas the English pound is 453.592 g), consisting of 12 (not 16) *unciae*.

lights: lights (unqualified) (*fara* or *lumina* or *luminaria*); the LP also has candelabra, candles, candlesticks, candlestick chandeliers, chandeliers, crowns, crown lamps, crown lights, crown which is a chandelier, dolphins, lamps, lanterns (see these words for the Latin equivalents). The translation aims to be consistent, even though the equivalents are not entirely satisfactory and it is far from certain that the LP is consistently using different terms for different objects. 'Dolphins' are evidently decorative features into each of which a wick was set. The other terms all denote lights which must be either freestanding (so specifically the 'candlesticks' at **61**:2) or suspended (at **34**:10 a 'light' hangs, as do 'chandeliers' on **48**:6). The 'chandeliers' (*canthara*) will all have been suspended if the Latin term is connected with *cantherius* (a rafter, a support, anything supported; used in classical Latin of vine-props and the vines supported on them). Krautheimer suggests that at the Lateran the 'chandelier' with 80 dolphins (**34**:11) must have been a huge structure standing in front of the altar; but since it weighed only 30 lb (unless this weight refers only to those parts of it actually made of gold) it could just as easily have been suspended. Where the word 'crown' occurs we may envisage some kind of circular structure with candle-holders set regularly around it. Whatever the distinctions, it will have been these items, so many of them of gold or silver (though bronze is also found), which will have struck the casual visitor to the churches in Rome when no liturgy was in progress as the most remarkable and expensive features.

liturgical books mentioned: antiphonal **72**:6; gospels **54**:10, **62**:2, **78**:1, **90**:10.

liturgical days mentioned: Sundays **53**:11, **63**:1, **78**:2,3, **90**:6; Christmas **9**:2, **83**:4, Eve: **61**:5; Epiphany **82**:3, **83**:4; Septuagesima **72**:6; [Sexagesima] **82**:5; Lent **9**:2; [Maundy Thursday] **82**:6; Easter **9**:2, **11**:2, **15**:2,3, **43**:1, **44**:3, **72**:6, **83**:5; Eastertide **34**:13; octave of Easter **81**:15; Whitsun, **72**:6; Ember days **17**:2; other fasting and non-fasting days **33**:2, **42**:6; feast days **86**:11; martyrs' feasts **53**:11; St Simeon (see *Hypapante*) **86**:14; St Valentine [14 Feb.] **83**:4; Annunciation [25 Mar.] **86**:14; Falling-asleep (Dormition) of St Mary [15 Aug.] **86**:14; Nativity of St Mary [8 Sept.] **86**:14; Exaltation of the Cross [14 Sept.] **86**:10; St Caecilia [22 Nov.] **61**:4; various litanies **62**:2, **72**:4, **79**:5, **86**:14.

liturgical texts mentioned: psalms **39**:5, [introit?] **45**:1, **54**:1, **72**:6, **82**:1; lessons **72**:6; hymns **30**:4, **31**:4, **51**:6, **62**:2, **72**:4; Behold the Lord and Master comes, etc. [Introit for Epiphany] **61**:5; Glory be to God on high **9**:2, **53**:11; prayers for the sacraments **51**:6; Epistle **45**:1; Alleluia **72**:6; Gospel **41**:1, **45**:1; prefaces **51**:6; Holy, holy, holy **8**:2; emperor's name **90**:10; and dispose our days **66**:3; mention of Passion **7**:2; a holy sacrifice etc. **47**:8; Lamb of God **86**:14.

magistrianus - **54**:3, **Appendix 3 54**:3 (Heliodorus and Demetrius), **86**:7 (Sergius); an official on the staff of the *magister officiorum* (the master of the imperial household, who had a wide range of duties: he was administrative controller of the secretariats (*scrinia*); he controlled the guards and the *agentes in rebus* (q.v.), supervised the public postal service, managed the emperor's timetable and regulated audiences with him; his control of the corps of interpreters gave him much influence in foreign affairs).

mandate; this translates two synonyms (cf. **85**:3) for a written instruction issued by the emperor: *iussio* (four times in **60**:7, then frequent) and *sacra* (**54**:4 = **Appendix 3 54**:4; **85**:3; **88**:5; **90**:3,6,8,11). The Latin *mandatum*

(**11**:2, **14**:2, **54**:3 = **Appendix 3 54**:3; **55**:2, **75**:2) is rendered 'order'. A written imperial order is also called *scriptio* ('writ') at **31**:6, **46**:2, more commonly, *auctoritas* ('warrant' **37**:3, **44**:2, **44**:4, **54**:5); the latter word is used also for papal orders (**47**:2, **54**:8, **76**:2 twice, **84**:4, **Appendix 3 54**:2). 'Instruction' renders *praeceptum* and *praeceptio*.

Manichaeans - **33**:2, **40**:2,3, **41**:2, **51**:1, **53**:5, **54**:9; holders of beliefs developed by Mani in the third century, in part from heterodox versions of Christianity. Adherents held a dualistic creed (divinity was imprisoned in matter created by the forces of darkness). Of the members, the lower grade of Hearers could hope for rebirth as members of the Elect by keeping certain moral rules (the most prominent Hearer in the west had, before his conversion, been St Augustine); for the Elect, redemption from transmigration was possible through more exacting forms of asceticism. The religion had been proscribed by Diocletian and frequently thereafter: this led to the book-burning by Gelasius, Symmachus, and Hormisdas recorded in the LP. These texts may have included hymns, the account of Mani's life preserved in Greek (first published in 1970), and the Κεφάλαια, a catechism of their doctrines which now survives only in Coptic. Symmachus' action followed an accusation by the emperor Anastasius that he was himself a Manichaean.

mansionarii - **83**:5, **84**:5, **85**:5; keepers of a church, sextons; it may reasonably be inferred that the author of lives 83-85 was one such.

manumissions (*manumissiones*) - **36**:3; the records of the freeing of slaves, but also any documents validated by the laying on of the hand.

mass (*missae*); first at **7**:2, then frequent; in late fourth-century Christian Latin (e.g. Egeria) *missa* is any service with a blessing by the bishop, but from the fifth or sixth century (not, however, in the Rule of St Benedict) its use comes to be limited to the eucharistic service of the Roman liturgy; in the LP this always seems to be the meaning and it is always plural; on four occasions the expression used is *sollemnia missarum* ('ceremonies of mass'). The meaning of 'second *missa*' at **70**:3 is unknown, since the LP does not otherwise use the singular to mean 'mass' until the late ninth century (*The Lives of the Ninth-Century Popes*, **108**:10).

master of the soldiers (*magister militum*) - **61**:1 (John the Bloody, *Sanguinarius*), **75**:2 (Donus); one of the commanders of the field armies, whether infantry or cavalry, with authority over regional army commanders ('dukes', q.v.).

matroneum - **53**:8 (at St Paul's); an area or section in a church for the use of women, but its precise nature is not clear; it may have been an enclosure for women, or perhaps the site where, across a chancel-screen, the clergy would accept the women's gifts.

medimnus - **34**:10,11,20,25; a measure of capacity, about 53 litres; strictly, for dry materials, but the LP is not strict (though at **34**:20 it is used for pepper).

metreta - **34**:11,18,25; strictly a measure of capacity for liquids, about 39 litres, and thence a jar of this capacity; but since the *metretae* at **34**:11 have a capacity of 10 medimni, and that at **34**:25 a capacity of only 2 *medimni*, the LP evidently means jars in general. Some of these appear to correspond to some of the Constantinian 'water-jars' (*hydriae*, **47**:6) melted down by Leo I; that the figures do not correspond shows that the LP has not tried to harmonize the source material.

mile (*miliarium*, strictly a 'milestone'; the word *milia* is used when describing the aqueduct at Naples, **34**:32); 5000 Roman feet; 1480 metres, somewhat shorter than the English mile (1609.3 metres).

missa(e); see on 'mass'.

modius - **67**:1; a measure of capacity for dry produce, about 9 litres, or one sixth of a *medimnus*.

Nestorian heresy - Nestorius (see 'patriarch' for references) proposed that there were two separate persons in Christ, one divine, one human.

nielloed letters (*litterae nigellae*) - **34**:17; niello is a method of ornamenting a surface of precious metal by engraving it and filling up the incised design with a black composition which gives it clarity; the process is similar to enamelling but the composition used need not be vitrified.

nomenclator - **81**:17, and (Sisinnius) **90**:3; an official who first appears in the late seventh century, but whose original functions are obscure; he may have been master of ceremonies at the papal court, and have dealt with petitions, visitors, etc.; by the tenth century he gained control of charitable services.

office (*scrinium*) - **36**:3, **90**:2,9; in the first passage may mean no more than archive (the word can mean dossier, record, register, as well as secretariat), but by life **90** the meaning is a building, the office of the *scriniarii* and notaries (and perhaps where the archives were kept); it was in the Lateran *Episcopium* near the main entrance and just off the reception hall. English 'office' is also used for *officium* in a liturgical sense at **72**:6 and for its near synonym *cursus* at **9**:2; also for *officium* in a hierarchical sense at **61**:3, **82**:4, **86**:5, and for its synonyms *honor* at **38**:2 and *dignitas* at **83**:1.

ordinator - **90**:4 (Sergius); assistant to the *nomenclator* (q.v.).

pallium; at **35**:2, **60**:8, **82**:4, this is a narrow band of white material hanging over the chest as a distinctive vestment of the pope and of certain other bishops to whom the pope granted it as a token of metropolitan status; at **34**:7, **43**:1 it is a vestment to cover a deacon's left hand or perhaps rather his forearm (like the later maniple), and is described as *linostima* ('half wool, half linen', i.e. with the warp of linen and the weft of wool); at **54**:10, **55**:7, **58**:2, **62**:3, **78**:2 perhaps cloths for covering an altar, or altar-frontals. The word is to be distinguished from 'pall' (*palla*, **13**:2, **44**:5); though this word can mean altar-cloth, the LP probably means the 'corporal' which came into contact with the consecrated bread and wine at mass.

paroecia - **8**:2; the territory of a bishop, i. e. the modern diocese (q.v.). But at **26**:2, **43**:1 the word has its later meaning and is translated 'parish'.

passio - **34**:24 (Laurence); evidently a depiction of incidents from the martyr's suffering and death—in this case very probably the story of Laurence being roasted on a grid-iron, which, whatever its origins, was known before the end of the fourth century to Damasus, Ambrose, and the poet Prudentius.

paten (*patena*); the plate for holding the eucharistic bread to be consecrated at mass; the large number recorded in the LP are all of gold or silver and in either case weigh on average about 24 lb; when the celebrant had to lift the paten he was assisted by deacons. According to the LP glass patens (**16:2** with **18:2**) were replaced by silver ones in the early third century. See also chrism-paten.

patriarch (*patriarcha*); the title used by the LP 23 times in these lives, mainly to refer to the bishop of Constantinople, but also to the bishops of the other major sees, Alexandria and Antioch (**81:15, 86:6**); the term is first used at **60:6** (in **59** Anthimus and Menas are merely styled 'bishop'); it is not used for the pope, though the Lateran is sometimes his 'patriarchate'. The following bishops of the patriarchal sees are mentioned: of Constantinople, Gregory of Nazianzus (379-381) **81:9** (unless the reference is to Gregory of Nyssa); John Chrysostom (398-404) **81:9**; Nestorius (428-431) and his heresy, **47:2,3, 48:1, 51:6, 80:2**; Flavian (447-449) **47:5**; Acacius (471-489) **49:3,4, 50:2,3, 51:2,3,4, 52:2, 54:2,6,8**; John the Cappadocian (518-520) **54:2,6**; Anthimus (536) **59:2,4,5, 60:6,7, 61:3,5**; Menas (536-552) **59:5, 60:6, 81:7**; Sergius (610-638) **76:3, 81:14, 82:2**; Pyrrhus (638-641 and 654) **75:3, 76:3, 81:14, 82:2**; Paul (641-653) **75:6, 76:1,3,4, 81:14, 82:2**; Peter (654-666) **77:2, 81:14, 82:2**; Theodore (677-679 and 686-687) **81:10**; George (679-682) **81:6,8,10,11,12,15, 82:2**; Cyrus (706-712) **90:5**; of Alexandria, Athanasius (328-373) **81:9**; Theophilus (384-412) **15:3**; Cyril (412-444) **81:9**; Dioscorus (444-451) **47:3**; Proterius (451-457) **49:4**; Timothy Salophaciolus (460-475, 477-482) **49:4**; John Talaia (482) **51:3**; Peter (Mongus, the Stammerer) (477, 482-489) **49:3,4, 50:2,3, 51:2,3,4, 54:2,8**; Cyrus (630/631-643/644) **76:3, 81:14, 82:2**; of Antioch, Macarius (? - 681) **81:6,8,10,12,14, 82:2,3**; Theophanes (681-before 685) **81:14,15, 82:2**.

patriarchate (*patriarchium*); see Episcopium.

patrician (*patricius*); a title of honour, the highest class of senatorial rank, bestowed sparingly by Constantine and later emperors on some holders of very high imperial offices (and their wives): Agapitus **55:2,5**, with others **Appendix 3 55:2,5**; Boethius and Symmachus **Appendix 3 55:5**; Belisarius **60:2-8 61:1**, and his wife Antonina **60:8**; the ex-king

Vitiges **61**:1; Cethegus, Albinus and Basilius **61**:7; Narses **62**:2 (in one MS); Romanus **66**:2; Eleutherius **70**:2, **71**:2; Isaac **73**:1,4, **75**:1,2; Theodore Calliopas **75**:2; Plato **76**:4; John Platyn **86**:3; Theophylact **87**:1; Theodore **90**:2,4; John Rizocopus **90**:4; Theophilus **90**:5; Scholasticius **90**:11; unnamed groups **73**:3, **81**:6, **90**:5.

patrimony (*patrimonium*) - **84**:2 (Sicily, Calabria), **85**:3,4 (Bruttium, Lucania, Sicily), **88**:3 (Cottian Alps); one of the districts into which the landed properties of the Roman church were grouped for administrative purposes, controlled by a *rector*.

praefectianus - **54**:3 = **Appendix 3 54**:3 (Heliodorus and Demetrius); probably 'official on the staff of a prefect', but possibly 'former prefect'.

praetorian prefect (the best MSS have merely the abbreviation *pp*, which probably no copyist understood; most MSS produce various unintelligent expansions) - **53**:10 (Albinus); the chief imperial minister in civil and especially financial matters (after the abolition of the praetorian guard in 312 he had no direct military responsibilites); there were four in the empire at this date, and the reference here will be to the prefect of Italy. Albinus (consul in 493, *patricius* by 503, see *PLRE* 2, 51-2) is not otherwise known to have held the prefecture, and since its regular abbreviation is *ppo* Mommsen suggested *pp* represented *praepositus*, but the prefecture remains far more probable for a man whose status was 'illustrious'.

praetorium - **48**:12; the use of the word already in the New Testament to mean the official residence of a governor in a Roman province leads to its use for an official residence for the pope; Hilarus' *praetorium* dedicated to St Stephen at or near the shrine of St Laurence (one of the main suburban pilgrimage centres) is provided lavishly with baths and libraries; cf. *Episcopium*.

prase - **34**:10,13,18,26, **48**:7,9, **55**:7, **58**:2; a green precious stone, not excluding the emerald, most commonly linked with the jacinth (*hyacinthus*), a blue precious stone (possibly a sapphire or amethyst rather than strictly the modern jacinth); they are used for decorating *scyphi*, chalices, censers, and even altars.

prefaces and prayers for the sacraments (*sacramentorum praefationes et orationes*) - **51**:6; although *praefatio* can mean anything proclaimed, and therefore an entire prayer, its use was affected by the meaning 'introduction'. In Cyprian (*de dominica oratione* 31), the 'dialogue' (Sursum corda etc.) is the *praefatio* and the whole eucharistic prayer following it is the *oratio*; but 'preface' soon came to mean at Rome the variable text after the introductory dialogue and before the Sanctus and the rest of the eucharistic prayer (*canon*, **66**:3, or *actio*, 'performance', **8**:2, **47**:8), which had few variations. It is not likely that the LP means that Gelasius composed the canon of the Roman mass, though it may mean that he composed 'prefaces' (in the later sense); *orationes* probably refers to the other variable prayers at mass (collect, etc.). Whether he had any role in compiling the work known as the Gelasian Sacramentary is much disputed (the MS of this is not earlier than the seventh century, and the name was not given it until the seventeenth century).

prefect of the city (*praefectus urbi*); a senator appointed by and responsible to the emperor, with wide judicial responsibilities in and around Rome; as such he will sometimes have been involved in the persecution and trials of Christians and his introduction into the legend at **22**:5 is not absurd, even if on the strength of only one good MS Duchesne omits him from the text.

primicerius notariorum - **36**:3; the senior clerk or chief secretary in the church (a title borrowed from the imperial administration); as one of the seven chief men of the papal court he was one of the most influential dignitaries; his deputy was the *secundicerius*.

property (*possessio*), the commonest and vaguest designation of land holdings in the LP's endowment lists. The average revenue of the 69 mentioned is 236 *solidi* (neglecting additional revenue paid in kind by 8 properties): compare 'farm' and 'estate'. For agricultural holdings *ager* ('land') and *casalia* ('farmsteads', once only, **79**:4) are also used.

rector - **85**:4 (Constantine); manager of a patrimony (q.v.).

regionary - **60**:8 (John), **90**:5 (Theophanius), the former certainly, the latter possibly, a subdeacon of the Roman church; but in later lives the term is used for *defensores* (e.g. *The Lives of the Eighth-Century Popes* **92**:4, **97**:5,10-11,21) and notaries (**97**:3, the future pope Hadrian I).

requiem - **82**:4; this translates *agenda*, which coupled with 'anniversary' can hardly mean 'funeral' and must mean an annual requiem mass; a mass for the faithful departed is very ancient, certainly much earlier than the LP. But the word 'requiem' is anachronistic; it is not used as early as the seventh century, and the mass texts beginning with that word may not have been in existence this early: none of the six MSS of the Roman Antiphonal of the Mass which predate the tenth century contains them.

rooms (*cellae*) - **34**:19; see on 'cellars'.

sacellarius - **75**:2 (Donus, imperial) and **90**:3 (Cosmas, papal); in the Byzantine empire, keeper of the privy purse (a post originally held by a eunuch), strictly the paymaster, cashier, treasurer concerned with day to day expenses, as opposed to the *arcarius* or treasurer; in practice, any finance minister, treasurer, cashier, or paymaster, even at a local level, sometimes specifically concerned with military supplies; the term then came to be used in papal administration (and in that of the patriarchate of Constantinople), where the incumbent was one of the seven 'chief men'.

sacerdos (plural ***sacerdotes***); in some ancient texts the word perhaps means no more than clergyman; in the LP and elsewhere it seems to refer indifferently to a priest or a bishop, i.e. to one who can preside at the eucharist; it is here left untranslated, and 'priest' represents *presbyter*.

saddle-cloth, official (*mappula*) - **85**:4, **90**:5; a white cloth used as insignia by the higher members of the Roman clergy when travelling on horseback.

scevrocarnalis - **86**:6; a word occurring nowhere else: is it a hybrid from a Greek form σκεβρί(ο)ν cited from the late seventh-century writer Leontius of Naples (*vita Symeonis Sali*, PG 93.1733C; the context suggests the meaning 'money-box' and a derivation from σκεῦος) and Latin *carnalis* (of flesh, i.e. of leather)? Later MSS emend to *cartalis* (for letters, strictly those on papyrus), which gives no doubt the intended sense, but is not what the LP presumably wrote.

scholasticus - **74**:1 (father of John IV); the meaning varies—scholar, student, schoolmaster, professor.

scribo - **61**:4 (Anthemus) and **75**:2 (Marinus); commander or officer of the regiments of *excubitores* (imperial guards, to whom might be entrusted 'delicate' tasks, e.g. Anthemus arresting pope Vigilius in 545).

scriniarius - **90**:3 (Sergius); a term derived from *scrinium* (see 'office'), borrowed by the church from the imperial administration and denoting a keeper of records, secretary; known holders were clearly more than humble clerks.

scyphus; see on *ama*.

secretarium - **64**:2, **66**:5, **86**:12 (all at St Peter's); probably this means 'area close to the shrine', though it might refer to the lower levels in general, or even to the sacristy or vestry of a church (the Greek διακονικόν); at **81**:7,10 the same word is used for 'council chamber'.

secundicerius - **90**:3 (George); deputy to the *primicerius* (q.v.), and one of the 'chief men' of the papal court.

service chalice (*calix ministerialis*); see on *ama*.

shell (*conca*); at **46**:6 perhaps (despite its weight) used for pouring water by hand at baptism; those at **48**:4 are evidently a much larger structural feature.

siliqua - **42**:6, **46**:3; one twenty-fourth of a gold *solidus*, then used to mean that fraction generally.

solidus; the standard gold coin from Constantine's time onwards, struck at 72 to the (Roman) lb; it would buy about 1000 lb bread or about 200 lb meat; a poor man might survive on less than 3 *solidi* a year.

spatharius - **76**:6 (unnamed), **86**:7-9 (Zacharias); member of an imperial bodyguard (named from *spatha*, a kind of sword), originally made up of eunuchs, but the title was considered a dignity by the seventh century, by when this bodyguard was ceremonial and its dignitaries might be employed on other missions; at the head of it was the *protospatharius* (here translated 'chief *spatharius*'), a post first mentioned outside the LP (where Zacharias holds it) in 718 or perhaps 692.

stag (*cervus*); the LP mentions 12, all of silver (average weight 57½ lb), in connexion with baptismal fonts. Primarily decorative, but with the allusion to Psalm 42 verse 1 ('Like as the hart desireth the water-brooks', where the Vulgate (Ps. 41) has *fontes aquarum*).

statio (**and 'stational'**) - 48:11, **54**:11, **78**:3; a meeting of the faithful for the liturgy under the presidency of the bishop, in a basilica or in one of the *tituli*, as determined or fixed in advance (this use of the word was known already in the third century, Cyprian, *Ep.* 43.2, Cornelius, *apud* Cyprian, *Ep.* 48.3); at the first occurrence of the word in the LP it is clear from what follows that in effect it means *titulus* (q.v.).

stauracis - **86**:10; silken material decorated with crosses.

stipend; here used to translate *roga*, pay or a grant of money for soldiers or others; for soldiers or the army at **70**:2 and **73**:1; elsewhere for the clergy, **70**:4, **71**:1,3, **73**:5, **74**:3, **77**:1, **79**:1, **81**:18, where it seems clear that the word is used for donatives given on special occasions, perhaps (hence 'entire') equivalent to the annual stipend of the recipients; many of the examples refer to bequests made at papal funerals (so too with different wording at **83**:5, **84**:5, **85**:5), but it is clear from **71**:1 (contrast **71**:3), **73**:5 (if *donum*, 'bounty' is an alternative for *roga* used almost immediately afterwards) and perhaps **79**:1 that these donatives were sometimes, perhaps regularly, given earlier—probably at the ordination of a new pope (compare the *congiaria* given by Roman emperors, whose amounts are recorded by the Chronographer of 354).

stole - **81**:13; translates *orarium*, a vestment which might not be worn by any below the rank of deacon; it was a long band of linen worn round the neck and shoulders, and hanging down the front of the body. Latin *stola* appears at **54**:10, here translated 'vesture'.

strategos; general, governor of a territory in the empire (Greek στρατηγός); **90:4** (Theodore, who at **90:2** is called 'patrician and general', *patricium et primi exercitus*, where the latter phrase seems to represent the Greek μονοστρατηγός); also **90:5** (Theophilus).

territory (*territurium*); the area assigned to a municipality for local government purposes.

Thracesian (*thracesius*) - **85:**1; name of one of the themes (Byzantine military districts created from the seventh century), located in the areas of the plain of Thrace nearest to Constantinople, first recorded in 687.

titulus; in effect the word came to mean a parish church, as opposed to the basilicas which did not serve the merely local community. Within the walls of Rome there were 25 *tituli* in existence by 499 at the latest, though not all are mentioned in the LP before 715; the major basilicas within the walls are excluded from this total, as of course are the suburban basilicas and cemeteries; the LP sometimes refers to *tituli* simply as 'basilicas'. By the late eighth century the number was down to 22 because 3 (including SS Silvester & Martin, and the *titulus Fasciolae*) had been reduced in status (see *LECP* at **97:** n. 113). This use of the word *titulus* is best connected with the meaning 'title-deeds', and explained as a development from the pre-Constantinian period: the Christians of Rome were already too numerous to meet in one place and had met in private houses whose title-deeds showed them to be the property of individuals. Such house-churches eventually came into the possession of the church and were gradually replaced by buildings of basilical style, but for purposes of identification the name of the original owner was retained. Gradually that owner's name would be taken to be that of a saint, sometimes by confusion with a genuine martyr of the same name. New foundations in the fourth and fifth centuries were also for convenience referred to as the *titulus* of the donor (e.g. Vestina, **42:**3-6), even when the custom of dedicating the building to another saint had become normal: in Vestina's case her foundation was dedicated to SS Gervasius & Protasius, the unknown martyrs whose relics St Ambrose had discovered, though it later came to be known by the supposed name of their father St Vitalis, whose relics had also been discovered by St Ambrose. In theory, the *tituli* retained control of their own endowments, separately from the central papal administration, but the reality may have been rather different, particularly after 498 when Symmachus wanted to centralize control of these endowments; some local parish clergy resisted, and this was a contributory cause to the friction of the next few years.

Tome (*tomus*) - **47**:2, **48**:1; strictly, any written work, but used specifically of Leo I's document against the monophysite doctrine taught by Eutyches (q.v.) at the time of the Council of Chalcedon in 451; monophysites maintain that Christ has not merely one person but also one nature (that of God), not two (God and Man), the opposite view from that of Nestorians (q.v.).

tower (with dolphins) - **48**:5,9; of silver, 60 and 25 lb respectively. The former is in a baptismal context and analogy with the towers with patens (see below) might suggest that it was a container for reserving sacred oils until they were next needed, when they would be transferred to chrism-patens (q.v.), but its weight makes this unlikely; the latter immediately follows lighting equipment, and given the meaning of 'dolphins' elsewhere in the LP (see on 'lights'), some kind of freestanding light may be intended in both cases.

tower (with paten) - **34**:18 (gold), **42**:4 (silver); the weights are not given separately from the patens; the nature of these items is unclear— perhaps some kind of decorative and protective covering for a paten; a container for reserving the eucharist for the communion of the sick is possible.

transfers (*traditiones*) - **36**:3; written deeds recording transfers of ownership.

tremiss (*tremissis*) - **34**:3,19,29,33, **35**:4, **39**:4, **42**:6, **46**:3; from the latter part of the fourth century a gold coin, at first three eighths but soon one third of a *solidus* (q.v.), and perhaps money of account slightly earlier.

Trullus - **81**:6, **82**:2; a cupola, hence a domed building, and specifically the name of a hall in the imperial palace at Constantinople.

Typus - **76**:1,4, **82**:4; prescribed formula, standard form of document; hence used to mean a written decision, decree or edict; the first occurrences refer to Constans II's edict of 648 on monothelete religious dogma (prepared by Paul patriarch of Constantinople, and forbidding all discussion of the number of Wills in Christ, see *Ecthesis*), the last to the decree of the same emperor to Maurus, archbishop of Ravenna, granting his church independent status.

uncia - **42**:6; one twelfth of a *libra* ('lb') or 27.29 g (the English ounce is 28.3495 g, the Troy ounce used for precious metals is 31.035 g); also used to express the fraction one twelfth.

viaticum - **40**:3, **46**:1; communion given to the dying, though the word was used originally in a broader sense for any rites connected with the dying.

vicarianus - **62**:1 (the father of Pelagius I); it is unclear if this means one on the staff of a *vicarius* (see 'diocese') or a former actual *vicarius*.

vicedominus - **61**:5 (Ampliatus, priest), **90**:4 (Saiulus, deacon); the major-domo or steward of the papal *Episcopium* (q.v.); see Noble (1984) 223-4. Bishops and laymen are later found as holders of the post. He was perhaps in charge of the *cubicularii* (chamberlains), and was one of the most important papal officials. Cf. *Ordo Romanus* I (late seventh century, ed. Andrieu, II. 70): 'Following the (pope's) horse, these are they that are mounted: the *vicedominus*, *vestiarius*, *nomenclator* and *sacellarius*'.

visitor (*visitator*) - **53**:3, **Appendix 2 52**:6, **Appendix 3 53**:3 (Peter of Altinum); a term used at least from the time of Gelasius to mean the temporary administrator of a vacant bishopric, as opposed to a *cardinalis* (licitly transferred from another see) or to the usual bishop of the see (Kuttner (1945) 134); the north African term in Augustine's time was *interventor* (*Ep.* 44. 8).

water-jars (*hydriae*) - **47**:6; see on *metretae*.

wills (*testamenta*) - **36**:3; strictly a *testamentum* records the appointment of an heir, but the document can include legacies, manumissions, appointment of guardians—in effect, a will (it can even mean a written deed of any kind).

INDEX OF CHURCHES MENTIONED

ROME: basilicas, *tituli* and monasteries inside the walls:

Ad Lunam monastery, **48:**12
St Agatha *dei Goti*, xliv, **66:**4
St Andrew *in Catabarbara*, xlii, **49:**1
SS XII Apostoli (SS Philip and James) (?basilica of Julius, xxxvii, **36:**2,
　　44:1, **45:**2, **57:**1, **61:**1, **Appendix 1 36**), xxix, **62:**3, **63:**1
St Bibiana (and St Paul), xlii, xlv, **49:**1, **82:**5
Boethian monastery, **80:**2
Boniface IV's monastery, **69:**3
St Caecilia *in Trastevere*, **61:**4
St Caesarius *in Palatio*, **86:**2
titulus Callisti (basilica of Julius; S Maria *in Trastevere*), xxxvii, **17:**3,
　　36:2, **Appendix 1 36**
SS Cosmas and Damian, basilica, xliii, **56:**2, **86:**13
SS Cosmas and Damian, oratory, **53:**9
basilica Crescentiana (S Sisto Vecchio), xxxviii, **41:**2
Holy Cross in Jerusalem, xxxii, **34:**22
St Erasmus, monastery, **79:**4
St Euphemia (and St Michael) *in Vico Patricio*, **53:**9, **86:**13
titulus Fasciolae (SS Nereus and Achilleus), **50:**1
St George (and St Sebastian) *in Velabro*, **82:**5
St Gregory (St Andrew), monastery, **66:**5
SS John and Paul, **53:**5,9, **59:**1
St Hadrian (*Curia Senatus*), xliv, **72:**6, **86:**14
Lateran (Constantinian) basilica, xv, xxx-xxxii, xxxvi, xxxix-xlii, xlv,
　　34:9-12, **37:**6, **44:**1,3, **46:**4, **47:**6, **48:**6,11, **53:**2,5, **54:**9,11, **57:**1,
　　61:5, **63:**1, **71:**1, **76:**3,8, **84:**1, **85:**1, **86:**10, **Appendix 3 54:**9,
　　Glossary (*s. vv.* altar, *fastigium*, lights);
　　vestiarium, xiv, xlv; obelisk, xvi;
　　Baptistery, xvi, xxx, xl-xli, **34:**13-15, **46:**7, **48:**2-5,12, **74:**2; oratory of
　　St Stephen, **48:**12; church of SS Venantius etc., **74:**2; oratories: of St
　　John the Baptist, **48:**2,5; of St John the Evangelist, **48:**2,5, **74:**2; of the
　　Holy Cross **48:**2-4;
　　monastery of Honorius (SS Andrew and Bartholomew), **72:**6;

143

oratories inside the *Episcopium*: St Sebastian, **75**:5; St Silvester, **86**:2
St Laurence *in Damaso*, xxxviii, **39**:2
St Laurence *in Lucina*, xl, **46**:6, **83**:2, **86**:14
St Lucy *in Selcis*, **72**:6
St Marcellus (*catabulum*), xxvii, **31**:3-5
St Mark, xxxvi, **35**:3-4, **87**:3
St Mary *ad martyres* (Pantheon), xlv, **69**:2, **78**:3, **83**:2
St Mary Major (*ad praesepe*) (Basilica of Liberius = St Vitus *in macello*?), xxxvii, xxxix, xli, **37**:7, **46**:3,7, **48**:1,11, **49**:1, **51**:1, **53**:2,9, **55**:7, **75**:2, **76**:6, **77**:2, **81**:18, **86**:14; oratory of SS Cosmas and Damian, **53**:9
St Maria Antiqua, **88**:2, **Glossary** (*s.v. Episcopium*)
St Maria *in Trastevere*, xxxvii
St Martin *ai monti* (*titulus* Equitii, Silvestri), xxx, **34**:3,33, **53**:9, **Appendix 2 52**:15
St Peter *ad vincula*, xl, **53**:5
Ptochium of Pelagius II, **65**:2
St Pudentiana, xxvii, **11**:4
SS Quattuor Coronati, **72**:4
St Sabina, xl, **46**:8
St Susanna, **86**:1,13
St Stephen, xli, **49**:1, **75**:4, **85**:1
titulus Vestinae (SS Gervasius and Protasius; S Vitale), xxxviii-xxix, **42**:3-7, **Glossary** (*s.v. titulus*)
xenodochium of Belisarius (S Maria *di Trevi*), **61**:2

ROME: basilicas and cemeteries outside the walls:

Cemetery *ad Ursum Pileatum* via Portuensis, **41**:3, **42**:8
St Agapitus via Tiburtina, **50**:1
St Agatha via Aurelia, **53**:8
St Agnes, mausoleum of Costantina, St Agnes *ad corpus*, via Nomentana, xxviii, xxx, xxxiii-xxxiv, xxxvii, xxxix, **34**:23, **37**:4,5,7, **42**:7, **44**:3, **53**:10, **72**:3
St Alexander via Nomentana, **7**:3
St Andrew via Labicana, **86**:13
Cemetery of Calepodius (of Julius I) via Aurelia, xxxvii, **17**:4, **36**:4, **Appendix 1 36**

83:2,5, **84**:5, **85**:5, **86**:4,10,11,16, **87**:3, **88**:1,6, **89**:2, **90**:2,8,12, **Appendix 2 52**:4, **Appendix 3 53**:4,6,12, **54**:12, **Glossary** (*s. vv. confessio, Episcopium, fastigium*);
oratories of the Holy Cross, St John the Evangelist and St John the Baptist, **53**:7; of St Mary, **88**:1;
church of S Andrew, **53**:6,7, **72**:2, **87**:3, **Appendix 3 53**:6;
oratories of SS Thomas, Cassian, Protus and Hyacinth, Apollinaris, Sossus in St Andrew's, **53**:6;
church of S Apollinaris *ad Palmata*, **72**:3,4;
monastery of SS John and Paul, **47**:7
St Peter via Portuensis, **79**:4
St Peter via Trebana, xliii, **53**:10
Cemetery of Praetextatus via Appia, **18**:4, **25**:4
SS Primus and Felician via Nomentana, **75**:4
Cemetery of Priscilla via Salaria, **30**:4, **31**:5, **34**:34, **37**:8, **40**:4, **45**:3, **55**:7
St Saturninus (cemetery of Thrason) via Salaria, **56**:2
St Sebastian (Catacombs) via Appia, xxiv, xxviii, xxxiv, **22**:4, **39**:2, **46**:7
St Stephen via Latina, xl, **47**:1
St Stephen via Tiburtina, **49**:1
SS Tiburtius and Valerian via Appia, **63**:5
St Valentine (cemetery of Julius I) via Flaminia, xxxvii, **36**:2, **75**:5, **83**:2, **Appendix 1 36**

ITALY BEYOND ROME

ALBANO: Constantinian basilica (cathedral of St Pancras), xxxv-xxxvi, **34**:30
St Peter, xliii, **54**:1
ANTIUM: St Hermes, **44**:2
S MARIA CAPUA VETERE: Constantinian basilica of the apostles, xxxvi, **34**:31
HORTA: monastery of St Juvenal, **61**:2
MONTE GARGANO: St Michael, **51**:1
NAPLES: Constantinian basilica (St Restituta), xxxvi, **34**:32
OSTIA: Constantinian basilica of SS Peter, Paul and John the Baptist, xxxv, **34**:28,29
St Aurea, xlv, **86**:13

MAPS

I IDENTIFIABLE CEMETERIES AND BASILICAS OUTSIDE THE WALLS OF ROME

MENTIONED IN THE L.P. TO A.D. 715

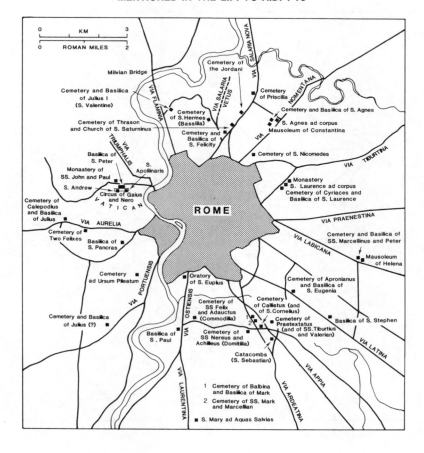

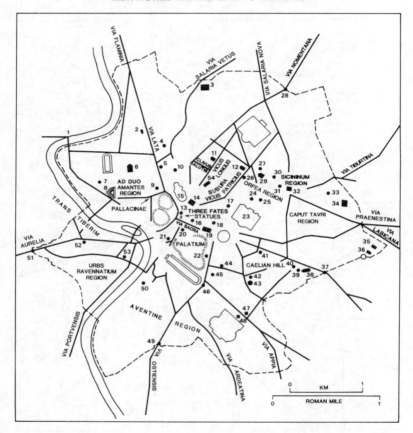

KEY TO MAP II

1. Porta S. Petri
2. S. Laurence in Lucina
3. Pincian Palace
4. Xenodochium of Belisarius
5. Catabulum (S. Marcellus)
6. Pantheon (S. Mary ad martyres)
7. S. Laurence in Damaso
8. Theatre of Pompey
9. Titulus of Mark
10. SS. Philip and James (XII Apostoli) (? = basilica of Julius in region VII near Trajan's forum)
11. Titulus Vestinae (S. Vitale)
12. S. Pudentiana
13. S. Hadrian
14. Temple of Mars Ultor
15. Forum of Trajan
16. SS. Cosmas and Damian
17. S. Peter ad vincula
18. Temple of Tellus
19. Temple of Venus and Rome
20. S. Maria Antiqua
21. SS. Sebastian and George in Velabro
22. S. Caesarius in Palatio
23. Baths of Trajan (or of Domitian)
24. S. Lucy in Selcis
25. Titulus of Equitius or Sivester (SS. Silvester and Martin; S. Martino ai monti)
26. S. Euphemia and S. Michael
27. Oratory of SS. Cosmas and Damian
28. Porta Nomentana
29. Basilica of S. Mary Major ad praesepe
30. S. Andrew
31. Basilica of Liberius?
32. Market of Livia
33. S. Bibiana (with adjacent church of S. Paul)
34. Licinian Palace?
35. Sessorian Palace
36. Basilica of Holy Cross in Jerusalem
37. Porta Asinaria or S. Iohannis
38. Constantinian or Lateran Basilica
39. Constantinian or Lateran Baptistery
40. Monastery of Honorius
41. SS. Quattuor Coronati
42. Monastery of S. Erasmus
43. S. Stephen
44. SS. John and Paul
45. Monastery of Gregory (of S. Andrew)
46. Arcus Stillans
47. Basilica Crescentiana (S. Sisto Vecchio)
48. Titulus Fasciolae (SS. Nereus and Achilleus)
49. Porta S. Pauli
50. S. Sabina
51. Porta S. Pancratii
52. Basilica of Julius = Titulus of Callistus = S. Maria in Trastevere
53. S. Caecilia
54. S. Agatha